2ND EDITION

Building Evolutionary Architectures

Automated Software Governance

*Neal Ford, Rebecca Parsons, Patrick Kua,
and Pramod Sadalage*

Beijing · Boston · Farnham · Sebastopol · Tokyo   

Building Evolutionary Architectures

by Neal Ford, Rebecca Parsons, Patrick Kua, and Pramod Sadalage

Copyright © 2023 Neal Ford, Rebecca Parsons, Patrick Kua, and Pramod Sadalage. All rights reserved.

Published by O'Reilly Media, Inc., 1005 Gravenstein Highway North, Sebastopol, CA 95472.

O'Reilly books may be purchased for educational, business, or sales promotional use. Online editions are also available for most titles (*http://oreilly.com*). For more information, contact our corporate/institutional sales department: 800-998-9938 or *corporate@oreilly.com*.

Acquisitions Editor: Melissa Duffield
Development Editor: Virginia Wilson
Production Editor: Christopher Faucher
Copyeditor: Audrey Doyle
Proofreader: Piper Editorial Consulting, LLC

Indexer: WordCo Indexing Services, Inc.
Interior Designer: David Futato
Cover Designer: Karen Montgomery
Illustrator: O'Reilly Media, Inc.

October 2017:   First Edition
December 2022:   Second Edition

Revision History for the Second Edition
2022-11-22:   First Release

See *http://oreilly.com/catalog/errata.csp?isbn=9781492097549* for release details.

978-1-492-09754-9

[LSI]

Table of Contents

Part II.   Structure

Part III.   Impact

Foreword to the First Edition

For a long time, the software industry followed the notion that architecture was something that ought to be developed and completed before writing the first line of code. Inspired by the construction industry, it was felt that the sign of a successful software architecture was something that didn't need to change during development, often a reaction to the high costs of scrap and rework that would occur due to a re-architecture event.

This vision of architecture was rudely challenged by the rise of agile software methods. The preplanned architecture approach was founded on the notion that requirements should also be fixed before coding began, leading to a phased (or waterfall) approach where requirements were followed by architecture which itself was followed by construction (programming). The agile world, however, challenged the very notion of fixed requirements, observing that regular changes in requirements were a business necessity in the modern world and providing project planning techniques to embrace controlled change.

In this new agile world, many people questioned the role of architecture. And certainly the preplanned architecture vision couldn't fit in with modern dynamism. But there is another approach to architecture, one that embraces change in the agile manner. In this perspective, architecture is a constant effort, one that works closely with programming so that architecture can react both to changing requirements and to feedback from programming. We've come to call this *evolutionary architecture*, to highlight that while the changes are unpredictable, the architecture can still move in a good direction.

At Thoughtworks, we've been immersed in this architectural worldview. Rebecca led many of our most important projects in the early years of this millennium and developed our technical leadership as our CTO. Neal has been a careful observer of our work, synthesizing and conveying the lessons we've learned. Pat has combined his project work with developing our technical leads. We've always felt that architecture is vitally important and can't be left to idle chance. We've made mistakes, but we've learned from them, growing a better understanding of how to build a codebase that can respond gracefully to the many changes in its purpose.

The heart of doing evolutionary architecture is to make small changes and put in feedback loops that allow everyone to learn from how the system is developing. The rise of Continuous Delivery has been a crucial enabling factor in making evolutionary architecture practical. The authorial trio use the notion of fitness functions to monitor the state of the architecture. They explore different styles of evolvability for architecture and emphasize the issues around long-lived data—often a topic that gets neglected. Conway's Law towers over much of the discussion, as it should.

While I'm sure we have much to learn about doing software architecture in an evolutionary style, this book marks an essential road map for the current state of understanding. As more people are realizing the central role of software systems in our 21st-century human world, knowing how best to respond to change while keeping on your feet will be an essential skill for any software leader.

— Martin Fowler
martinfowler.com
September 2017

Foreword to the Second Edition

A metaphor attempts to describe similarities between two unrelated things in order to clarify their essential elements. A good example of this is with software architecture. We commonly attempt to describe software architecture by comparing it to the structure of a building. The things that make up the structure of a building—its outer walls, inner walls, roof, room size, number of floors, even the location of the building—all relate to structural elements of software architecture—databases, services, communication protocols, interfaces, deployment location (cloud, on-premises), and so on. The old view is that in both cases these are things that, once in place, are very hard to change later. And that's exactly where the building metaphor breaks down.

Today, the building metaphor for software architecture is no longer a valid one. While it's still useful to explain what software architecture is to a nontechnical person in terms of comparing the *structure* of a system, software architecture must be malleable enough to change quickly, which is very different from a physical building. Why must software architecture be so malleable? Because businesses are in a constant state of rapid change, undergoing mergers, acquisitions, new business lines, cost-cutting measures, organizational structures, and so on. However, so is technology, with new frameworks, technical environments, platforms, and products. To properly align with the business and technology environment, software architecture must change as well, and at the same rapid pace. A good example is a major acquisition by a large company. Aside from the myriad business concerns and changes, the software architectures supporting the major business applications must be able to scale to meet the additional customer base and must be both adaptable and extensible to accommodate new business functionality and practices.

Many companies already know this but struggle with one thing: how do you make software architecture malleable enough to withstand a fast rate of business and technology change? The answers are found in this book you are about to read. This second edition builds on the concepts of guided and incremental change introduced in the first edition to provide you with the latest techniques, knowledge, and tips on fitness functions, automated architectural governance, and evolutionary data to make sure your software architectures are agile enough to keep up with the constant change we are all experiencing today.

— Mark Richards
developertoarchitect.com
October 2022

Preface

When we wrote the first edition of *Building Evolutionary Architectures* in 2017, the idea of evolving software architecture was still somewhat radical. During one of her first presentations about the subject, Rebecca was approached afterward by someone accusing her of being professionally irresponsible for suggesting that software architecture *can* evolve over time—after all, the architecture is the thing that never changes.

However, as reality teaches us, systems must evolve to meet new demands of their users and to reflect changes in the constantly shifting software development ecosystem.

When the first edition was published, few tools existed to take advantage of the techniques we describe. Fortunately, the software development world keeps evolving, including many more tools to make building evolutionary architectures easier.

The Structure of This Book

We changed the structure from the first edition to more clearly delineate the two main topics: the engineering practices for evolving software systems and the structural approaches that make it easier.

In Part I, we define the various mechanisms and engineering practices that teams can use to implement the goals of evolutionary architecture, including techniques, tools, categories, and other information readers need to understand this topic.

Software architecture also involves *structural design*, and some design decisions make evolution (and governance) easier. We cover this in Part II, which also includes coverage of architecture styles as well as design principles around coupling, reuse, and other pertinent structural considerations.

Virtually nothing in software architecture exists in isolation; many principles and practices in evolutionary architecture involve the holistic entanglement of many parts of the software development process, which we cover in Part III.

Case Studies and PenultimateWidgets

We highlight a number of case studies in this book. All four authors were (and some still are) consultants while working on the material in this book, and we used our real-world experience to derive many of the case studies that appear here. While we can't divulge the details for particular clients, we wanted to provide some relevant examples to make the topic less abstract. Thus, we adopted the idea of a surrogate company, PenultimateWidgets, as the "host" for all our case studies.

In the second edition, we also solicited case studies from our colleagues, which further highlight examples of applying the techniques we discuss. Throughout the book, each case study appears as one from PenultimateWidgets, but each comes from a real project.

Conventions Used in This Book

The following typographical conventions are used in this book:

Italic
Indicates new terms, URLs, email addresses, filenames, and file extensions.

`Constant width`
Used for program listings, as well as within paragraphs to refer to program elements such as variable or function names, databases, data types, environment variables, statements, and keywords.

`Constant width bold`
Shows commands or other text that should be typed literally by the user.

`Constant width italic`
Shows text that should be replaced with user-supplied values or by values determined by context.

 This element signifies a tip or suggestion.

This element signifies a general note.

 This element indicates a warning or caution.

Using Code Examples

Supplemental material (code examples, exercises, etc.) is available for download at *http://evolutionaryarchitecture.com*.

If you have a technical question or a problem using the code examples, please send email to *bookquestions@oreilly.com*.

This book is here to help you get your job done. In general, if example code is offered with this book, you may use it in your programs and documentation. You do not need to contact us for permission unless you're reproducing a significant portion of the code. For example, writing a program that uses several chunks of code from this book does not require permission. Selling or distributing examples from O'Reilly books does require permission. Answering a question by citing this book and quoting example code does not require permission. Incorporating a significant amount of example code from this book into your product's documentation does require permission.

We appreciate, but generally do not require, attribution. An attribution usually includes the title, author, publisher, and ISBN. For example: "*Building Evolutionary Architectures*, 2nd edition, by Neal Ford, Rebecca Parsons, Patrick Kua, and Pramod Sadalage (O'Reilly). Copyright 2023 Neal Ford, Rebecca Parsons, Patrick Kua, and Pramod Sadalage, 978-1-492-09754-9."

If you feel your use of code examples falls outside fair use or the permission given above, feel free to contact us at *permissions@oreilly.com*.

O'Reilly Online Learning

O'REILLY® For more than 40 years, *O'Reilly Media* has provided technology and business training, knowledge, and insight to help companies succeed.

Our unique network of experts and innovators share their knowledge and expertise through books, articles, and our online learning platform. O'Reilly's online learning platform gives you on-demand access to live training courses, in-depth learning paths, interactive coding environments, and a vast collection of text and video from O'Reilly and 200+ other publishers. For more information, visit *https://oreilly.com*.

How to Contact Us

Please address comments and questions concerning this book to the publisher:

O'Reilly Media, Inc.
1005 Gravenstein Highway North
Sebastopol, CA 95472
800-998-9938 (in the United States or Canada)
707-829-0515 (international or local)
707-829-0104 (fax)

We have a web page for this book, where we list errata, examples, and any additional information. You can access this page at *https://oreil.ly/evolutionary-arch-2e*.

Email *bookquestions@oreilly.com* to comment or ask technical questions about this book.

For news and information about our books and courses, visit *https://oreilly.com*.

Find us on LinkedIn: *https://linkedin.com/company/oreilly-media*.

Follow us on Twitter: *https://twitter.com/oreillymedia*.

Watch us on YouTube: *https://youtube.com/oreillymedia*.

Additional Information

The authors maintain a companion website for this book at *http://evolutionaryarchitecture.com*.

Acknowledgments

The authors would like to give vociferous thanks to our colleagues who provided the outlines and inspirations for the many fitness function case studies presented within. In no particular order, thanks to Carl Nygard, Alexandre Goedert, Santhoshkumar Palanisamy, Ravi Kumar Pasumarthy, Indhumathi V., Manoj B. Narayanan, Neeraj Singh, Sirisha K., Gireesh Chunchula, Madhu Dharwad, Venkat V., Abdul Jeelani, Senthil Kumar Murugesh, Matt Newman, Xiaojun Ren, Archana Khanal, Heiko Gerin, Slin Castro, Fernando Tamayo, Ana Rodrigo, Peter Gillard-Moss, Anika Weiss,

Bijesh Vijayan, Nazneen Rupawalla, Kavita Mittal, Viswanath R., Dhivya Sadasivam, Rosi Teixeira, Gregorio Melo, Amanda Mattos, and many others whose names we failed to capture.

Neal would like to thank all the attendees of the various conferences at which he has spoken over the last few years to help hone and revise this material in person and especially online, due to the unusual circumstances of a global pandemic. Thanks to all the front-line workers who stepped up bravely to help us all through this difficult time. He would also like to thank the technical reviewers who went above and beyond to provide excellent feedback and advice. Neal would also like to thank his cats, Amadeus, Fauci, and Linda Ruth, for providing useful distractions that often led to insights. Cats never dwell on the past or future; they are always in the current moment, so he uses his time with them to join their presence in the here and now. Thanks also to our outdoor neighborhood "cocktail club," which started as a community way to see friends and has evolved into the neighborhood brain trust. And finally, Neal would like to thank his long-suffering wife, who endures his travel, and then the abrupt absence of travel, and other professional indignities with a smile.

Rebecca would like to thank all the colleagues, conference attendees and speakers, and authors who have, over the years, contributed ideas, tools, and methods and asked clarifying questions about the field of evolutionary architecture. She echoes Neal's thanks to the technical reviewers for their careful reading and commentary. Further, Rebecca would like to thank her coauthors for all the enlightening conversations and discussions while working together on this book. In particular, she thanks Neal for the great discussion, or perhaps debate, they had several years ago regarding the distinction between emergent and evolutionary architecture. These ideas have come a long way since that first conversation.

Patrick would like to thank all his colleagues and customers at ThoughtWorks, who have driven the need and provided the test bed to articulate the ideas in building evolutionary architecture. He also would like to echo Neal's and Rebecca's thanks to the technical reviewers, whose feedback helped to improve the book immensely. Finally, he would like to thank his coauthors for the past several years and for the opportunity to work closely together on this topic, despite the numerous time zones and flights that made meeting in person the rare occasion.

Pramod would like to thank all his colleagues and clients who have always provided the space and time to explore new ideas and to push new ideas and thinking. He would like to thank his coauthors for thoughtful discussions ensuring that all aspects of architecture are considered. He also would like to thank the reviewers—Cassandra Shum, Henry Matchen, Luca Mezzalira, Phil Messenger, Vladik Khononov, Venkat Subramanium, and Martin Fowler—for thoughtful comments that helped the authors immensely. And finally, he would like to thank his daughters, Arula and Arhana, for the joy they bring into his life, and his wife, Rupali, for all her love and support.

Mechanics

Evolutionary architecture consists of broad areas of inquiry: *mechanics* and *structure*.

The *mechanics* of evolutionary architecture concern the engineering practices and verification that allow an architecture to evolve, which overlap architectural governance. This covers engineering practices, testing, metrics, and a host of other moving parts that make evolving software possible. Part I defines and presents numerous examples of the mechanics of evolutionary architecture.

The other aspect of *Building Evolutionary Architectures* concerns the structure or topology of software systems. Do some architecture styles better facilitate building systems that are easier to evolve? Are there structural decisions in architecture that should be avoided to make evolution easier? We answer these and other questions in Part II, which concerns structuring architecture for evolution.

Many of the facets of building evolutionary architectures combine both mechanics and structure; Part III of the book is titled "Impact." It includes many case studies, provides advice, and covers patterns and antipatterns as well as other considerations architects and teams need to be aware of to make evolution possible.

CHAPTER 1

Evolving Software Architecture

Building systems that age gracefully and effectively is one of the enduring challenges of software development generally and software architecture specifically. This book covers two fundamental aspects of how to build evolvable software: utilizing effective engineering practices derived from the agile software movement and structuring architecture to facilitate change and governance.

Readers will grow to understand the state of the art in how to manage change in architecture in a deterministic way, unifying previous attempts at providing protection for architecture characteristics and actionable techniques to improve the ability to change architecture without breaking it.

The Challenges of Evolving Software

> *bit rot*: also known as *software rot*, *code rot*, *software erosion*, *software decay*, or *software entropy*, is either a slow deterioration of software quality over time or its diminishing responsiveness that will eventually lead to software becoming faulty.

Teams have long struggled with building high-quality software that *remains* high quality over time, including adages that reflect this difficulty, such as the varied definitions of *bit rot* shown above. At least two factors drive this struggle: the problems of policing all the various moving parts in complex software, and the dynamic nature of the software development ecosystem.

Modern software consists of thousands or millions of individual parts, each of which may be changed along some set of dimensions. Each of those changes has predictable and sometimes unpredictable effects. Teams that attempt manual governance eventually become overwhelmed by the sheer volume of parts and combinatorial side effects.

Managing the myriad interactions of software would be bad enough against a static backdrop, but that doesn't exist. The software development ecosystem consists of all the tools, frameworks, libraries, and best practices—the accumulated state of the art in software development at any given snapshot in time. This ecosystem forms an equilibrium—much like a biological system—that developers can understand and build things within. However, that equilibrium is *dynamic*—new things come along constantly, initially upsetting the balance until a new equilibrium emerges. Visualize a unicyclist carrying boxes: *dynamic* because the unicyclist continues to adjust to stay upright, and *equilibrium* because they continue to maintain balance. In the software development ecosystem, each new innovation or practice may disrupt the status quo, forcing the establishment of a new equilibrium. Metaphorically, we keep tossing more boxes onto the unicyclist's load, forcing them to reestablish balance.

In many ways, architects resemble our hapless unicyclist, constantly both balancing and adapting to changing conditions. The engineering practices of Continuous Delivery represent such a tectonic shift in the equilibrium: incorporating formerly siloed functions such as operations into the software development lifecycle enabled new perspectives on what *change* means. Enterprise architects can no longer rely on static, five-year plans because the entire software development universe will evolve in that time frame, rendering every long-term decision potentially moot.

Disruptive change is hard to predict even for savvy practitioners. The rise of containers via tools like Docker (*https://www.docker.com*) is an example of an unknowable industry shift. However, we can trace the rise of containerization via a series of small, incremental steps. Once upon a time, operating systems, application servers, and other infrastructure were commercial entities, requiring licensing and great expense. Many of the architectures designed in that era focused on efficient use of shared resources. Gradually, Linux became good enough for many enterprises, reducing the *monetary* cost of operating systems to zero. Next, DevOps practices like automatic machine provisioning via tools like Puppet (*https://puppet.com*) and Chef (*https://www.chef.io*) made Linux *operationally* free. Once the ecosystem became free and widely used, consolidation around common portable formats was inevitable: thus, Docker. But containerization couldn't have happened without all the evolutionary steps leading to that end.

The software development ecosystem constantly evolves, which leads to new architectural approaches. While many developers suspect that a cabal of architects retreat to an ivory tower to decide what the *Next Big Thing* will be, the process is much more organic. New capabilities constantly arise within our ecosystem, providing new ways to combine with existing and other new features to enable new capabilities. For example, consider the recent rise of microservices architectures. As open source operating systems became popular, combined with Continuous Delivery–driven engineering practices, enough clever architects figured out how to build more scalable systems that they eventually needed a name: thus, microservices.

Why We Didn't Have Microservices in the Year 2000

Consider an architect with a time machine who travels back in time to the year 2000 and approaches the head of operations with a new idea.

"I have a great new concept for an architecture that allows fantastic isolation between each of the capabilities—it's called *microservices*; we'll design each service around business capabilities and keep things highly decoupled."

"Great," says the head of operations. "What do you need?"

"Well, I'm going to need about 50 new computers, and of course 50 new operating system licenses, and another 20 computers to act as isolated databases, along with licenses for those. When do you think I can get all that?"

"Please leave my office."

While microservices might have seemed like a good idea even back then, the ecosystem wasn't available to support it.

A portion of an architect's job is structural design to solve particular problems—you have a problem, and you've decided that software will solve it. When considering structural design, we can partition it into two areas: the *domain (or requirements)* and *architecture characteristics*, as illustrated in Figure 1-1.

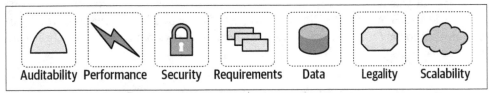

Figure 1-1. The entire scope of software architecture encompasses requirements plus architecture characteristics: the "-ilities" of software

The requirements shown in Figure 1-1 represent whatever problem domain the software solution addresses. The other parts are variously known as *architecture characteristics* (our preferred term), *nonfunctional requirements*, *system quality attributes*, *cross-cutting requirements*, and a host of other names. Regardless of the name, they represent critical capabilities required for project success, both for initial release and long-term maintainability. For example, architecture characteristics such as *scale* and *performance* may form success criteria for a market, whereas others such as *modularity* contribute to *maintainability* and *evolvability*.

Software is rarely static; it continues to evolve as teams add new features, integration points, and a host of other common changes. What architects need are protection mechanisms for architecture characteristics, similar to unit tests but focused on architecture characteristics, which change at a different rate and are sometimes subject to forces that are different from the domain. For example, technical decisions within a company may drive a database change that is independent of the domain solution.

This book describes the mechanisms and design techniques for adding the same kind of continual assurance about architectural governance that high-performing teams now have about other aspects of the software development process.

Architectural decisions are ones in which each choice offers significant trade-offs. Throughout this book, when we refer to the role of *architect*, we encompass anyone who makes architectural decisions, regardless of their title in an organization. Additionally, important architecture decisions virtually always require collaboration with other roles.

Evolutionary Architecture

Both the mechanisms for evolution and the decisions architects make when designing software derive from the following definition:

> An evolutionary software architecture supports *guided*, *incremental* change across *multiple dimensions*.

The definition consists of three parts, which we describe in more detail below.

Guided Change

Once teams have chosen important characteristics, they want to *guide* changes to the architecture to protect those characteristics. For that purpose, we borrow a concept from evolutionary computing called *fitness functions*. A fitness function is an objective function used to summarize how close a prospective design solution is to achieving the set aims. In evolutionary computing, the fitness function determines whether an algorithm has improved over time. In other words, as each variant of an algorithm is generated, the fitness functions determine how "fit" each variant is, based on how the designer of the algorithm defined "fit."

We have a similar goal in evolutionary architecture: as architecture evolves, we need mechanisms to evaluate how changes impact the important characteristics of the architecture and prevent degradation of those characteristics over time. The fitness function metaphor encompasses a variety of mechanisms we employ to ensure architecture doesn't change in undesirable ways, including metrics, tests, and other verification tools. When an architect identifies an architectural characteristic they want to protect as things evolve, they define one or more fitness functions to protect that feature.

Historically, a portion of architecture has often been viewed as a governance activity, and architects have only recently accepted the notion of enabling change through architecture. Architectural fitness functions allow decisions in the context of the organization's needs and business functions, while making the basis for those decisions explicit and testable. Evolutionary architecture is not an unconstrained, irresponsible approach to software development. Rather, it is an approach that balances the need for rapid change and the need for rigor around systems and architectural characteristics. The fitness function drives architectural decision making, guiding the architecture while allowing the changes needed to support changing business and technology environments.

We use *fitness functions* to create evolutionary guidelines for architectures; we cover them in detail in Chapter 2.

Incremental Change

Incremental change describes two aspects of software architecture: how teams build software incrementally and how they deploy it.

During development, an architecture that allows small, incremental changes is easier to evolve because developers have a smaller scope of change. For deployment, incremental change refers to the level of modularity and decoupling for business features and how they map to architecture. An example is in order.

Let's say that PenultimateWidgets, a large seller of widgets, has a catalog page backed by a microservices architecture and modern engineering practices. One of the page's features enables users to rate different widgets with star ratings. Other services within PenultimateWidgets' business also need ratings (customer service representatives, shipping provider evaluation, etc.), so they all share the star rating service. One day, the star rating team releases a new version alongside the existing one that allows half-star ratings—a small but significant upgrade. The other services that require ratings aren't required to move to the new version but to gradually migrate as convenient. Part of PenultimateWidgets' DevOps practices include architectural monitoring of not only the services but also the routes between services. When the operations group observes that no one has routed to a particular service within a given time interval, they automatically disintegrate that service from the ecosystem.

This is an example of incremental change at the architectural level: the original service can run alongside the new one as long as other services need it. Teams can migrate to new behavior at their leisure (or as need dictates), and the old version is automatically garbage collected.

Making incremental change successful requires coordination of a handful of Continuous Delivery practices. Not all of these practices are required in all cases; rather, they commonly occur together in the wild. We discuss how to achieve incremental change in Chapter 3.

Multiple Architectural Dimensions

> There are no separate systems. The world is a continuum. Where to draw a boundary around a system depends on the purpose of the discussion.
>
> —Donella H. Meadows

Classical Greek physicists gradually learned to analyze the universe based on fixed points, culminating in classical mechanics (*https://oreil.ly/jHoLH*). However, more precise instruments and more complex phenomena gradually refined that definition toward relativity in the early 20th century. Scientists realized that what they previously viewed as isolated phenomena in fact interact relative to one another. Since the 1990s, enlightened architects have increasingly viewed software architecture as multidimensional. Continuous Delivery expanded that view to encompass operations. However, software architects often focus primarily on *technical* architecture—how the software components fit together—but that is only one dimension of a software project. If architects want to create an architecture that can evolve, they must consider *all* the interconnected parts of the system that change affects. Just like we know from physics that everything is relative to everything else, architects know there are many dimensions to a software project.

To build evolvable software systems, architects must think beyond just the technical architecture. For example, if the project includes a relational database, the structure and relationship between database entities will evolve over time as well. Similarly, architects don't want to build a system that evolves in a manner that exposes a security vulnerability. These are all examples of *dimensions* of architecture—the parts of architecture that fit together in often orthogonal ways. Some dimensions fit into what are often called *architectural concerns* (the list of "-ilities" referred to earlier), but *dimensions* are actually broader, encapsulating things traditionally outside the purview of technical architecture. Each project has dimensions the architect role must consider when thinking about evolution. Here are some common dimensions that affect evolvability in modern software architectures:

Technical
> The implementation parts of the architecture: the frameworks, dependent libraries, and implementation language(s).

Data
> Database schemas, table layouts, optimization planning, and so on. The database administrator generally handles this type of architecture.

Security
> Defines security policies and guidelines, and specifies tools to help uncover deficiencies.

Operational/System
> Concerns how the architecture maps to existing physical and/or virtual infrastructure: servers, machine clusters, switches, cloud resources, and so on.

Each of these perspectives forms a *dimension* of the architecture—an intentional partitioning of the parts supporting a particular perspective. Our concept of architectural dimensions encompasses traditional architectural characteristics ("-ilities") plus any other role that contributes to building software. Each of these forms a perspective on architecture that we want to preserve as our problem evolves and the world around us changes.

When architects think in terms of architectural dimensions, it provides a mechanism by which they can analyze the evolvability of different architectures by assessing how each important dimension reacts to change. As systems become more intertwined with competing concerns (scalability, security, distribution, transactions, etc.), architects must expand the dimensions they track on projects. To build an evolvable system, architects must think about how the system might evolve across all the important dimensions.

The entire architectural scope of a project consists of the software requirements plus the other dimensions. We can use fitness functions to protect those characteristics as the architecture and the ecosystem evolve together through time, as illustrated in Figure 1-2.

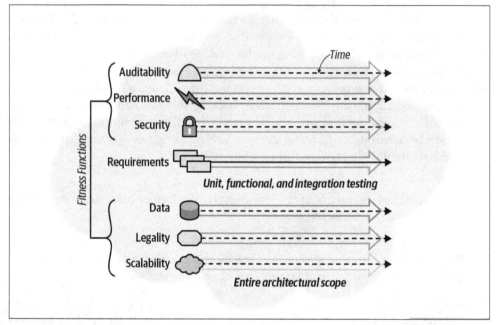

Figure 1-2. An architecture consists of requirements and other dimensions, each protected by fitness functions

In Figure 1-2, the architects have identified *auditability*, *data*, *security*, *performance*, *legality*, and *scalability* as the additional architectural characteristics important for this application. As the business requirements evolve over time, each of the architectural characteristics utilizes fitness functions to protect its integrity as well.

While the authors of this text stress the importance of a holistic view of architecture, we also realize that a large part of evolving architecture concerns technical architecture patterns and related topics like coupling and cohesion. We discuss how technical architecture coupling affects evolvability in Chapter 5 and the impacts of data coupling in Chapter 6.

Coupling applies to more than just structural elements in software projects. Many software companies have recently discovered the impact of team structure on surprising things like architecture. We discuss all aspects of coupling in software, but the team impact comes up so early and often that we need to discuss it here.

Evolutionary architecture helps answer two common questions that arise among architects in the modern software development ecosystem: *How is long-term planning possible when everything changes all the time?* and *Once I've built an architecture, how can I prevent it from degrading over time?* Let's explore these questions in more detail.

How Is Long-Term Planning Possible When Everything Changes All the Time?

The programming platforms we use exemplify constant evolution. Newer versions of a programming language offer better APIs to improve the flexibility of or applicability to new problems; newer programming languages offer a different paradigm and different set of constructs. For example, Java was introduced as a C++ replacement to ease the difficulty of writing networking code and to improve memory management issues. When we look at the past 20 years, we observe that many languages still continually evolve their APIs while totally new programming languages appear to regularly attack newer problems. The evolution of programming languages is demonstrated in Figure 1-3.

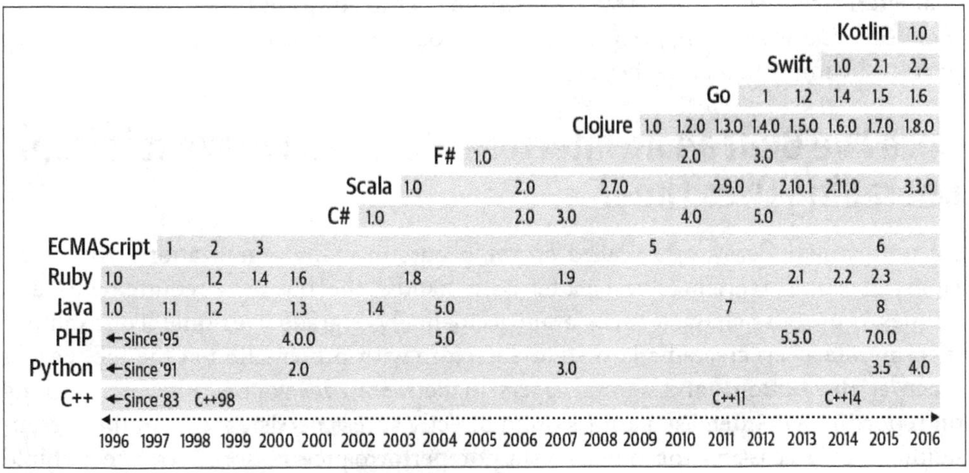

The evolution of popular programming languages, shown as a timeline from 1996 to 2016:

- **Kotlin:** 1.0
- **Swift:** 1.0, 2.1, 2.2
- **Go:** 1, 1.2, 1.4, 1.5, 1.6
- **Clojure:** 1.0, 1.2.0, 1.3.0, 1.4.0, 1.5.0, 1.6.0, 1.7.0, 1.8.0
- **F#:** 1.0, 2.0, 3.0
- **Scala:** 1.0, 2.0, 2.7.0, 2.9.0, 2.10.1, 2.11.0, 3.3.0
- **C#:** 1.0, 2.0, 3.0, 4.0, 5.0
- **ECMAScript:** 1, 2, 3, 5, 6
- **Ruby:** 1.0, 1.2, 1.4, 1.6, 1.8, 1.9, 2.1, 2.2, 2.3
- **Java:** 1.0, 1.1, 1.2, 1.3, 1.4, 5.0, 7, 8
- **PHP:** Since '95, 4.0.0, 5.0, 5.5.0, 7.0.0
- **Python:** Since '91, 2.0, 3.0, 3.5, 4.0
- **C++:** Since '83, C++98, C++11, C++14

(Years axis: 1996 1997 1998 1999 2000 2001 2002 2003 2004 2005 2006 2007 2008 2009 2010 2011 2012 2013 2014 2015 2016)

Figure 1-3. The evolution of popular programming languages

Regardless of the particular aspect of software development—the programming platform, languages, operating environment, persistence technologies, cloud offerings, and so on—we expect constant change. Although we cannot predict when changes in the technical or domain landscape will occur, or which changes will persist, we know change is inevitable. Consequently, we should architect our systems knowing the technical landscape will change.

If the ecosystem constantly changes in unexpected ways, and if predictability is impossible, what is the *alternative* to fixed plans? Enterprise architects and other developers must learn to adapt. Part of the traditional reasoning behind making long-term plans was financial; software changes were expensive. However, modern engineering practices invalidate that premise by making change less expensive through the automation of formerly manual processes and other advances such as DevOps.

For years, many smart developers recognized that some parts of their systems were harder to modify than others. That's why *software architecture* is defined as "the parts that are hard to change later." This convenient definition partitioned the things you *can* modify without much effort from truly difficult changes. Unfortunately, this definition also evolved into a blind spot when thinking about architecture: developers' assumption that change is difficult becomes a self-fulfilling prophecy.

Several years ago, some innovative software architects revisited the "hard to change later" problem: what if we build changeability *into* the architecture? In other words, if *ease of change* is a bedrock principle of the architecture, then change is no longer difficult. Building evolvability into architecture in turn allows a whole new set of behaviors to emerge, upsetting the dynamic equilibrium again.

Even if the ecosystem doesn't change, what about the gradual erosion of architectural characteristics that occurs? Architects design architectures but then expose them to the messy real world of *implementing* things atop the architecture. How can architects protect the important parts they have defined?

Once I've Built an Architecture, How Can I Prevent It from Degrading Over Time?

An unfortunate decay, often called *bit rot*, occurs in many organizations. Architects choose particular architectural patterns to handle the business requirements and "-ilities," but those characteristics often accidentally degrade over time. For example, if an architect has created a layered architecture with presentation at the top, persistence at the bottom, and several layers in between, developers who are working on reporting will often ask permission to directly access persistence from the presentation layer, bypassing the other layers, for performance reasons. Architects build layers to isolate change. Developers then bypass those layers, increasing coupling and invalidating the reasoning behind the layers.

Once they have defined the important architectural characteristics, how can architects *protect* those characteristics to ensure they don't erode? Adding *evolvability* as an architectural characteristic implies protecting the other characteristics as the system evolves. For example, if an architect has designed an architecture for scalability, they don't want that characteristic to degrade as the system evolves. Thus, *evolvability* is a meta-characteristic, an architectural wrapper that protects all the other architectural characteristics.

The mechanism of evolutionary architecture heavily overlaps with the concerns and goals of architectural governance—defined principles around design, quality, security, and other quality concerns. This book illustrates the many ways that evolutionary architecture approaches enable automating architectural governance.

Why Evolutionary?

A common question about evolutionary architecture concerns the name itself: why call it *evolutionary* architecture and not something else? Other possible terms include *incremental, continual, agile, reactive*, and *emergent*, to name just a few. But each of these terms misses the mark. The definition of evolutionary architecture that we state here includes two critical characteristics: incremental and guided.

The terms *continual, agile*, and *emergent* all capture the notion of change over time, which is clearly a critical characteristic of an evolutionary architecture, but none of these terms explicitly captures any notion of *how* an architecture changes or what the desired end-state architecture might be. While all the terms imply a changing environment, none of them covers what the architecture should look like. The *guided* part of our definition reflects the architecture we want to achieve—our end goal.

We prefer the word *evolutionary* over *adaptable* because we are interested in architectures that undergo fundamental evolutionary change, not ones that have been patched and adapted into increasingly incomprehensible accidental complexity. *Adapting* implies finding some way to make something work regardless of the elegance or longevity of the solution. To build architectures that truly evolve, architects must support genuine change, not jury-rigged solutions. Going back to our biological metaphor, *evolutionary* concerns the process of having a system that is fit for purpose and can survive the ever-changing environment in which it operates. Systems may have individual adaptations, but as architects, we should care about the overall evolvable system.

Another useful comparison architects can make is between *evolutionary architecture* and *emergent design*, and why there is not such a thing as an "emergent architecture." One common misconception about agile software development is the alleged lack of architecture: "Let's just start coding and the architecture will emerge as we go." However, this depends on how simple the problem is. Consider a physical building. If you need to build a dog house, you don't need an architecture; you can go to the hardware store and buy lumber and bang it together. If, on the other hand, you need to build a 50-floor office building, architecture is definitely required! Similarly, if you are building a simple catalog system for a small number of users, you likely don't need a lot of up-front planning. However, if you are designing a software system that needs strict performance for a large number of users, planning is necessary! The purpose of agile architecture isn't *no* architecture; it's *no useless* architecture: don't go through bureaucratic processes that don't add value to the software development process.

Another complicating factor in software architecture is the different types of essential complexity architects must design for. When evaluating trade-offs, it's often not the easy *simple* versus *complex* system distinction but rather systems that are complex in different ways. In other words, each system has a unique set of criteria for success. While we discuss architectural styles such as microservices, each style is a starting point for a complex system that grows to look like no other.

Similarly, if an architect builds a very simple system, they can afford to pay little attention to architectural concerns. However, sophisticated systems require purposeful design, and they need a starting point. *Emergence* suggests that you can start with nothing, whereas architecture provides the scaffolding or structure for all the other parts of the system; something must be in place to begin.

The concept of *emergence* also implies that teams can slowly crescendo their design toward the ideal architectural solution. However, like building architecture, there is no perfect architecture, only different ways architects deal with trade-offs. Architects can implement most problems in a wide variety of different architecture styles and be successful. However, some of them will fit the problem better, offering less resistance and fewer workarounds.

One key to evolutionary architecture is the balance between how much structure and governance is necessary to support long-term goals and needless formality and friction.

Summary

Useful software systems aren't static. They must grow and change as the problem domain changes and the ecosystem evolves, providing new capabilities and complexities. Architects and developers can gracefully evolve software systems, but they must understand both the necessary engineering practices to make that happen and how best to structure their architecture to facilitate change.

Architects are also tasked with governing the software they design, along with many of the development practices used to build it. Fortunately, the mechanisms we uncover to allow easier evolution also provide ways to automate important software governance activities. We take a deep dive into the mechanics of how to make this happen in the next chapter.

CHAPTER 2

Fitness Functions

The mechanics of evolutionary architecture cover the tools and techniques developers and architects use to build systems that can evolve. An important gear in that machinery is the protection mechanism called a *fitness function*, the architectural equivalent of a unit test for the domain part of an application. This chapter defines fitness functions and explains the categories and usage of this important building block.

> An evolutionary architecture supports *guided*, incremental change across multiple dimensions.

As noted in our definition, the word *guided* indicates that some objective exists that architecture should move toward or exhibit. We borrow a concept from evolutionary computing called fitness functions, which are used in genetic algorithm design to define success.

Evolutionary computing includes a number of mechanisms that allow a solution to gradually emerge via mutation—small changes in each generation of the software. The evolutionary computing world defines a number of types of mutations. For example, one mutation is called a *roulette mutation*: if the algorithm utilizes constants, this mutation will choose new numbers as if from a roulette wheel in a casino. For example, suppose a developer is designing a genetic algorithm to solve the traveling salesperson problem (*https://oreil.ly/jtqHZ*) to find the shortest route between a number of cities. If the developer notices that smaller numbers supplied by the roulette mutation yield better results, they may build a fitness function to guide the "decision" during mutation. Thus, fitness functions are used to evaluate how close a solution is to ideal.

What Is a Fitness Function?

We borrow this concept of fitness functions from the evolutionary computing world to define an architectural fitness function:

> An architectural fitness function is any mechanism that provides an objective integrity assessment of some architectural characteristic(s).

Architectural fitness functions form the primary mechanisms for implementing evolutionary architecture.

As the *domain* part of our solution evolves, teams have developed a wide variety of tools and techniques to manage integrating new features without breaking existing ones: unit, functional, and user acceptance testing. In fact, most companies bigger than a certain size have an entire department dedicated to managing domain evolution, called *quality assurance*: ensuring that existing functionality isn't negatively affected by changes.

Thus, well-functioning teams have mechanisms for managing evolutionary change to the problem domain: adding new features, changing behaviors, and so on. The domain is typically written in a fairly coherent technology stack: *Java*, *.NET*, or a host of other platforms. Thus, teams can download and use testing libraries suited to their combination of technology stacks.

Fitness functions are to architecture characteristics as unit tests are to the domain. However, teams cannot download a single tool for the wide variety of validations possible for architecture characteristics. Rather, fitness functions encompass a wide variety of tools in different parts of the ecosystem, depending on the architecture characteristics the team is governing, as illustrated in Figure 2-1.

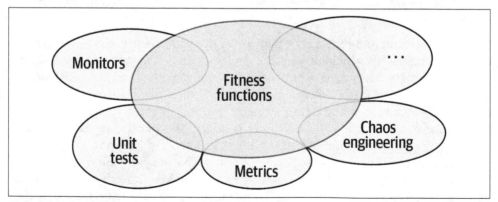

Figure 2-1. Fitness functions encompass a wide variety of tools and techniques

As shown in Figure 2-1, architects can use many different tools to define fitness functions:

Monitors

DevOps and operational tools such as monitors allow teams to verify concerns such as performance, scalability, and so on.

Code metrics

Architects can embed metrics checks and other verifications within unit tests to validate a wide variety of architecture concerns, including design criteria (many examples follow in Chapter 4).

Chaos engineering

This recently developed branch of engineering practices artificially stresses remote environments by injecting faults to force teams to build resiliency into their systems.

Architecture testing frameworks

In recent years, testing frameworks dedicated to testing architecture structure have appeared, allowing architects to encode a wide variety of validations into automated tests.

Security scanning

Security—even if supervised by another part of the organization—affects design decisions that architects make and thus falls under the umbrella of concerns that architects want to govern.

Before we define the categories of fitness functions and other factors, an example will help make the concept less abstract. The *component cycle* is a common antipattern across all platforms with components. Consider the three components in Figure 2-2.

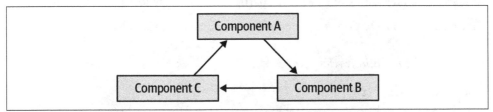

Figure 2-2. A cycle exists when components have a cyclic dependency

Architects consider the cyclic dependency shown in Figure 2-2 an antipattern because it presents difficulties when a developer tries to reuse one of the components—each of the entangled components must also come along. Thus, in general, architects want to keep the number of cycles low. However, the universe is actively fighting the architect's desire to prevent this problem via convenience tools. What happens when a developer references a class whose namespace/package they haven't referenced yet in a modern IDE? It pops up an auto-import dialog to automatically import the necessary package.

Developers are so accustomed to this affordance that they swat it away as a reflex action, never actually paying attention. Most of the time, auto-importing is a great convenience that doesn't cause any problems. However, once in a while, it creates a component cycle. How do architects prevent this?

Consider the set of packages illustrated in Figure 2-3.

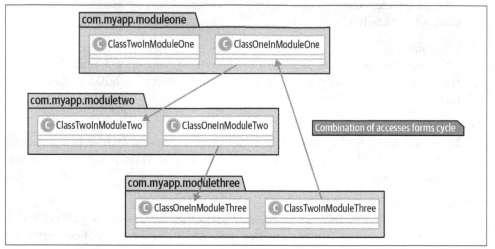

Figure 2-3. Component cycles represented as packages in Java

ArchUnit (*https://www.archunit.org*) is a testing tool inspired by (and using some of the facilities of) JUnit, but it's used to test various architecture features, including validations to check for cycles within a particular scope, as illustrated in Figure 2-3.

An example of how to prevent cycles using ArchUnit appears in Example 2-1.

Example 2-1. Preventing cycles using ArchUnit

```
public class CycleTest {
    @Test
    public void test_for_cycles() {
        slices().
          matching("com.myapp.(*)..").
          should().beFreeOfCycles()
    }
}
```

In this example, the testing tool "understands" cycles. An architect who wants to prevent cycles from gradually appearing in their codebase can wire this testing into a continuous build process and never have to worry about cycles again. We will show more examples of using ArchUnit and similar tools in Chapter 4.

We first define fitness functions more rigorously, and then examine conceptually how they guide the evolution of the architecture.

Don't mistake the *function* part of our definition as implying that architects must express all fitness functions in code. Mathematically speaking, a function takes an input from some allowed set of input values and produces an output in some allowed set of output values. In software, we also generally use the term *function* to refer to something implementable in code. However, as with acceptance criteria in agile software development, the fitness functions for evolutionary architecture may not be implementable in software (e.g., a required manual process for regulatory reasons). An architectural fitness function is an *objective* measure, but architects may implement that measure in a wide variety of ways.

As discussed in Chapter 1, real-world architecture consists of many different dimensions, including requirements around performance, reliability, security, operability, coding standards, and integration, to name a few. We want a fitness function to represent each requirement for the architecture, requiring us to find (and sometimes create) ways to measure things we want to govern. We'll look at a few examples and then consider the different kinds of functions more broadly.

Performance requirements make good use of fitness functions. Consider a requirement that all service calls must respond within 100 ms. We can implement a test (i.e., fitness function) that measures the response to a service request and fails if the result is greater than 100 ms. To this end, every new service should have a corresponding performance test added to its test suite (you'll learn more about triggering fitness functions in Chapter 3). Performance is also a good example of the vast number of ways architects can think about common measures. For example, *performance* may suggest request/response timing, as measured by a mentoring tool, or another metric such as *first contentful paint*, a mobile device performance metric provided by Lighthouse (*https://oreil.ly/7EHeZ*). The purpose of a performance fitness function is not to measure *all* types of performance but ones that architects deem important for governance.

Fitness functions also can be used to maintain coding standards. A common code metric is cyclomatic complexity (*https://oreil.ly/rYeYV*), a measure of function or method complexity available for all structured programming languages. An architect may set a threshold for an upper value, guarded by a unit test running in continuous integration, using one of the many tools available to evaluate that metric.

Despite need, developers cannot always implement some fitness functions completely because of complexity or other constraints. Consider something like a failover for a database from a hard failure. While the recovery itself might be fully automated (and should be), triggering the test itself is likely best done manually. Additionally, it might be far more efficient to determine the success of the test manually, although developers should still encourage scripts and automation.

These examples highlight the myriad forms that fitness functions can take, the immediate response to failure of a fitness function, and even when and how developers might run them. While we can't necessarily run a single script and say "our architecture currently has a composite fitness score of 42," we can have precise and unambiguous conversations about the state of the architecture. We can also entertain discussions about the changes that might occur on the architecture's fitness.

Finally, when we say an evolutionary architecture is guided by the fitness function, we mean we evaluate individual architectural choices against the individual and the system-wide fitness functions to determine the impact of the change. The fitness functions collectively denote what matters to us in our architecture, allowing us to make the kinds of trade-off decisions that are both crucial and vexing during the development of software systems.

You may think, "Wait! We've been running code metrics as part of continuous integration for years—this isn't new!" You would be correct: the idea of validating parts of software as part of an automated process is as old as automation. However, we formerly considered all the different architecture verification mechanisms as separate—code quality versus DevOps metrics versus security, and so on. Fitness functions unify many existing concepts into a single mechanism, allowing architects to think in a uniform way about many existing (often ad hoc) "nonfunctional requirements" tests. Collecting important architecture thresholds and requirements as fitness functions allows for a more concrete representation for previously fuzzy, subjective evaluation criteria. We leverage a large number of existing mechanisms to build fitness functions, including traditional testing, monitoring, and other tools. Not all tests are fitness functions, but some tests are—if the test helps verify the integrity of architectural concerns, we consider it a fitness function.

Categories

Fitness functions exist across a variety of categories related to their scope, cadence, result, invocation, proactivity, and coverage.

Scope: Atomic Versus Holistic

Atomic fitness functions run against a singular context and exercise one particular aspect of the architecture. An excellent example of an atomic fitness function is a unit test that verifies some architectural characteristic, such as modular coupling (we show an example of this type of fitness function in Chapter 4). Thus, some application-level testing falls under the heading of fitness functions, but not all unit tests serve as fitness functions—only the ones that verify architecture characteristic(s). The example in Figure 2-3 represents an *atomic* fitness function: it checks only for the presence of cycles between components.

For some architectural characteristics, developers must test more than each architectural dimension in isolation. *Holistic* fitness functions run against a shared context and exercise a combination of architectural aspects. Developers design holistic fitness functions to ensure that combined features that work atomically don't break in real-world combinations. For example, imagine an architecture has fitness functions around both security and scalability. One of the key items the security fitness function checks is staleness of data, and a key item for the scalability tests is number of concurrent users within a certain latency range. To achieve scalability, developers implement caching, which allows the atomic scalability fitness function to pass. When caching isn't turned on, the security fitness function passes. However, when run holistically, enabling caching makes data too stale to pass the security fitness function, and the holistic test fails.

We obviously cannot test every possible combination of architecture elements, so architects use holistic fitness functions selectively to test important interactions. This selectivity and prioritization also allows architects and developers to assess the difficulty in implementing a particular testing scenario, thus allowing an assessment of how valuable that characteristic is. Frequently, the interactions between architectural concerns determine the quality of the architecture, which holistic fitness functions address.

Cadence: Triggered Versus Continual Versus Temporal

Execution cadence is another distinguishing factor between fitness functions. *Triggered* fitness functions run based on a particular event, such as a developer executing a unit test, a deployment pipeline running unit tests, or a QA person performing exploratory testing. This encompasses traditional testing, such as unit, functional, and behavior-driven development (BDD) testing, among others.

Continual tests don't run on a schedule but instead execute constant verification of architectural aspect(s), such as transaction speed. For example, consider a microservices architecture in which the architects want to build a fitness function around transaction time—how long it takes for a transaction to complete, on average. Building any kind of triggered test provides sparse information about real-world behavior. Thus, architects build a continual fitness function that simulates a transaction in production while all the other real transactions run, often using a technique called synthetic transactions. This allows developers to verify behavior and gather real data about the system "in the wild."

Synthetic Transactions

How do teams measure complex, real-world interactions between services in a microservices architecture? One common technique employs *synthetic transactions*. For this practice, requests into the system have a flag that indicates that a particular transaction may be synthetic. It follows exactly the normal course of interactions in the architecture (often tracked via a correlation ID for forensic analysis) until the last step, where the system evaluates the flag and doesn't commit the transaction as a real one. This allows architects and DevOps to learn exactly how their complex system performs.

No advice about synthetic transactions is complete without mentioning the tale of hundreds of appliances showing up accidentally because someone forgot to flip the "synthetic" flag, which can itself be governed by a fitness function—make sure that any fitness function identified as a synthetic transaction (e.g., via an annotation) has the flag set.

Notice that using a monitoring tool does not imply that you have a fitness function, which must have *objective outcomes*. Rather, using a monitoring tool *in which the architect has created an alarm for deviations outside the objective measure of the metric* converts the mere use of monitors into a fitness function.

Monitoring-driven development (MDD) (*https://oreil.ly/2fPIe*) is another testing technique gaining popularity. Rather than relying solely on tests to verify system results, MDD uses monitors in production to assess both technical and business health. These continual fitness functions are necessarily more dynamic than standard triggered tests and fall into the broader category called *fitness function-driven architecture*, discussed in more detail in Chapter 7.

While most fitness functions trigger either on change or continually, in some cases architects may want to build a time component into assessing fitness, leading to a *temporal* fitness function. For example, if a project uses an encryption library, the architect may want to create a temporal fitness function as a reminder to check if important updates have been performed. Another common use of this type of fitness function is a *break upon upgrade* test. In platforms like Ruby on Rails, some developers can't wait for the tantalizing new features coming in the next release, so they add a feature to the current version via a *back port*, a custom implementation of a future feature. Problems arise when the project finally upgrades to the new version because the back port is often incompatible with the "real" version. Developers use *break upon upgrade* tests to wrap back-ported features to force re-evaluation when the upgrade occurs.

Another common use of a temporal fitness function comes from an important but not urgent requirement that arises on virtually every project eventually. Many developers have experienced the pain of upgrading more than one major version number of a core framework or library their project depends upon—so many changes occur between major point releases, it's often quite difficult to leap versions. However, upgrading a core framework is time-consuming and not deemed as critical, making it more likely to accidentally slip too far behind. Architects can use a temporal fitness function in conjunction with a tool like Dependabot (*https://github.com/dependabot*) or snyk (*https://snyk.io*), which tracks releases, versions, and security patches for software, to create increasingly insistent reminders to upgrade once the corporate criteria (e.g., first patch release) have been met.

Case Study: Triggered or Continuous?

Often the choice of *continuous* versus *triggered* fitness function comes down to trade-offs between the approaches. Many developers in distributed systems such as microservices want the same kind of dependency check but on allowed communication between services rather than cycles. Consider the set of services illustrated in Figure 2-4, a more advanced version of the cyclic dependency fitness function shown in Figure 2-3.

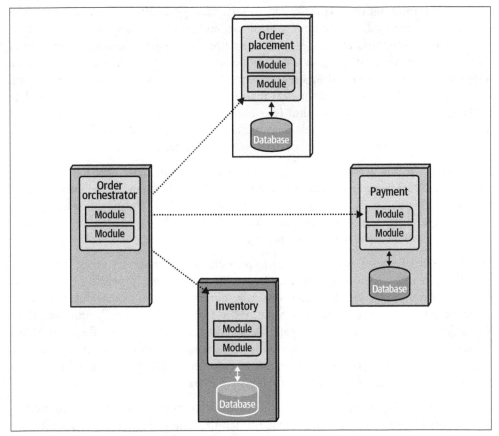

Figure 2-4. Set of orchestrated microservices, where communication should not exist between nonorchestrator services

In Figure 2-4, the architect has designed the system so that the orchestrator service contains the state of the workflow. If any of the services communicates with each other, bypassing the orchestrator, the team won't have accurate information about the workflow state.

In the case of dependency cycles, metrics tools exist to allow architects to do compile-time checks. However, services aren't constrained to a single platform or technology stack, making it highly unlikely that someone has already built a tool that exactly matches a particular architecture. This is an example of what we alluded to earlier—often, architects must build their own tools rather than rely on third parties. For this particular system, the architect can build either a *continuous* or a *triggered* fitness function.

In the continuous case, the architect must ensure that each of the services provides monitoring information (typically via a particular port) that broadcasts who the service calls during the course of workflows. Either the orchestrator service or a utility service monitors those messages to ensure that illegal communication doesn't occur. Alternatively, rather than using monitors, the team could use asynchronous message queues, have each domain service publish a message to the queue indicating collaboration messages, and allow the orchestrator to listen to that queue and validate collaborators. This fitness function is continuous because the receiving service can react immediately to disallowed communication. For example, perhaps this fault indicates a security concern or other detrimental side effect.

The benefit of this version of the fitness function is immediate reaction: architects and other interested parties know immediately when governance has been violated. However, this solution adds runtime overhead: monitors and/or message queues require operation resources, and this level of observability may have a negative impact on performance, scalability, and so on.

Alternatively, the team may decide to implement a triggered version of this fitness function. In this case, on a regular cadence, the deployment pipeline calls a fitness function that harvests logfiles and investigates communication to determine if it is all appropriate. We show an implementation of this fitness function in "Communication Governance in Microservices" on page 66. The benefit of this fitness function is lack of possible runtime impact—it runs only when triggered and looks at log records. However, teams shouldn't use a triggered version for critical governance issues such as security where the time lag may have negative impacts.

As in all things in software architecture, the decision between triggered and continuous fitness functions will often provide different trade-offs, making this a case-by-case decision.

Result: Static Versus Dynamic

Static fitness functions have a fixed result, such as the binary *pass/fail* of a unit test. This type encompasses any fitness function that has a predefined desirable value: binary, a number range, set inclusion, and so on. Metrics are often used for fitness functions. For example, an architect may define acceptable ranges for average cyclomatic complexity of methods in the codebase.

Dynamic fitness functions rely on a shifting definition based on extra context, often real-time content. For example, consider a fitness function to verify scalability along with request/response responsiveness for a number of users. As the number of concurrent users rises, the architects will allow responsiveness to degrade slightly, but they don't want it to degrade past the point where it will become a problem. Thus, a responsiveness fitness function will take into account the number of concurrent users and adjust the evaluation accordingly.

Notice that *dynamic* and *objective* do not conflict—fitness functions must evaluate to an objective outcome, but that evaluation may be based on dynamic information.

Invocation: Automated Versus Manual

Architects like automated things—part of incremental change includes automation, which we delve into deeply in Chapter 3. Thus, it's not surprising that developers will execute most fitness functions within an automated context: continuous integration, deployment pipelines, and so on. Indeed, developers and DevOps have performed a tremendous amount of work under the auspices of Continuous Delivery to automate many parts of the software development ecosystem previously thought impossible.

However, as much as we'd like to automate every single aspect of software development, some parts of software development resist automation. Sometimes architects cannot automate away a critical dimension within a system, such as legal requirements or exploratory testing, which leads to manual fitness functions. Similarly, a project may have aspirations to become more evolutionary but not yet have appropriate engineering practices in place. For example, perhaps most QA is still manual on a particular project and must remain so for the near future. In both of these cases (and others), we need *manual* fitness functions that are verified by a person-based process.

The path to better efficiency eliminates as many manual steps as possible, but many projects still require manual procedures. We still define fitness functions for those characteristics and verify them using manual stages in deployment pipelines (covered in more detail in Chapter 3).

Proactivity: Intentional Versus Emergent

While architects will define most fitness functions at project inception as they elucidate the characteristics of the architecture, some fitness functions will emerge during development of the system. Architects never know all the important parts of the architecture at the beginning (the classic *unknown unknowns* problem we address in Chapter 7), and thus must identify fitness functions as the system evolves. Architects write *intentional* fitness functions at project inception and as part of a formal governance process, sometimes in collaboration with other architect roles such as enterprise architects.

Fitness functions not only verify the initial assumptions by architects on projects, but they also provide ongoing governance. Thus, it's common for architects to notice some behavior that would benefit from better governance, leading to an *emergent* fitness function. Architects should keep a wary eye open for misbehavior in a project, especially those that can be verified via fitness functions, and add them aggressively.

These two sometimes form a spectrum, beginning as intentional protection for some aspect but evolving into a more nuanced or even different fitness function over time. Just like unit tests, fitness functions become part of the team's codebase. Thus, as architectural requirements change and evolve, the corresponding fitness functions must change similarly.

Coverage: Domain-Specific Fitness Functions?

We are sometimes asked if some particular problem domains tend toward certain architectural fitness functions. While nothing is impossible in software architecture and you might use the same automated testing framework to implement some fitness functions, generally fitness functions are used only for abstract architectural principles, not with the problem domain. What we see in practice if you use the same test automation tools is a separation of tests. One set of tests will focus on testing domain logic (e.g., traditional unit or end-to-end tests) and another set of tests on fitness functions (e.g., performance or scalability tests).

This separation is utilitarian to avoid duplication and misguided effort. Remember, fitness functions are another verification mechanism in projects and are meant to coexist alongside other (domain) verifications. To avoid duplicating efforts, teams are wise to keep fitness functions to pure architecture concerns and allow the other verifications to handle domain issues. For example, consider *elasticity*, which describes a website's ability to handle sudden bursts of users. Notice that we can talk about elasticity in purely architectural terms—the website in question could be a gaming site, a catalog site, or a streaming movie site. Thus, this part of the architecture is governed by a fitness function. In contrast, if a team needed to verify something like a change of address, that requires domain knowledge and would fall to traditional verification mechanisms. Architects can use this as a litmus test to determine where the verification responsibility lies.

Thus, even within common domains (such as finance), it is difficult to predict a standard set of fitness functions. What each team ultimately views as important and valuable varies to an annoyingly wide degree between teams and projects.

Who Writes Fitness Functions?

Fitness functions represent the architectural analog to unit tests and should be treated similarly in terms of development and engineering practices. In general, architects write fitness functions as they determine the objective measures for important architecture characteristics. Both architects and developers maintain the fitness functions, including preserving a passing state at all times—passing fitness functions are an objective measure of an architecture's fitness.

Architects *must* collaborate with developers in the definition and understanding of both the purpose and utility of fitness functions, which add an extra layer of verification to the overall quality of the system. As such, they will occasionally fail as changes violate governance rules—a good thing! However, developers must understand the purpose of the fitness function so that they can repair the fault and continue the build process. Collaboration between the two roles is critical so that developers don't misunderstand the governance as a burden rather than a useful constraint to preserve important features.

 Keep knowledge of key and relevant fitness functions alive by posting the results of executing fitness functions somewhere visible or in a shared space so that developers remember to consider them in day-to-day coding.

Where Is My Fitness Function Testing Framework?

For testing the problem domain, developers have a wide variety of *platform-specific* tools because the domain is purposefully written in a particular platform/technology stack. For example, if the primary language is Java, developers can choose from a wide array of unit, functional, user acceptance, and other testing tools and frameworks. Consequently, architects look for the same level of "turnkey" support for architecture fitness functions—which generally doesn't exist. We cover a few easy-to-download-and-run fitness function tools in Chapter 4, but such tools are sparse compared to domain testing libraries. This is due mostly to the highly varied nature of fitness functions, as illustrated in Figure 2-1: operational fitness functions require monitoring tools, security fitness functions require scanning tools, quality checks require code-level metrics, and so on. In many cases, a particular tool doesn't exist for your particular blend of architectural forces. However, as we illustrate in future chapters, architects can use a bit of programming "glue" to compose useful fitness functions with little effort, just not as little as downloading a prebuilt framework.

Outcomes Versus Implementations

It is important for architects to focus on the outcomes—the objective measures for architecture characteristics—rather than implementation details. Architects often write fitness functions in technology stacks other than the main domain platform, or utilize DevOps tools or any other convenient process that enables them to objectively measure something of interest. The important metaphorical analogy with *function* in the term *fitness function* implies something that takes inputs and produces outputs without side effects. Similarly, a fitness function measures an *outcome*—an objective evaluation of some architecture characteristic.

Throughout the book, we show examples of fitness function implementations, but it is important for readers to focus on the outcome and *why* we measure something rather than *how* an architect makes a particular measurement.

PenultimateWidgets and the Enterprise Architecture Spreadsheet

When the architects for PenultimateWidgets decided to build a new project platform, they first created a spreadsheet of all the desirable characteristics: scalability, security, resiliency, and a host of other "-ilities." But then they faced an age-old question: if they built the new architecture to support those features, how can they ensure it maintains that support? As developers add new features, how would they keep unexpected degradation of these important characteristics from occurring?

The solution was to create fitness functions for each of the concerns in the spreadsheet, reformulating some of them to meet objective evaluation criteria. Rather than occasional, ad hoc verification of their important criteria, they wired the fitness functions into their deployment pipeline (discussed more fully in Chapter 3).

Although software architects are interested in exploring evolutionary architectures, we aren't attempting to model biological evolution. Theoretically, we could build an architecture that randomly changed one of its bits (mutation) and redeployed itself. After a few million years, we would likely have a very interesting architecture. However, we don't have millions of years to wait.

We want our architecture to evolve in a guided way, so we place constraints on different aspects of the architecture to rein in undesirable evolutionary directions. A good example is dog breeding: by selecting the characteristics we want, we can create a vast number of differently shaped canines in a relatively short amount of time.

We can also think about the *system-wide fitness function* as a collection of fitness functions with each function corresponding to one or more dimensions of the architecture. Using a system-wide fitness function aids our understanding of necessary trade-offs when individual elements of the fitness function conflict with one another. As is common with multifunction optimization problems, we might find it impossible to optimize all values simultaneously, forcing us to make choices. For example, in the case of architectural fitness functions, issues like performance might conflict with security due to the cost of encryption. This is a classic example of the bane of architects everywhere—the *trade-off*. Trade-offs dominate much of an architect's headaches during the struggle to reconcile opposing forces, such as scalability and performance. However, architects have a perpetual problem of comparing these different characteristics because they fundamentally differ (an apples to oranges comparison) and all stakeholders believe their concern is paramount. System-wide fitness functions allow architects to think about divergent concerns using the same unifying mechanism of fitness functions, capturing and preserving the important architectural characteristics. The relationship between the system-wide fitness function and its constituent smaller fitness functions is illustrated in Figure 2-5.

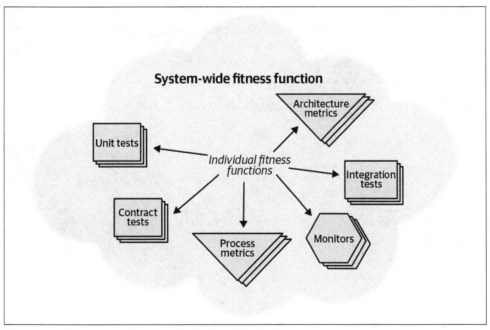

Figure 2-5. System-wide versus individual fitness functions

The system-wide fitness function is crucial for an architecture to be evolutionary, as we need some basis to allow architects to compare and evaluate architectural characteristics against one another. Unlike with the more directed fitness functions, architects likely will never try to "evaluate" the system-wide fitness function. Rather, it provides guidelines for prioritizing decisions about the architecture in the future. While fitness functions may not help resolve the trade-off, they help architects more clearly understand the forces at play, with objective measures, so that they can reason about the necessary system-wide trade-offs.

> A system is never the sum of its parts. It is the product of the interactions of its parts.
>
> —Dr. Russel Ackoff

Without guidance, evolutionary architecture becomes simply reactionary architecture. Thus, for architects, a crucial early architectural decision for any system is to define important dimensions such as scalability, performance, security, data schemas, and so on. Conceptually, this allows architects to weigh the importance of a fitness function based on its importance to the system's overall behavior.

Summary

The original seed of the idea of applying fitness functions to software architecture occurred to Rebecca when she realized she could use some of her experience derived from another technical domain (evolutionary computing) and apply it to software: fitness functions. Architects have verified parts of architecture forever, but they haven't previously unified all the different verification techniques into a single overarching concept. Treating all these different governance tools and techniques as fitness functions allows teams to unify around execution.

We cover more aspects of operationalizing fitness functions in the next chapter.

CHAPTER 3

Engineering Incremental Change

In 2010, Jez Humble and Dave Farley released *Continuous Delivery* (*http://continuous delivery.com*), a collection of practices to enhance engineering efficiency in software projects. They provided the *mechanism* for building and releasing software via automation and tools but not the *structure* of how to design evolvable software. Evolutionary architecture assumes these engineering practices as being prerequisites but addresses how to utilize them to help design evolvable software.

Our definition of evolutionary architecture is one that supports guided, incremental change across multiple dimensions. By incremental change, we mean the architecture should facilitate change through a series of small changes. This chapter describes architectures that support incremental change along with some of the engineering practices used to achieve incremental change, an important building block of evolutionary architecture. We discuss two aspects of incremental change: *development*, which covers how developers build software, and *operational*, which covers how teams deploy software.

This chapter covers the characteristics, engineering practices, team considerations, and other aspects of building architectures that support incremental change.

Incremental Change

Here is an example of the operational side of incremental change. We start with the fleshed-out example of incremental change from Chapter 1, which includes additional details about the architecture and deployment environment. PenultimateWidgets, our seller of widgets, has a catalog page backed by a microservices architecture and engineering practices, as illustrated in Figure 3-1.

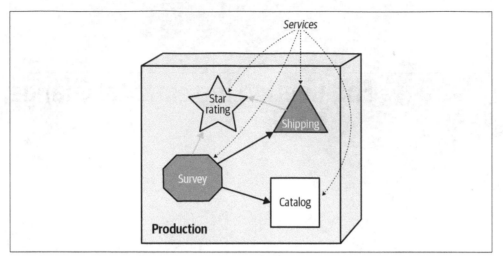

Figure 3-1. Initial configuration of PenultimateWidgets' component deployment

PenultimateWidgets' architects have implemented microservices that are operationally isolated from other services. Microservices implement a *share nothing* architecture: each service is operationally distinct to eliminate technical coupling and therefore promote change at a granular level. PenultimateWidgets deploys all its services in separate containers to trivialize operational changes.

The website allows users to rate different widgets with star ratings. But other parts of the architecture also need ratings (customer service representatives, shipping provider evaluation, etc.), so they all share the star rating service. One day, the star rating team releases a new version alongside the existing one that allows half-star ratings—a significant upgrade, as shown in Figure 3-2.

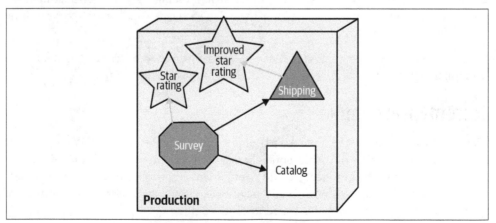

Figure 3-2. Deploying with an improved star rating service showing the addition of the half-star rating

The services that utilize ratings aren't required to migrate to the improved rating service but can gradually transition to the better service when convenient. As time progresses, more parts of the ecosystem that need ratings move to the enhanced version. One of PenultimateWidgets' DevOps practices is architectural monitoring—monitoring not only the services but also the routes between services. When the operations group observes that no one has routed to a particular service within a given time interval, they automatically disintegrate that service from the ecosystem, as shown in Figure 3-3.

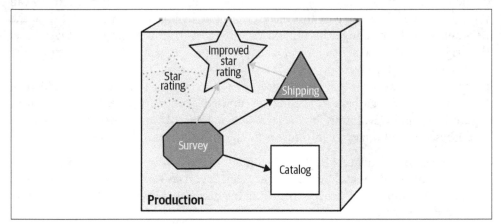

Figure 3-3. All services now use the improved star rating service

The mechanical ability to evolve is one of the key components of an evolutionary architecture. Let's dig one level deeper in the abstraction above.

PenultimateWidgets has a fine-grained microservices architecture, where each service is deployed using a container—such as Docker (*https://www.docker.com*)—and using a service template to handle infrastructure coupling. Applications within Penultima-teWidgets consist of routes between instances of running services—a given service may have multiple instances to handle operational concerns like on-demand scalability. This allows architects to host different versions of services in production and control access via routing. When a deployment pipeline deploys a service, it registers itself (location and contract) with a service discovery tool. When a service needs to find another service, it uses the discovery tool to learn the location and version suitability via the contract.

When the new star rating service is deployed, it registers itself with the service discovery tool and publishes its new contract. The new version of the service supports a broader range of values—specifically, half-point values—than the original. That means the service developers don't have to worry about restricting the supported values. If the new version requires a different contract for callers, it is typical to handle that within the service rather than burden callers with resolving which version to call. We cover that contract strategy in "Version Services Internally" on page 171.

When the team deploys the new service, they don't want to force the calling services to upgrade to the new service immediately. Thus, the architect temporarily changes the star-service endpoint into a proxy that checks to see which version of the service is requested and routes to the requested version. No existing services must change to use the rating service as they always have, but new calls can start taking advantage of the new capability. Old services aren't forced to upgrade and can continue to call the original service as long as they need it. As the calling services decide to use the new behavior, they change the version they request from the endpoint. Over time, the original version falls into disuse, and at some point, the architect can remove the old version from the endpoint when it is no longer needed. Operations is responsible for scanning for services that no other services call anymore (within some reasonable threshold) and for garbage collecting the unused services. The example shown in Figure 3-3 shows evolution in the abstract; a tool that implements this style of cloud-based evolutionary architecture is Swabbie (*https://oreil.ly/WvKxj*).

All the changes to this architecture, including the provisioning of external components such as the database, happen under the supervision of a deployment pipeline, removing the responsibility of coordinating the disparate moving parts of the deployment from DevOps.

Once they have defined fitness functions, architects must ensure that they are evaluated in a timely manner. Automation is the key to continual evaluation. A *deployment pipeline* is often used to evaluate tasks like this. Using a deployment pipeline, architects can define which, when, and how often fitness functions execute.

Deployment Pipelines

Continuous Delivery describes the deployment pipeline mechanism. Similar to a continuous integration server, a deployment pipeline "listens" for changes, then runs a series of verification steps, each with increasing sophistication. Continuous Delivery practices encourage using a deployment pipeline as the mechanism to automate common project tasks, such as testing, machine provisioning, deployments, and so forth. Open source tools such as GoCD (*https://www.go.cd*) facilitate building these deployment pipelines.

Continuous Integration Versus Deployment Pipelines

Continuous integration is a well-known engineering practice in agile projects that encourages developers to integrate as early and as often as possible. To facilitate continuous integration, tools such as ThoughtWorks CruiseControl (*http://cruisecontrol.sourceforge.net*), Jenkins (*https://www.jenkins.io*), and other commercial and open

---

source offerings have emerged. Continuous integration provides an "official" build location, and developers enjoy the concept of a single mechanism to ensure working code. However, a continuous integration server also provides a perfect time and place to perform common project tasks such as unit testing, code coverage, metrics, functional testing, and…fitness functions! For many projects, the continuous integration server includes a list of tasks to perform whose successful culmination indicates build success. Large projects eventually build an impressive list of tasks.

Deployment pipelines encourage developers to split individual tasks into *stages*. A deployment pipeline includes the concept of multistage builds, allowing developers to model as many post–check-in tasks as necessary. This ability to separate tasks discretely supports the broader mandates expected of a deployment pipeline—to verify production readiness—compared to a continuous integration server primarily focused on integration. Thus, a deployment pipeline commonly includes application testing at multiple levels, automated environment provisioning, and a host of other verification responsibilities.

Some developers try to "get by" with a continuous integration server but soon find they lack the level of separation of tasks and feedback necessary.

A typical deployment pipeline automatically builds the deployment environment (a container like Docker (*https://www.docker.com*) or a bespoke environment generated by a tool like Puppet (*https://puppet.com*), or Chef (*https://www.chef.io/chef*)) as shown in Figure 3-4.

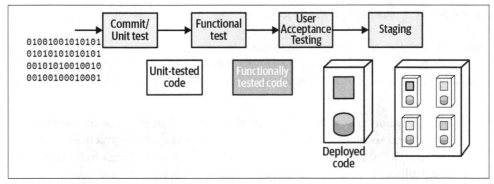

Figure 3-4. Deployment pipeline stages

By building the deployment image that the deployment pipeline executes, developers and operations have a high degree of confidence: the host computer (or virtual machine) is declaratively defined, and it's a common practice to rebuild it from nothing.

The deployment pipeline also offers an ideal way to execute the fitness functions defined for an architecture: it applies arbitrary verification criteria, has multiple stages to incorporate differing levels of abstraction and sophistication of tests, and runs every single time the system changes in any way. A deployment pipeline with fitness functions added is shown in Figure 3-5.

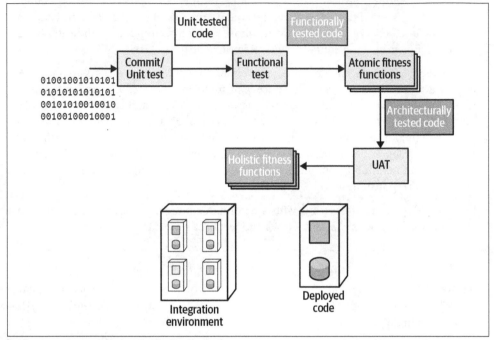

Figure 3-5. A deployment pipeline with fitness functions added as stages

Figure 3-5 shows a collection of atomic and holistic fitness functions, with the latter in a more complex integration environment. Deployment pipelines can ensure the rules defined to protect architectural dimensions execute each time the system changes.

In Chapter 2, we described PenultimateWidgets' spreadsheet of requirements. Once the team adopted some of the Continuous Delivery engineering practices, they realized that the architecture characteristics for the platform work better in an automated deployment pipeline. To that end, service developers created a deployment pipeline to validate the fitness functions created both by the enterprise architects and by the service team. Now, each time the team makes a change to the service, a barrage of tests validate both the correctness of the code and its overall fitness within the architecture.

Another common practice in evolutionary architecture projects is continuous deployment—using a deployment pipeline to put changes into production contingent on successfully passing the pipeline's gauntlet of tests and other verifications. While continuous deployment is ideal, it requires sophisticated coordination: developers must ensure changes deployed to production on an ongoing basis don't break things.

To solve this coordination problem, a *fan-out* operation is commonly used in deployment pipelines in which the pipeline runs several jobs in parallel, as shown in Figure 3-6.

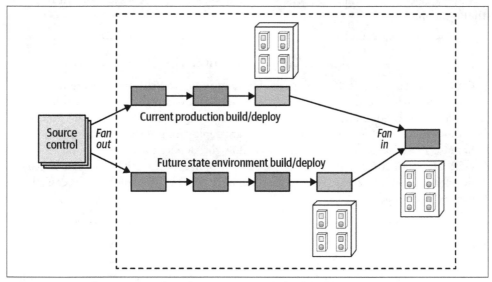

Figure 3-6. Deployment pipeline fan-out to test multiple scenarios

As shown in Figure 3-6, when a team makes a change, they have to verify two things: they haven't negatively affected the current production state (because a successful deployment pipeline execution will deploy code into production) and their changes were successful (affecting the future state environment). A deployment pipeline fan-out allows tasks (testing, deployment, etc.) to execute in parallel, saving time. Once the series of concurrent jobs illustrated in Figure 3-6 completes, the pipeline can evaluate the results and, if everything is successful, perform a *fan-in*, consolidating to a single thread of action to perform tasks like deployment. Note that the deployment pipeline may perform this combination of *fan-out* and *fan-in* numerous times whenever the team needs to evaluate a change in multiple contexts.

Another common issue with continuous deployment is business impact. Users don't want a barrage of new features showing up on a regular basis and would rather have them staged in a more traditional way, such as in a "Big Bang" deployment. A common way to accommodate both continuous deployment and staged releases is to use feature toggles (*https://oreil.ly/0sMvU*). A feature toggle is typically a condition in code that enables or disables a feature, or switches between two implementations (e.g., new and old). The simplest implementation of a feature toggle is an if-statement that inspects an environment variable or configuration value and shows or hides a feature based on the value of that environment variable. You also can have more complex feature toggles that provide the ability to reload configurations and enable or disable features at runtime. By implementing code behind feature toggles, developers can safely deploy new changes to production without worrying that users see their changes prematurely. In fact, many teams performing continuous deployment utilize feature toggles so that they can separate operationalizing new features from releasing them to consumers.

QA in Production

One beneficial side effect of habitually building new features using feature toggles is the ability to perform QA tasks in production. Many companies don't realize they can use their production environment for exploratory testing. Once a team becomes comfortable using feature toggles, they can deploy those changes to production because most feature toggle frameworks allow developers to route users based on a wide variety of criteria (IP address, access control list [ACL], etc.). If a team deploys new features within feature toggles to which only the QA department has access, they can test in production.

Using deployment pipelines in engineering practices, architects can easily apply project fitness functions. Figuring out which stages are needed is a common challenge for developers designing a deployment pipeline. However, once the fitness functions inside a deployment pipeline are in place, architects and developers have a high level of confidence that evolutionary changes won't violate the project guidelines. Architectural concerns are often poorly elucidated and sparsely evaluated, often subjectively; creating them as fitness functions allows better rigor and therefore better confidence in the engineering practices.

Case Study: Adding Fitness Functions to PenultimateWidgets' Invoicing Service

Our exemplar company, PenultimateWidgets, has an architecture that includes a service to handle invoicing. The invoicing team wants to replace outdated libraries and approaches but wants to ensure these changes don't impact other teams' ability to integrate with them.

The invoicing team identified the following needs:

Scalability
    While performance isn't a big concern for PenultimateWidgets, the company handles invoicing details for several resellers, so the invoicing service must maintain availability service-level agreements.

Integration with other services

Several other services in the PenultimateWidgets ecosystem use invoicing. The team wants to make sure integration points don't break while making internal changes.

Security

Invoicing means money, and security is an ongoing concern.

Auditability

Some state regulations require that changes to taxation code be verified by an independent accountant.

The invoicing team uses a continuous integration server and recently upgraded to on-demand provisioning of the environment that runs their code. To implement evolutionary architecture fitness functions, they implement a deployment pipeline to replace the continuous integration server, allowing them to create several stages of execution, as shown in Figure 3-7.

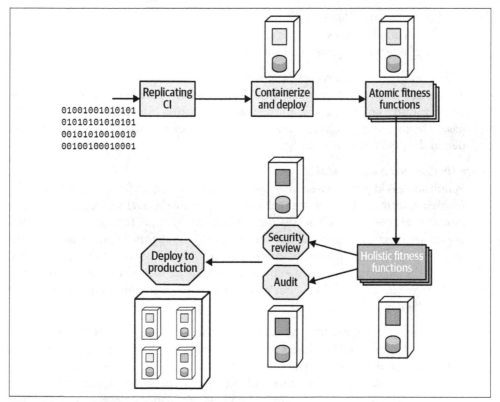

Figure 3-7. PenultimateWidgets' deployment pipeline

PenultimateWidgets' deployment pipeline consists of six stages:

Stage 1: Replicate CI
The first stage replicates the behavior of the former CI server, running unit and functional tests.

Stage 2: Containerize and deploy
Developers use the second stage to build containers for their service, allowing deeper levels of testing, including deploying the containers to a dynamically created test environment.

Stage 3: Execute atomic fitness functions
In the third stage, atomic fitness functions, including automated scalability tests and security penetration testing, are executed. This stage also runs a metrics tool that flags any code within a certain package that developers changed, pertaining to auditability. While this tool doesn't make any determinations, it assists a later stage in narrowing in on specific code.

Stage 4: Execute holistic fitness functions
The fourth stage focuses on holistic fitness functions, including testing contracts to protect integration points and some further scalability tests.

Stage 5a: Conduct a security review (manual)
This stage includes a manual stage by a specific security group within the organization to review, audit, and assess any security vulnerabilities in the codebase. Deployment pipelines allow the definition of manual stages, triggered on demand by the relevant security specialist.

Stage 5b: Conduct audits (manual)
PenultimateWidgets is based in a state that mandates specific auditing rules. The invoicing team builds this manual stage into their deployment pipeline, which offers several benefits. First, treating auditing as a fitness function allows developers, architects, auditors, and others to think about this behavior in a unified way—a necessary evaluation to determine the system's correct function. Second, adding the evaluation to the deployment pipeline allows developers to assess the engineering impact of this behavior compared to other automated evaluations within the deployment pipeline.

For example, if the security review happens weekly but auditing happens only monthly, the bottleneck to faster releases is clearly the auditing stage. By treating both security and audit as stages in the deployment pipeline, decisions concerning both can be addressed more rationally: Is it of value to the company to increase release cadence by having consultants perform the necessary audit more often?

Stage 6: Deploy

The last stage is deployment into the production environment. This is an auto-mated stage for PenultimateWidgets and is triggered only if the two upstream manual stages (*security review* and *audit*) report success.

Interested architects at PenultimateWidgets receive an automatically generated report each week about the success/failure rate of the fitness functions, helping them gauge health, cadence, and other factors.

Case Study: Validating API Consistency in an Automated Build

PenultimateWidgets architects have designed an API encapsulating the internal com-plexity of their accounting systems into a cleaner interface that the remainder of the company (and partner companies) use. Because they have many integration consum-ers, when rolling out changes they want to be careful not to create inconsistencies or breakages with previous versions.

To that end, the architects designed the deployment pipeline shown in Figure 3-8.

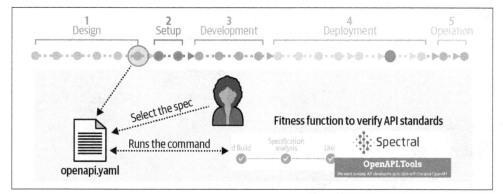

Figure 3-8. A consistency fitness function as part of a deployment pipeline

In Figure 3-8, the five stages of the deployment pipeline are:

Stage 1: Design

Design artifacts, including new and changed entries for the integration API.

Stage 2: Setup

Set up the operational tasks required to run the rest of the tests and other verifications in the deployment pipeline, including tasks such as containerization and database migrations.

Stage 3: Development

Develop the testing environment for unit, functional, and user acceptance test-ing, as well as architectural fitness functions.

Stage 4: Deployment
> If all upstream tasks were successful, deploy to production under a feature toggle that controls the exposure of new features to users.

Stage 5: Operation
> Maintain continuous fitness functions and other monitors.

In the case of API changes, the architects designed a multipart fitness function. Stage 1 of the verification chain starts with the design and definition of the new API, published in *openapi.yaml*. The team verifies the structure and other aspects of the new specification using Spectral (*https://oreil.ly/SHsZo*) and OpenAPI.Tools (*https://openapi.tools*).

The next stage in the deployment pipeline appears at the start of the development phase, illustrated in Figure 3-9.

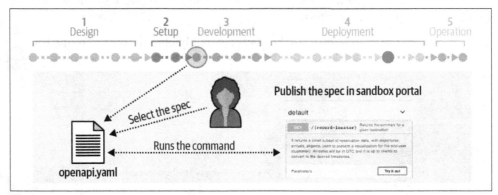

Figure 3-9. Second stage of consistency verification

In Stage 2, shown in Figure 3-9, the deployment pipeline selects the new specification and publishes it to a sandbox environment to allow testing. Once the sandbox environment is live, the deployment pipeline runs a series of unit and functional tests to verify the changes. This stage verifies that the applications underlying the APIs still function consistently.

Stage 3, shown in Figure 3-10, tests integration architecture concerns using Pact (*https://docs.pact.io*), a tool that allows cross-service integration testing to ensure integration points are preserved, an implementation of a common concept known as consumer-driven contracts.

Consumer-driven contracts (*https://oreil.ly/syKlD*), which are atomic integration architecture fitness functions, are a common practice in microservices architectures. Consider the illustration shown in Figure 3-11.

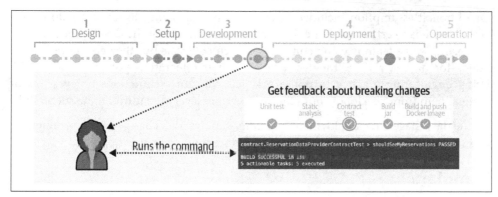

Figure 3-10. Third stage of consistency verification, for integration architecture

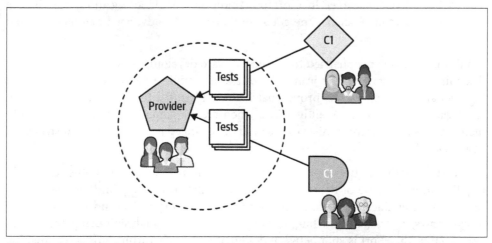

Figure 3-11. Consumer-driven contracts use tests to establish contracts between a provider and consumer(s)

In Figure 3-11, the *provider* team is supplying information (typically data in a lightweight format like JSON) to each of the consumers, *C1* and *C2*. In consumer-driven contracts, the consumers of information put together a suite of tests that encapsulate what they need from the provider and hand off those tests to the provider, who promises to keep the tests passing at all times. Because the tests cover the information needed by the consumer, the provider can evolve in any way that doesn't break these fitness functions. In the scenario shown in Figure 3-11, the *provider* runs tests on behalf of all three consumers in addition to their own suite of tests. Using fitness functions like this is informally known as an *engineering safety net*. Maintaining integration protocol consistency shouldn't be done manually when it is easy to build fitness functions to handle this chore.

One implicit assumption included in the incremental change aspect of evolutionary architecture is a certain level of engineering maturity among the development teams. For example, if a team is using consumer-driven contracts but they also have broken builds for days at a time, they can't be sure their integration points are still valid. Using engineering practice to police practices via fitness functions relieves lots of manual pain from developers but requires a certain level of maturity to be successful.

In the last stage, the deployment pipeline deploys the changes into production, allowing A/B testing and other verification before it officially goes live.

Summary

A couple of us worked in engineering disciplines outside software, such as Neal, who started his university career in the more traditional engineering discipline. Before switching to computer science, he got a good dose of the advanced mathematics that structural engineers use.

Traditionally, many people tried to equate software development to other engineering disciplines. For example, the *waterfall process* of complete design up front followed by mechanical assembly has proved particularly ill-suited to software development. Another question that frequently arises: when are we going to get the same kind of mathematics in software, similar to the kind of advanced math they have in structural engineering?

We don't think that software *engineering* will rely on math as much as other engineering disciplines because of the distinct differences between *design* and *manufacturing*. In structural engineering, manufacturing is intensely expensive and unforgiving of design flaws, necessitating a huge catalog of predictive analysis during the design phase. Thus, the effort is split between design and manufacturing. Software, however, has a completely different balance. Manufacturing in software equals compilation and deployment, activities that we have increasingly learned to automate. Thus, in software, virtually all the effort lies with design, not manufacturing; design encompasses coding and virtually every other thing we think of as "software development."

However, the things we manufacture are also vastly different. Modern software consists of thousands or millions of moving parts, all of which can be changed virtually arbitrarily. Fortunately, teams can make that design change and virtually instantly redeploy (in essence, remanufacture) the system.

The keys to a true software engineering discipline lie in incremental change with automated verification. Because our manufacturing is essentially free but extremely variable, the secret to sanity in software development lies with confidence in making changes, backed up by automated verification—incremental change.

CHAPTER 4

Automating Architectural Governance

Architects are tasked with designing the structure of software systems as well as defining many of the development and engineering practices. However, another important job for architects is *governing* aspects of the building of software, including design principles, good practices, and identified pitfalls to avoid.

Traditionally, architects had few tools to allow them to enforce their governance policies outside manual code reviews, architecture review boards, and other inefficient means. However, with the advent of automated fitness functions, we provide architects with new sets of capabilities. In this chapter, we describe how architects can use the fitness functions created to evolve software to also create automated governance policies.

Fitness Functions as Architectural Governance

The idea that led to this book was the metaphorical mash-up between software architecture and practices from the development of genetic algorithms described in Chapter 2, focusing on the core idea of how architects can create software projects that successfully evolve rather than degrade over time. The results of that initial idea blossomed into the myriad ways we describe fitness functions and their application.

However, while it wasn't part of the original conception, we realized that the mechanics of evolutionary architecture heavily overlap *architectural governance*, especially the idea of *automating* governance, which itself represents the evolution of software engineering practices.

In the early 1990s, Kent Beck led a group of forward-looking developers who uncovered one of the driving forces of software engineering advances in the last three decades. He and the developers worked on the C3 project (whose domain isn't important). The team was well versed in the current trends in software development processes but were unimpressed—it seemed that none of the processes that were popular at the time yielded any kind of consistent success. Thus, Kent started the idea of eXtreme Programming (XP) (*http://www.extremeprogramming.org*): based on past experience, the team took things they knew worked well and did them in the most extreme way. For example, their collective experience was that projects that have higher test coverage tended to have higher-quality code, which led them to evangelize test-driven development, which guarantees that all code is tested because the tests precede the code.

One of their key observations revolved around integration. At that time, a common practice on most software projects was to conduct an *integration phase*. Developers were expected to code in isolation for weeks or months at a time, then merge their changes during an integration phase. In fact, many version control tools popular at that time forced this isolation at the developer level. The practice of an integration phase was based on the many manufacturing metaphors often misapplied to software. The XP developers noted a correlation from past projects that more frequent integration led to fewer issues, which led them to create continuous integration: every developer commits to the main line of development at least once a day.

What continuous integration and many of the other XP practices illustrated is the power of automation and incremental change. Teams that use continuous integration not only spend less time performing merge tasks regularly, they spend less time overall. When teams use continuous integration, merge conflicts arise and are resolved as quickly as they appear, at least once a day. Projects using a final integration phase allow the combinatorial mass of merge conflicts to grow into a Big Ball of Mud, which they must untangle at the end of the project.

Automation isn't important only for integration; it is also an optimizing force for engineering. Before continuous integration, teams required developers to spend time performing a manual task (integration and merging) over and over; continuous integration (and its associated cadence) automated most of that pain away.

We relearned the benefits of automation in the early 2000s during the DevOps revolution. Teams ran around the operations center installing operating systems, applying patches, and performing other manual tasks, allowing important problems to fall through the cracks. With the advent of automated machine provisioning via tools such as Puppet (*https://puppet.com*) and Chef (*https://oreil.ly/jGABa*), teams can automate infrastructure and enforce consistency.

In many organizations, we observed the same ineffective manual practices recurring with architecture: architects were attempting to perform governance checks via code reviews, architecture review boards, and other manual, bureaucratic processes—and important things fell through the cracks. By tying fitness functions to continuous integration, architects can convert metrics and other governance checks into a regularly applied integrity validation.

In many ways, the marriage of fitness functions and incremental change via continuous integration represents the evolution of engineering practices. Just as teams utilized incremental change for integration and DevOps, we increasingly see the same principles applied to architecture governance.

Fitness functions exist for every facet of architecture, from low-level, code-based analysis up to enterprise architecture. We organize our examples of automating architectural governance in the same manner, starting from the code level, then extending through the software development stack. We cover a number of fitness functions; the illustration in Figure 4-1 provides a road map.

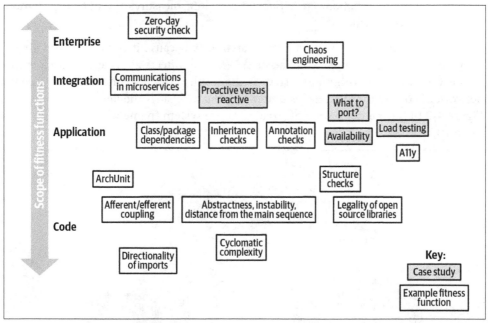

Figure 4-1. Overview of fitness functions

We start at the bottom of the map in Figure 4-1 with code-based fitness functions and make our way gradually to the top.

Code-Based Fitness Functions

Software architects have a fair amount of envy for other engineering disciplines that have built up numerous analysis techniques for predicting how their designs will function. We don't (yet) have anywhere near the level of depth and sophistication of engineering mathematics, especially about architectural analysis.

However, we do have a few tools that architects can use, generally based on code-level metrics. The next few sections highlight some metrics that illustrate something of interest in architecture.

Afferent and Efferent Coupling

In 1979, Edward Yourdon and Larry Constantine published *Structured Design: Fundamentals of a Discipline of Computer Program and Systems Design* (Prentice-Hall), defining many core concepts, including the metrics afferent and efferent coupling. *Afferent* coupling measures the number of *incoming* connections to a code artifact (component, class, function, etc.). *Efferent* coupling measures the *outgoing* connections to other code artifacts.

Coupling in architecture is of interest to architects because it constrains and affects so many other architecture characteristics. When architects allow any component to connect to any other with no governance, the result is often a codebase with a dense network of connections that defies understanding. Consider the illustration shown in Figure 4-2 of the metrics output of a real software system (name withheld for obvious reasons).

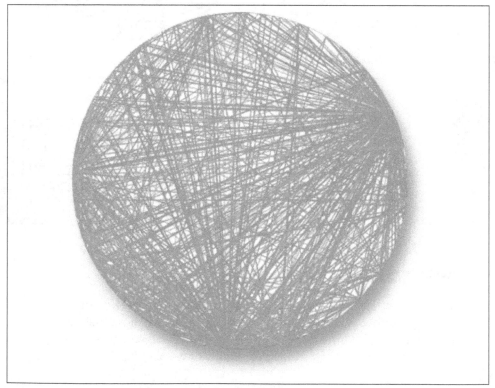

Figure 4-2. Component-level coupling in a Big-Ball-of-Mud architecture

In Figure 4-2, components appear on the perimeter as single dots, and connectivity between components appears as lines, where the boldness of the line indicates the strength of the connection. This is an example of a dysfunctional codebase—changes in any component may ripple out to many other components.

Virtually every platform has tools that allow architects to analyze the coupling characteristics of code in order to assist in restructuring, migrating, or understanding a codebase. Many tools exist for various platforms that provide a matrix view of class and/or component relationships, as illustrated in Figure 4-3.

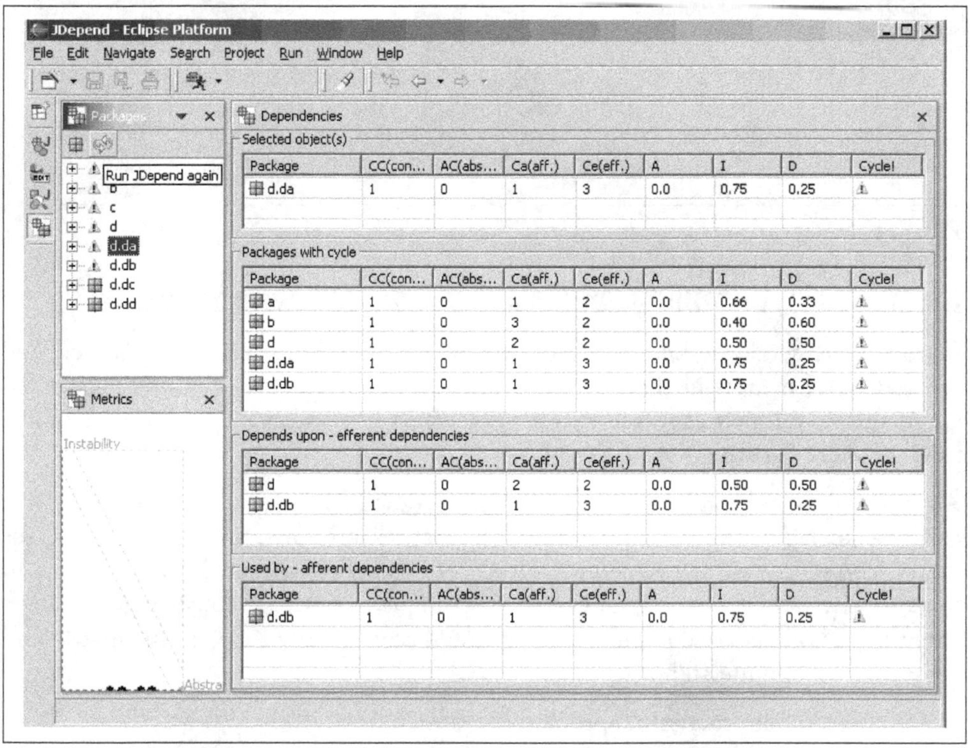

JDepend - Eclipse Platform

File Edit Navigate Search Project Run Window Help

Packages

- Run JDepend again
- b
- c
- d
- d.da
- d.db
- d.dc
- d.dd

Metrics

Instability

Dependencies

Selected object(s)

Package	CC(con...	AC(abs...	Ca(aff.)	Ce(eff.)	A	I	D	Cycle!
d.da	1	0	1	3	0.0	0.75	0.25	

Packages with cycle

Package	CC(con...	AC(abs...	Ca(aff.)	Ce(eff.)	A	I	D	Cycle!
a	1	0	1	2	0.0	0.66	0.33	
b	1	0	3	2	0.0	0.40	0.60	
d	1	0	2	2	0.0	0.50	0.50	
d.da	1	0	1	3	0.0	0.75	0.25	
d.db	1	0	1	3	0.0	0.75	0.25	

Depends upon - efferent dependencies

Package	CC(con...	AC(abs...	Ca(aff.)	Ce(eff.)	A	I	D	Cycle!
d	1	0	2	2	0.0	0.50	0.50	
d.db	1	0	1	3	0.0	0.75	0.25	

Used by - afferent dependencies

Package	CC(con...	AC(abs...	Ca(aff.)	Ce(eff.)	A	I	D	Cycle!
d.db	1	0	1	3	0.0	0.75	0.25	

Abstra

Figure 4-3. JDepend in Eclipse analysis view of coupling relationships

In Figure 4-3, the Eclipse plug-in provides a tabular view of the output of JDepend, which includes coupling analysis per package, along with some aggregate metrics highlighted in the next section.

A number of other tools provide this metric and many of the others we discuss. Notably, IntelliJ (*https://www.jetbrains.com/idea*) for Java, Sonar Qube (*https://www.sonarqube.org*), JArchitect (*https://www.jarchitect.com*), and others, based on your preferred platform or technology stack. For example, IntelliJ includes a structure dependency matrix showing a variety of coupling characteristics, as illustrated in Figure 4-4.

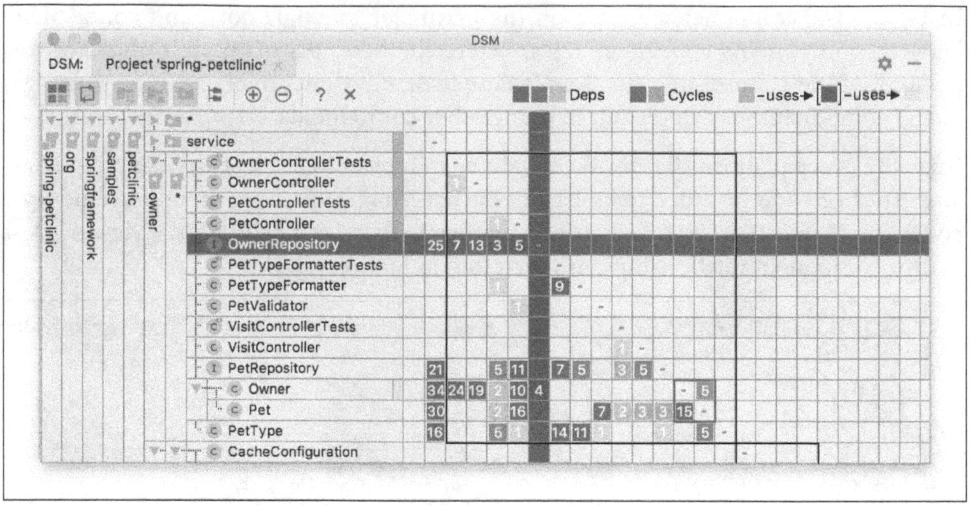

Figure 4-4. Dependency structure matrix from IntelliJ

Abstractness, Instability, and Distance from the Main Sequence

Robert Martin, a well-known figure in the software architecture world, created some derived metrics in the late 1990s which are applicable to any object-oriented language. These metrics—abstractness and instability—measure the balance of the internal characteristics of a codebase.

Abstractness is the ratio of abstract artifacts (abstract classes, interfaces, etc.) to concrete artifacts (implementation classes). It represents a measure of *abstract* versus *implementation*. Abstract elements are features of a codebase that allow developers to better understand the overall function. For example, a codebase consisting of a single `main()` method and 10,000 lines of code would score nearly zero on this metric and be quite hard to understand.

The formula for abstractness appears in Equation 4-1.

Equation 4-1. Abstractness

$$A = \frac{\Sigma\, m_a}{\Sigma\, m_c + \Sigma\, m_a}$$

In the equation, m_a represents *abstract* elements (interfaces or abstract classes) within the codebase, and m_c represents *concrete* elements. Architects calculate *abstractness* by calculating the ratio of the sum of abstract artifacts to the sum of the concrete ones.

Another derived metric, *instability*, is the ratio of efferent coupling to the sum of both efferent and afferent coupling, shown in Equation 4-2.

Equation 4-2. Instability

$$I = \frac{C_e}{C_e + C_a}$$

In the equation, C_e represents *efferent* (or outgoing) coupling, and C_a represents *afferent* (or incoming) coupling.

The *instability* metric determines the volatility of a codebase. A codebase that exhibits high degrees of instability breaks more easily when changed because of high coupling. Consider two scenarios, each with C_a of 2. In the first scenario, $C_e = 0$, yielding an instability score of zero. In the second scenario, $C_e = 3$, yielding an instability score of 3/5. Thus, the measure of instability for a component reflects how many potential changes might be forced by changes to related components. A component with an instability value near 1 is highly unstable, and a value close to 0 may be either stable or rigid: it is stable if the module or component contains mostly abstract elements and rigid if it is composed of mostly concrete elements. However, the trade-off for high stability is lack of reuse—if every component is self-contained, duplication is likely.

A component with an I value close to 1, we can agree, is highly instable. However, a component with an I value close to 0 may be either stable or rigid. However, if it contains mostly concrete elements, it is rigid.

Thus, in general, it is important to look at the values of I and A together rather than in isolation; they are combined in the next metric, *distance from the main sequence*.

One of the few holistic metrics architects have for architectural structure is *normalized distance from the main sequence*, a derived metric based on *instability* and *abstractness*, shown in Equation 4-3.

Equation 4-3. Normalized distance from the main sequence

$$D = |A + I - 1|$$

In the equation, $A = abstractness$ and $I = instability$.

The *normalized distance from the main sequence* metric imagines an ideal relationship between abstractness and instability; components that fall near this idealized line exhibit a healthy mixture of these two competing concerns. For example, graphing a particular component allows developers to calculate the *distance from the main sequence* metric, illustrated in Figure 4-5.

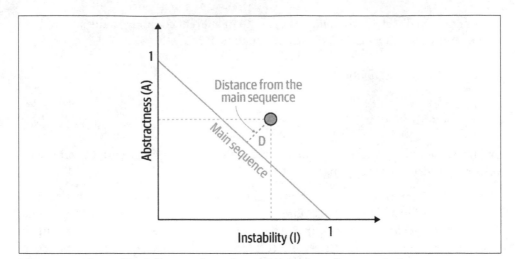

Figure 4-5. Normalized distance from the main sequence for a particular component

In Figure 4-5, developers graph the candidate component, then measure the distance from the idealized line. The closer to the line, the better balanced the component. Components that fall too far into the upper-right corner enter into what architects call the *zone of uselessness*: code that is too abstract becomes difficult to use. Conversely, code that falls into the lower-left corner enters the *zone of pain*: code with too much implementation and not enough abstraction becomes brittle and hard to maintain, as illustrated in Figure 4-6.

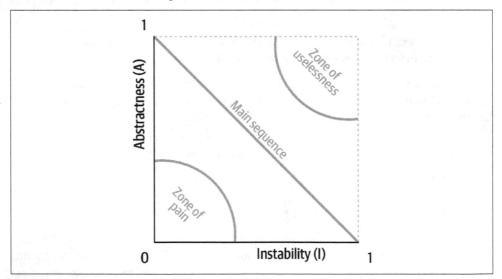

Figure 4-6. Zones of uselessness and pain

This kind of analysis is useful for architects for either evaluation (e.g., to migrate from one architecture style to another) or to set up as a fitness function. Consider the screenshot shown in Figure 4-7, using the commercial tool NDepend (*https:// www.ndepend.com*) applied to the NUnit open source testing tool (*https://nunit.org*).

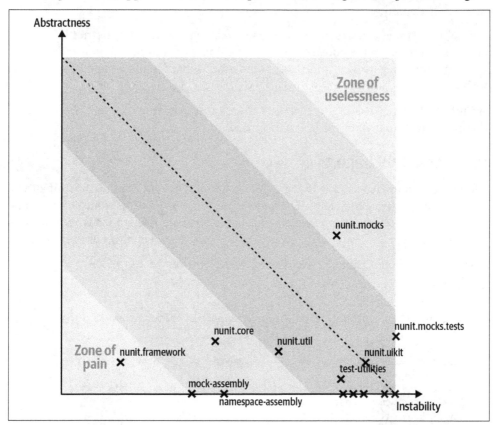

Figure 4-7. NDepend output for distance from the main sequence for the NUnit testing library

In Figure 4-7, the output illustrates that most of the code falls near the *main sequence* line. The mocks components are tending toward the *zone of uselessness*: too much abstractness and instability. That makes sense for a set of mocking components, which tend to use indirection to achieve their results. More worrying, the framework code has slipped into the *zone of pain*: too little abstractness and instability. What does this code look like? Many overly large methods without enough reuse.

How can an architect pull the troublesome code back toward the main sequence line? By using refactoring tools in an IDE: find the large methods that drive this measure and start extracting parts to increase abstractness. As you perform this exercise, you will find duplication among the extracted code, allowing you to remove it and improve instability.

Before performing a restructuring exercise, architects should use metrics like this to analyze and improve the codebase prior to moving it. Just as in building architecture, moving something with an unstable foundation is harder than moving something with a solid one.

Architects also can use this metric as a fitness function to make sure the codebase doesn't degrade to this degree in the first place.

Directionality of Imports

Closely related to the example in Figure 2-3, teams should govern the directionality of imports. In the Java ecosystem, JDepend (*https://oreil.ly/6fYd2*) is a metrics tool that analyzes the coupling characteristics of packages. Because JDepend is written in Java, it has an API that developers can leverage to build their own analysis via unit tests.

Consider the fitness function in Example 4-1, expressed as a JUnit test (*http://junit.org*).

Example 4-1. JDepend test to verify the directionality of package imports

```
public void testMatch() {
    DependencyConstraint constraint = new DependencyConstraint();

    JavaPackage persistence = constraint.addPackage("com.xyz.persistence");
    JavaPackage web = constraint.addPackage("com.xyz.web");
    JavaPackage util = constraint.addPackage("com.xyz.util");

    persistence.dependsUpon(util);
    web.dependsUpon(util);

    jdepend.analyze();

    assertEquals("Dependency mismatch",
            true, jdepend.dependencyMatch(constraint));
}
```

In Example 4-1, we define the packages in our application and then define the rules about imports. If a developer accidentally writes code that imports into util from persistence, this unit test will fail before the code is committed. We prefer building unit tests to catch architecture violations over using strict development guidelines (with the attendant bureaucratic scolding): it allows developers to focus more on the domain problem and less on plumbing concerns. More importantly, it allows architects to consolidate rules as executable artifacts.

Cyclomatic Complexity and "Herding" Governance

A common code metric is cyclomatic complexity, a measure of function or method complexity available for all structured programming languages, that has been around for decades.

An obvious measurable aspect of code is complexity, defined by the *cyclomatic complexity* metric.

Cyclomatic complexity (CC) (*https://oreil.ly/mAHFZ*) is a code-level metric designed to provide an object measure for the complexity of code, at the function/method, class, or application level, developed by Thomas McCabe Sr. in 1976.

It is computed by applying graph theory to code, specifically decision points, which cause different execution paths. For example, if a function has no decision statements (such as if statements), then CC = 1. If the function had a single conditional, then CC = 2 because two possible execution paths exist.

The formula for calculating the cyclomatic complexity for a single function or method is $CC = E - N + 2$, where N represents *nodes* (lines of code) and E represents *edges* (possible decisions). Consider the C-like code shown in Example 4-2.

Example 4-2. Sample code for cyclomatic complexity evaluation

```
public void decision(int c1, int c2) {
    if (c1 < 100)
        return 0;
    else if (c1 + C2 > 500)
        return 1;
    else
        return -1;
}
```

The cyclomatic complexity for Example 4-2 is 3 (=3 − 2 + 2); the graph appears in Figure 4-8.

The number 2 appearing in the cyclomatic complexity formula represents a simplification for a single function/method. For fan-out calls to other methods (known as *connected components* in graph theory), the more general formula is $CC = E - N + 2P$, where P represents the number of connected components.

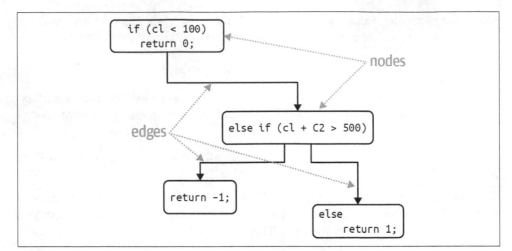

Figure 4-8. Cyclomatic complexity for the decision function

Architects and developers universally agree that overly complex code represents code smell; it harms virtually every one of the desirable characteristics of codebases: modularity, testability, deployability, and so on. Yet, if teams don't keep an eye on gradually growing complexity, that complexity will dominate the codebase.

What's a Good Value for Cyclomatic Complexity?

A common question we receive when talking about this subject is: what's a good threshold value for CC? Of course, like all answers in software architecture: it depends! Specifically it depends on the complexity of the problem domain. One of the weaknesses of metrics like this is the inability to distinguish between *essential* and *accidental* complexity. For example, if you have an algorithmically complex problem, the solution will yield complex functions. One of the key aspects of CC for architects to monitor is whether functions are complex because of the problem domain or because of poor coding, and alternatively, whether the code is partitioned poorly. In other words, could a large method be broken down into smaller, logical chunks, distributing the work (and complexity) into more well-factored methods?

In general, the industry thresholds for CC suggest that a value under 10 is acceptable, barring other considerations such as complex domains. We consider that threshold very high and would prefer code to fall under 5, indicating cohesive, well-factored code. A metrics tool in the Java world, Crap4j (*http://www.crap4j.org*), attempts to determine how poor (crappy) your code is by evaluating a combination of CC and code coverage; if CC grows to over 50, no amount of code coverage can rescue that code from crappiness. The most terrifying professional artifact Neal ever encountered was a single C function that served as the heart of a commercial software package whose CC was over 800! It was a single function with over 4,000 lines of code, including the liberal use of GOTO statements (to escape impossibly deeply nested loops).

Engineering practices like test-driven development have the accidental (but positive) side effect of generating smaller, less complex methods on average for a given problem domain. When practicing TDD, developers try to write a simple test, then write the smallest amount of code to pass the test. This focus on discrete behavior and good test boundaries encourages well-factored, highly cohesive methods that exhibit low CC.

CC is a good example of a metric architects might want to govern; no one benefits from overly complex codebases. However, what happens on projects where this value has been ignored for a long time?

Rather than set a hard threshold for a fitness function value, you can *herd* teams toward better values. For example, let's say that you decided as an organization that the absolute upper limit for CC should be 10, yet when you put that fitness function in place most of your projects fail. Instead of abandoning all hope, you can set up a cascading fitness function that issues a warning for anything past some threshold, which eventually escalates into an error over time. This gives teams time to address technical debt in a controlled, gradual way.

Gradually narrowing to desired values for a variety of metrics-based fitness functions allows teams to both address existing technical debt and, by leaving the fitness functions in place, prevent future degradation. This is the essence of preventing bit rot via governance.

Turnkey Tools

Because all architectures differ, architects struggle to find ready-made tools for complex problems. However, the more common the ecosystem, the more likely you are to find suitable, somewhat generic tools. Here are a few exemplars.

Legality of Open Source Libraries

PenultimateWidgets was working on a project that contained some patented proprietary algorithms, along with a few open source libraries and frameworks. The lawyers became concerned about the development team accidentally using a library whose license requires its users to adopt the same extremely liberal license, which PenultimateWidgets obviously didn't want for their code.

So, the architects gathered up all the licenses from the dependencies and allowed the lawyers to approve them. Then, one of the lawyers asked an awkward question: what happens if one of these dependencies updates the terms of their license during a routine software update? And, being a good lawyer, they had a good example of this happening in the past with some user interface libraries. How can the team make sure that one of the libraries doesn't update a license without them realizing it?

First, the architects should check to see if a tool already exists to do this; as of this writing, the tool Black Duck (*https://oreil.ly/C7bol*) performs exactly this task. However, at the time, PenultimateWidgets' architects couldn't find a tool to suffice.

Thus, they built a fitness function using the following steps:

1. Note the location of each license file within the open source download package in a database.

2. Along with the library version, save the contents (or a hash) of the full license file.

3. When a new version number is detected, the tool reaches into the download package, retrieves the license file, and compares it to the currently saved version.

4. If the versions (or hash) don't match, fail the build and notify the lawyer.

Note that we didn't try to assess the difference between library versions, or build some incredible artificial intelligence to analyze it. As is often the case, the fitness function notifies us of unexpected changes. This is an example of both an *automated* and a *manual* fitness function: the detection of change was automated, but the reaction to the change—approval by the lawyers of the changed library—remains as a manual intervention.

A11y and Other Supported Architecture Characteristics

Sometimes, knowing what to search for leads architects to the correct tool. "A11y" is developer shorthand for *accessibility* (derived from *a*, 11 letters, and *y*), which determines how well an application supports people with differing capabilities.

Because many companies and government agencies require accessibility, tools to validate this architecture characteristic have blossomed, including tools such as Pa11y (*https://pa11y.org*), which allows command-line scanning for static web elements to ensure accessibility.

ArchUnit

ArchUnit is a testing tool inspired by and using some of the helpers created for JUnit. However, it is designed for testing architecture features rather than general code structure. We already showed an example of an ArchUnit fitness function in Figure 2-3; here are some more examples of the kinds of governance available.

Package dependencies

Packages delineate components in the Java ecosystem, and architects frequently want to define how packages should be "wired" together. Consider the example components illustrated in Figure 4-9.

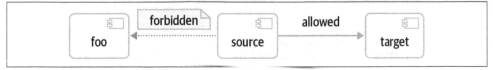

Figure 4-9. Declarative package dependencies in Java

The ArchUnit code that enforces the dependencies shown in Figure 4-9 appears in Example 4-3.

Example 4-3. Package dependency governance

```
noClasses().that().resideInAPackage("..source..")
    .should().dependOnClassesThat().resideInAPackage("..foo..")
```

ArchUnit uses the Hamcrest matchers (*https://oreil.ly/fuVil*) used in JUnit to allow architects to write very language-like assertions, as shown in Example 4-3, enabling them to define which components may or may not access other components.

Another common governable concern for architects are component dependencies, as illustrated in Figure 4-10.

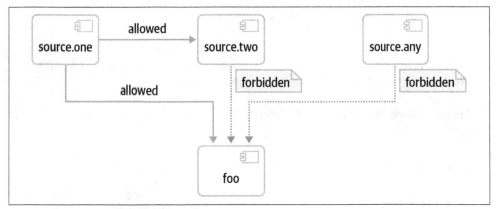

Figure 4-10. Package dependency governance

In Figure 4-10, the *foo* shared library should be accessible from `source.one` but not from other components; an architect can specify the governance rule via ArchUnit as in Example 4-4.

Example 4-4. Allowing and restricting package access

```
classes().that().resideInAPackage("..foo..")
    .should().onlyHaveDependentClassesThat()
        .resideInAnyPackage("..source.one..", "..foo..")
```

Example 4-4 shows how an architect can control compile-time dependencies between projects.

Class dependency checks

Similar to the rules concerning packages, architects often want to control architectural aspects of class design. For example, an architect may want to restrict dependencies between components to prevent deployment complications. Consider the relationship between classes in Figure 4-11.

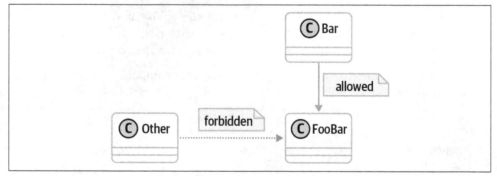

Figure 4-11. Dependency checks allowing and disallowing access

ArchUnit allows an architect to codify the rules shown in Figure 4-11 via Example 4-5.

Example 4-5. Class dependency rules in ArchUnit

```
classes().that().haveNameMatching(".*Bar")
    .should().onlyHaveDependentClassesThat().haveSimpleName("Bar")
```

ArchUnit allows architects fine-grained control over the "wiring" of components within an application.

Inheritance checks

Another dependency supported by object-oriented programming languages is inheritance; from an architecture perspective, it is a specialized form of coupling. In a classic example of the perpetual answer "it depends!" the question of whether inheritance is an architectural headache depends on how teams deploy the affected components: if the inheritance is contained with a single component, it has no architectural side effects. On the other hand, if inheritance stretches across component and/or deployment boundaries, architects must take special action to make sure the coupling remains intact.

Inheritance is often an architectural concern; an example of the type of structure requiring governance appears in Figure 4-12.

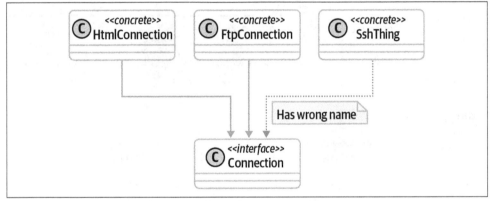

Figure 4-12. Governing inheritance dependencies

Architects can express the rules appearing in Figure 4-12 through the code in Example 4-6.

Example 4-6. Inheritance governance rule expressed in ArchUnit

```
classes().that().implement(Connection.class)
    .should().haveSimpleNameEndingWith("Connection")
```

Annotation checks

A common way architects indicate intent in supported platforms is through *tagging annotations* (or attributes, depending on your platform). For example, an architect may intend for a particular class to only act as an orchestrater for other services—the intent is that it never takes on nonorchestration behavior. Using an annotation allows the architect to verify intent and correct usage.

ArchUnit allows architects to validate this kind of usage, as shown in Figure 4-13.

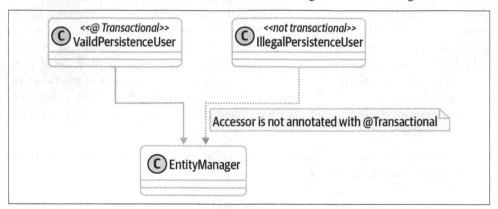

Figure 4-13. Governing proper annotation use

Architects can codify the governance rules implied in Figure 4-13 as shown in Example 4-7.

Example 4-7. Governance rules for annotations

```
classes().that().areAssignableTo(EntityManager.class)
    .should().onlyHaveDependentClassesThat().areAnnotatedWith(Transactional.class)
```

In Example 4-7, the architect wants to ensure that only annotated classes are allowed to utilize the EntityManager class.

Layer checks

One of the most common usages of a governance tool like ArchUnit is to allow architects to enforce design decisions. Architects often make decisions such as separation of concerns that cause short-term inconvenience for developers but have long-term benefits in terms of evolution and isolation. Consider the illustration in Figure 4-14.

The architect has built a layered architecture to isolate changes between layers. In such an architecture, dependencies should exist only between adjacent layers; the more layers couple to a particular layer, the more rippling side effects occur because of change.

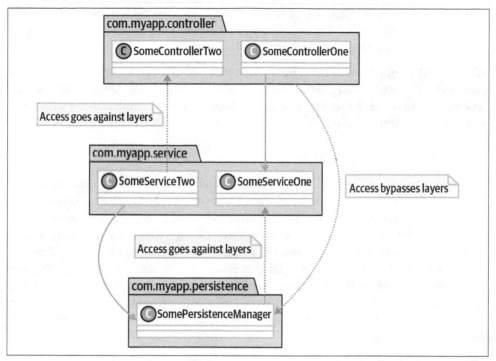

Figure 4-14. Using components to define a layered architecture

A layer governance check fitness function expressed in ArchUnit appears in Example 4-8.

Example 4-8. Layered architecture governance checks

```
layeredArchitecture()
    .consideringAllDependencies()
    .layer("Controller").definedBy("..controller..")
    .layer("Service").definedBy("..service..")
    .layer("Persistence").definedBy("..persistence..")

    .whereLayer("Controller").mayNotBeAccessedByAnyLayer()
    .whereLayer("Service").mayOnlyBeAccessedByLayers("Controller")
    .whereLayer("Persistence").mayOnlyBeAccessedByLayers("Service")
```

In Example 4-8, an architect defines layers and access rules for those layers.

Many of you as architects have written the native language versions of many of the principles expressed in the preceding examples in some wiki or other shared information repository—and they were read by no one! It's great for architects for express principles, but principles without enforcement are aspirational rather than governance. The layered architecture in Example 4-8 is a great example—while an architect may write a document describing layers and the underlying separation of concerns principle, unless a fitness function validates it, an architect can never have confidence that developers will follow the principles.

We've spent a lot of time highlighting ArchUnit, as it is the most mature of many governance-focused testing frameworks. It is obviously applicable only in the Java ecosystem. Fortunately, NetArchTest (*https://oreil.ly/mviqT*) replicates the same style and basic capabilities of ArchUnit but for the .NET platform.

Linters for Code Governance

A common question we field from salivating architects from platforms other than Java and .NET is whether there is a tool for platform *X* to ArchUnit that is equivalent. While tools as specific as ArchUnit are rare, most programming languages include a *linter*, a utility that scans source code to find coding antipatterns and deficiencies. Generally, the linter lexes and parses the source code, providing plug-ins by developers to write checks for syntax. For example, ESLint (*https://eslint.org*), the linting tool for JavaScript (technically, the linter for ECMAScript), allows developers to write syntax rules requiring (or not) semicolons, nominally optional braces, and so on. They can also write rules about what function-calling policies architects want to enforce and other governance rules.

Most platforms have linters; for example, C++ is served by Cpplint (*https://oreil.ly/zs9pY*), Staticcheck (*https://staticcheck.io*) is available for the Go language. There's even a variety of linters for SQL, including sql-lint (*https://oreil.ly/T4OB9*). While they are not as convenient as ArchUnit, architects can still code many structural checks into virtually any codebase.

Case Study: Availability Fitness Function

A common conundrum appears for many architects: should we use a legacy system as an integration point or build a new one? If a particular solution hasn't been tried before, how can architects make objective decisions?

PenultimateWidgets faced this problem when integrating with a legacy system. To that end, the team created a fitness function to stress-test the legacy service, as shown in Figure 4-15.

After setting up the ecosystem, the team measured the percentage of errors compared to total responses from the third-party system using the monitoring tool.

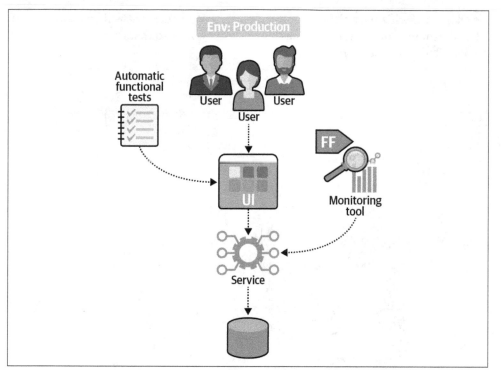

Figure 4-15. Availability verification fitness function

The results of the experiment showed them that the legacy system had no trouble with availability, with plenty of overhead to handle the integration point.

This objective outcome allowed the team to state with confidence that the legacy integration point was sufficient, freeing the resources otherwise dedicated to rewriting that system. This example illustrates how fitness functions help move software development from a gut-feel craft to a measurable engineering discipline.

Case Study: Load-Testing Along with Canary Releases

PenultimateWidgets has a service that currently "lives" in a single virtual machine. However, under load, this single instance struggles to keep up with necessary scalability. As a quick fix, the team implements auto-scaling for the service, replicating the single instance with several instances as a stopgap measure because a busy annual sale is fast approaching. However, the skeptics on the team wanted to know how they could prove that the new system was working under load.

The architects on the project created a fitness function tied to a feature flag that allows *canary releases* or *dark launches*, which release new behaviors to a small subset of users to test the potential overall impact of the change. For example, when developers of a highly scalable website release a new feature that will consume a lot of bandwidth, they often want to release the change slowly so that they can monitor the impact. This setup appears in Figure 4-16.

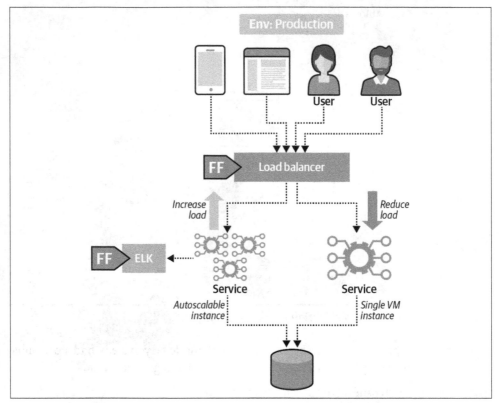

Figure 4-16. Canary-releasing auto-scaling to provide support and increase confidence

For the fitness function shown in Figure 4-16, the team initially released the auto-scaling instances to a small group, then increased the number of users as their monitoring showed continued good performance and support.

This solution will act as scaffolding to allow limited-term expansion while the team develops a better solution. Having the fitness function in place and regularly executed allows the team a better feel for how long this stopgap solution will last.

Case Study: What to Port?

One particular PenultimateWidgets application has been a workhorse, developed as a Java Swing application over the better part of a decade and continually growing new features. The company decided to port it to the web application. However, now the business analysts face a difficult decision: how much of the existing sprawling functionality should they port? And, more practically, in what order should they implement the ported features of the new application to deliver the most functionality quickly?

One of the architects at PenultimateWidgets asked the business analysts what the most popular features were, and they had no idea! Even though they have been specifying the details of the application for years, they had no real understanding of how users used the application. To learn from users, the developers released a new version of the legacy application with logging enabled to track which menu features users actually used.

After a few weeks, they harvested the results, providing an excellent road map of what features to port and in what order. They discovered that the invoicing and customer lookup features were most commonly used. Surprisingly, one subsection of the application that had taken great effort to build had very little use, leading the team to decide to leave that functionality out of the new web application.

Fitness Functions You're Already Using

Outside of new tools such as ArchUnit, many of the tools and approaches we outline aren't new. However, teams use them sparsely and inconsistently, on an ad hoc basis. Part of our insight surrounding the *fitness function* concept unifies a wide variety of tools into a single perspective. Thus, chances are good that you are already using a variety of fitness functions on your projects, and you just don't call them that yet.

Fitness functions include metrics suites such as SonarCube; linting tools such as esLint, pyLint, and cppLint; and a whole family of source-code verification tools, such as PMD.

Just because a team uses monitors to observe traffic doesn't make those measures a fitness function. Setting an *objective measure* associated with an alert converts measurements into fitness functions.

 To convert a metric or measurement into a fitness function, define *objective measures* and provide fast feedback for acceptable use.

Using these tools every once in a while doesn't make them fitness functions; wiring them into continuous verification does.

Integration Architecture

While many fitness functions apply to individual applications, they exist in all parts of the architectural ecosystem—any part that may benefit from governance. Inevitably, the more examples move away from application-specific concerns, the fewer generic solutions exist. Integration architecture by its nature integrates different specific parts, defying generic advice. However, some general patterns exist for integration architecture fitness functions.

Communication Governance in Microservices

Many architects see the cycle test shown in Figure 2-3 and fantasize about the same kind of test for distributed architectures such as microservices. However, this desire intersects with the heterogeneous nature of architecture problems. Testing for component cycles is a compile-time check, requiring a single codebase and tool in the appropriate language. However, in microservices, a single tool won't suffice: each service might be written in a different tech stack, in different repositories, using different communication protocols, and many other variables. Thus, finding a turnkey tool for fitness functions for microservices is unlikely.

Architects often need to write their own fitness functions, but creating an entire framework isn't necessary (and is too much work). Many fitness functions consist of 10 or 15 lines of "glue" code, often in a different technology stack than the solution.

Consider the governance problem of governing calls between microservices, illustrated in Figure 4-17. The architect designed the `OrderOrchestrator` as the sole state owner of the workflow. However, if the domain services communicate with each other, the orchestrator can't maintain correct state. Thus, an architect might want to govern the communication between services: domain services can only communicate with the orchestrator.

However, if an architect can ensure a consistent interface between systems (such as logging in a parsable format), they can write a few lines of code in a scripting language to build a governance fitness function. Consider a log message that includes the following information:

- Service name
- Username
- IP address
- Correlation ID

- Message received time in UTC
- Time taken
- Method name

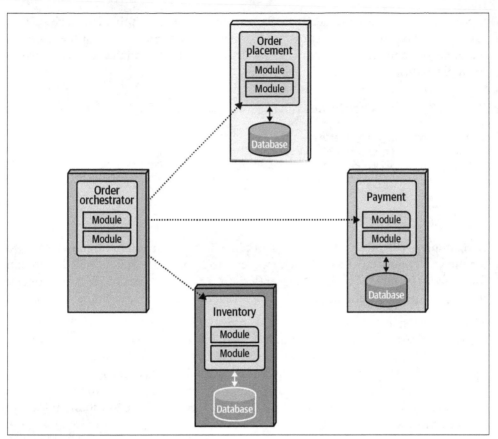

Figure 4-17. Governing communication between microservices

For example, a particular log message might resemble the one shown in Example 4-9.

Example 4-9. Sample microservices log format

```
["OrderOrchestrator", "jdoe", "192.16.100.10", "ABC123",
  "2021-11-05T08:15:30-05:00", "3100ms", "updateOrderState()"]
```

First, an architect can create a fitness function for each project that mandates out-putting log messages in the format shown in Example 4-9, regardless of technology stack. This fitness function may be attached to the common container image shared by services.

Second, the architect writes a simple fitness function in a scripting language such as Ruby or Python to harvest the log messages, parse the common format mandated in Example 4-9, and check for approved (or disapproved) communication, as shown in Example 4-10.

Example 4-10. Checking communication between services

```
list_of_services.each { |service|
    service.import_logsFor(24.hours)
    calls_from(service).each { |call|
        unless call.destination.equals("orchestrator")
          raise FitnessFunctionFailure.new()
     }
   }
```

In Example 4-10, the architect writes a loop that iterates over all the logfiles harvested for the last 24 hours. For each log entry, they check to ensure that the call destination for each call is only the orchestrator service, not any of the domain services. If one of the services has violated this rule, the fitness function raises an exception.

You may recognize some parts of this example from Chapter 2 in the discussion of *triggered* versus *continual* fitness functions; this is a good example of two different ways to implement a fitness function with differing trade-offs. The example shown in Example 4-10 represents a *reactive* fitness function—it reacts to the governance check after a time interval (in this case, 24 hours). However, another way to implement this fitness function is *proactively*, based on real-time monitors for communication, catching violations as they occur.

Each approach has trade-offs. The reactive version doesn't impose any overhead on the runtime characteristics of the architecture, whereas monitors can add a small amount of overhead. However, the proactive version catches violations right away rather than a day later.

Thus, the real trade-off between the two approaches may come down to the criticality of the governance. For example, if the unauthorized communication creates an immediate issue (such as a security concern), architects should implement it proactively. If, however, the purpose is only structural governance, creating the log-based reactive fitness function has less chance of impacting the running system.

Case Study: Choosing How to Implement a Fitness Function

Testing the problem domain is mostly straightforward: as developers implement features in code, they incrementally test those features using one or more testing frameworks. However, architects may find even simple fitness functions have a variety of implementations.

Consider the example shown in Figure 4-18.

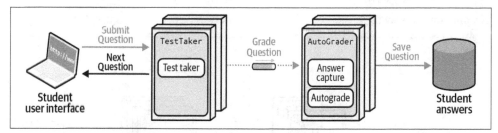

Figure 4-18. Grading message governance

In Figure 4-18, a student answers test questions presented by the `TestTaker` service, which in turn passes messages asynchronously to `AutoGrader`, which persists the graded test answers. Reliability is a key requirement for this system—the system should never "drop" any answers during this communication. How could an architect design a fitness function for this problem?

At least two solutions present themselves, differing mostly by what trade-offs each offers. Consider the solution illustrated in Figure 4-19.

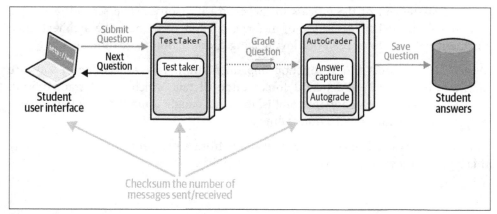

Figure 4-19. Counting the number of messages sent and received

If we can assume a modern microservices architecture, concerns such as message ports are typically managed at the container. A simple way to implement the fitness function shown in Figure 4-19 is to instrument the container to check the number of incoming and outgoing messages, and raise an alarm if the numbers don't match.

This is a simple fitness function, as it is atomic at the service/container level and architects can enforce it via consistent infrastructure. However, it doesn't guarantee end-to-end reliability, only service-level reliability.

An alternative way to implement the fitness function appears in Figure 4-20.

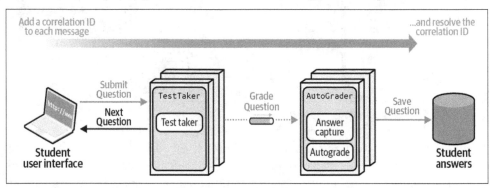

Figure 4-20. Using correlation IDs to ensure reliability

In Figure 4-20, the architect uses *correlation IDs*, a common technique that tags each request with a unique identifier to allow traceability. To ensure message reliability, each message is assigned a correlation ID at the start of the request, and each ID is checked at the end of the process to make sure it resolved. The second technique provides more holistic assurance of message reliability, but now the architect must maintain state for the entire workflow, making coordination more difficult.

Which is the correct fitness function implementation? Like everything in software architecture, *it depends*! External forces often dictate which set of trade-offs an architect chooses; the important point is not to get caught up in thinking that there is only one way to implement a fitness function.

The chart shown in Figure 4-21 is an example from a real project that set up exactly this type of fitness function to ensure data reliability.

Ratio of "No. of non-missed exits event for the day"/"total number of exits for the day"			
Trend Reports in Google Data studio[#]			
effectiveDa...	total_exits_per_day	successful_exits_per_day	service_level_indicator
1. Mar 28, 2022	5	5	1
2. Mar 27, 2022	4	4	1
3. Mar 25, 2022	17	16	0.94
4. Mar 24, 2022	1	1	1
5. Mar 23, 2022	9	9	1
6. Mar 22, 2022	4	4	1
7. Mar 21, 2022	10	10	1
8. Mar 20, 2022	1	1	1
9. Mar 18, 2022	10	10	1
10. Mar 17, 2022	24	24	1
11. Mar 16, 2022	1	1	1
12. Mar 15, 2022	6	6	1
13. Mar 14, 2022	4	4	1
14. Mar 13, 2022	1	1	1

1 - 25 / 25 〈 〉

Figure 4-21. Chart showing the reliability of messages in an orchestrated workflow

As you can see, the fitness function exposed the fact that some messages were *not* passing through, encouraging the team to perform forensic analysis as to why (and leaving the fitness function in place to ensure future problems don't arise).

DevOps

While most of the fitness functions we cover pertain to architectural structure and related concepts, like software architecture itself, governance concerns may touch all parts of the ecosystem, including a family of DevOps-related fitness functions.

These are fitness functions and not just operational concerns for two reasons. First, they intersect software architecture and the operational concern—changes to the architecture may impact the operational parts of the system. Second, they represent governance checks with objective outcomes.

Chaos Engineering

When engineers designed Netflix's distributed architecture, they designed it to run on the Amazon Cloud. But they were concerned what sort of odd behavior could occur because they had no direct control over their operations, such as high latency, availability, elasticity, and so on. To assuage their fears, they created the Chaos Monkey, eventually followed by an entire open source Simian Army (*https://oreil.ly/qNHLF*).

While the original monkey was meant for chaos and randomness, the fleshed out Simian Army included some specialization:

Chaos Monkey

The Chaos Monkey can "infiltrate" an Amazon data center and make unexpected things happen: latency can go up, reliability can go down, and other chaos can ensue. By designing with the Chaos Monkey in mind, each team must build resilient services that can withstand the imposed chaos.

Chaos Gorilla

The Chaos Gorilla can knock out an entire Amazon data center, suddenly feigning an overall data outage.

Chaos Kong

As if the Chaos Gorilla doesn't sound dire enough, Chaos Kong can knock out an entire availability zone, making a portion of the cloud ecosystem seem to disappear. In a tribute to the effectiveness of chaos engineering generally and the Simian Army specifically, a few years ago (*https://oreil.ly/2pv4V*) a lack of automation caused an Amazon engineer to accidentally shut down all of Amazon East (the engineer fat-fingered a command so that instead of kill 10, it was kill 100). However, during that outage, Netflix stayed operational—its architects had been forced by the Chaos Gorilla to write around that eventuality.

Doctor Monkey

The Doctor Monkey can check on the general health of a service—CPU utilization, disk space, and so on—and raise alarms if a resource has become constrained.

Latency Monkey

One of the constant headaches of cloud-based resources, especially in the early days, was high latency resolving resources. While the original Chaos Monkey also randomly affected latency, the Latency Monkey was built to stress this common fault specifically.

Janitor Monkey

Netflix has an evolutionary ecosystem: new services gradually appear that replace and enhance existing ones, but the fluidity of change doesn't mandate that teams use the new capabilities as soon as they appear. Rather, they can take on new capabilities when it becomes convenient to use that service. Because many of its services don't have a formal release cycle, it created the possibility for *orphaned* services—services still running in the cloud without any users left, as they all moved to a better version. The Janitor Monkey governs this problem by searching for services still running in the cloud but without any other services routing to it, and disintegrating that orphan from the cloud, saving the fungible cloud resources it was consuming.

Conformity Monkey

> The Conformity Monkey provides a platform for Netflix architects to implement specific governance fitness functions. For example, architects might be concerned that all REST endpoints support the proper verbs, exhibit correct error handling, and support metadata properly, and therefore they might build a tool that runs continually to call REST endpoints (just as normal clients would) to verify the results.

Security Monkey

> As the name implies, the Security Monkey is a specialized version of the Conformity Monkey, focused on security issues specifically. For example, it scans for open debug ports, missing authentication, and other automatable verifications.

The Simian Army was open source and eventually was deprecated as the Netflix engineers built more advanced governance mechanisms. However, some of the monkeys found new homes. For example, the extremely useful Janitor Monkey has been reborn as Swabbie (*https://oreil.ly/WvKxj*), as part of a suite of open source cloud-based fitness functions.

The principle behind chaos engineering is compelling: it's not a question of *if* your system will eventually have a fault of some kind but rather *when*. By designing (and governing) known eventualities, architects and operations can collaborate on more robust systems.

Note that the Chaos Monkey wasn't a testing tool run on a schedule—it ran continuously within Netflix's ecosystem. Not only did this force developers to build systems that could withstand problems, it tested the system's validity continually. Having this constant verification built into the architecture allowed Netflix to build one of the most robust systems in the world. The Simian Army is an excellent example of a holistic, continual, operational fitness function. It ran against multiple parts of the architecture at once, ensuring architectural characteristics (resiliency, scalability, etc.) would be maintained.

Enterprise Architecture

Most of the fitness functions we have shown so far have concerned application or integration architecture, but they are applicable at any part of an architecture that could benefit from governance. One place in particular where enterprise architects have a big impact on the rest of the ecosystem is when they define *platforms* within their ecosystem to encapsulate business functionality. This effort aligns with our stated desire to keep implementation details at the smallest possible scope.

Consider the example shown in Figure 4-22.

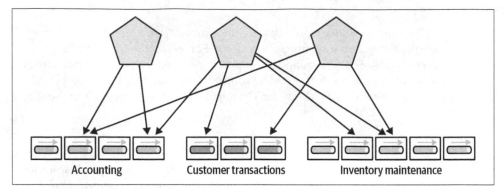

Figure 4-22. Applications as ad hoc compositions of services

In Figure 4-22, applications (shown at the top) consume services from a variety of different parts of the enterprise. Having fine-grained access from applications to services results in implementation details regarding how the parts interact with one another leak into the application, in turn making them more brittle.

Realizing this, many enterprise architects design platforms to encapsulate business functionality behind managed contracts, as illustrated in Figure 4-23.

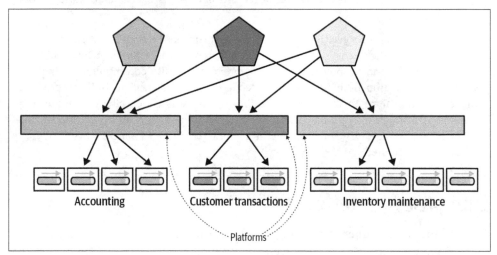

Figure 4-23. Building platforms to hide implementation details

In Figure 4-23, the architects build platforms to hide the way the organization solves problems, instead building a consistent, hopefully slow-changing API that describes the facilities other parts of the ecosystem need via contracts for the platform. By encapsulating the implementation details at the platform level, architects decrease the spread of implementation coupling, in turn making a less brittle architecture.

Enterprise architects define the APIs for these platform and fitness functions to govern the capabilities, structure, and other governable aspects of the platform and its implementation. This, in turn, provides another benefit by keeping enterprise architects *away* from making technology choices! Instead, they focus on capabilities rather than how to implement them, which solves two problems.

First, enterprise architects are typically far away from implementation details, and thus are not as up-to-date on cutting-edge changes, in the technology landscape and within their own ecosystem; they often suffer from the Frozen Caveman antipattern.

Frozen Caveman Antipattern

A behavioral antipattern commonly observed in the wild, the *Frozen Caveman Antipattern*, describes an architect who always reverts to their pet irrational concern for every architecture. For example, one of Neal's colleagues worked on a system that featured a centralized architecture. Yet, each time they delivered the design to the client architects, the persistent question was "But what if we lose Italy?" Several years before, a freak communication problem had prevented headquarters from communicating with its stores in Italy, causing great inconvenience. While the chances of a reoccurrence were extremely small, the architects had become obsessed about this particular architectural characteristic.

Generally, this antipattern manifests in architects who have been burned in the past by a poor decision or unexpected occurrence, making them particularly cautious in the future. While risk assessment is important, it should be realistic as well. Understanding the difference between genuine versus perceived technical risk is part of the ongoing learning process for architects. Thinking like an architect requires overcoming these "frozen caveman" ideas and experiences, seeing other solutions, and asking more relevant questions.

However out of date they may be on current implementation trends, enterprise architects understand best the long-term strategic goals of the organization, which they can codify in fitness functions. Rather than specify technology choices, they instead define concrete fitness functions at the platform level, ensuring that the platform continues to support the appropriate characteristics and behavior. This further explains our advice to decompose architecture characteristics until you can objectively measure them—things that can be measured can be governed.

Also, allowing enterprise architects to focus on building fitness functions to manage strategic vision frees domain and integration architects to make technology decisions with consequences, protected by the guardrails implemented as fitness functions. This, in turn, allows organizations to grow their next generation of enterprise architects, by allowing lower-tier roles to make decisions and work through the trade-offs.

We have advised several companies that have an enterprise architecture role of *evolutionary architect*, tasked with looking around the organization for opportunities to find and implement fitness functions (often harvested from a specific project and made more generic) and to build reusable ecosystems with appropriate quantum boundaries and contracts to ensure loose coupling between platforms.

Case Study: Architectural Restructuring While Deploying 60 Times per Day

GitHub (*http://github.com*) is a well-known developer-centric website with aggressive engineering practices, deploying 60 times per day, on average. GitHub describes a problem in its blog "Move Fast and Fix Things" (*https://oreil.ly/zJQ1x*) that will make many architects shudder in horror. It turns out that GitHub has long used a shell script wrapped around command-line Git to handle merges, which works correctly but doesn't scale well enough. The Git engineering team built a replacement library for many command-line Git functions called libgit2 and implemented their merge functionality there, thoroughly testing it locally.

But now they must deploy the new solution into production. This behavior has been part of GitHub since its inception and has worked flawlessly. The last thing the developers want to do is introduce bugs in existing functionality, but they must address technical debt as well.

Fortunately, GitHub developers created Scientist (*https://oreil.ly/bl2hN*), an open source framework written in Ruby that provides holistic, continual testing to vet changes to code. Example 4-11 gives us the structure of a `Scientist` test.

Example 4-11. Scientist setup for an experiment

```
require "scientist"

class MyWidget
  include Scientist

  def allows?(user)
    science "widget-permissions" do |e|
      e.use { model.check_user(user).valid? } # old way
      e.try { user.can?(:read, model) } # new way
    end # returns the control value
  end
end
```

In Example 4-11, the developer encapsulates the existing behavior with the `use` block (called the *control*) and adds the experimental behavior to the `try` block (called the *candidate*). The `science` block handles the following details during the invocation of the code:

Decides whether to run the `try` *block*

Developers configure Scientist to determine how the experiment runs. For example, in this case study—the goal of which was to update the merge functionality—1% of random users tried the new merge functionality. In either case, Scientist *always* returns the results of the use block, ensuring the caller always receives the existing behavior in case of differences.

Randomizes the order in which use *and* try *blocks run*

Scientist does this to prevent accidentally masking bugs due to unknown dependencies. Sometimes the order or other incidental factors can cause false positives; by randomizing their order, the tool makes those faults less likely.

Measures the durations of all behaviors

Part of Scientist's job is A/B performance testing, so monitoring performance is built in. In fact, developers can use the framework piecemeal—for example, they can use it to measure calls without performing experiments.

Compares the result of try *to the result of* use

Because the goal is refactoring existing behavior, Scientist compares and logs the results of each call to see if differences exist.

Swallows (but logs) any exceptions raised in the try *block*

There's always a chance that new code will throw unexpected exceptions. Developers never want end users to see these errors, so the tool makes them invisible to the end user (but logs them for developer analysis).

Publishes all this information

Scientist makes all its data available in a variety of formats.

For the merge refactoring, the GitHub developers used the following invocation to test the new implementation (called `create_merge_commit_rugged`), as shown in Example 4-12.

Example 4-12. Experimenting with a new merge algorithm

```
def create_merge_commit(author, base, head, options = {})
  commit_message = options[:commit_message] || "Merge #{head} into #{base}"
  now = Time.current

  science "create_merge_commit" do |e|
    e.context :base => base.to_s, :head => head.to_s, :repo => repository.nwo
    e.use { create_merge_commit_git(author, now, base, head, commit_message) }
    e.try { create_merge_commit_rugged(author, now, base, head, commit_message) }
  end
end
```

In Example 4-12, the call to `create_merge_commit_rugged` occurred in 1% of invocations, but, as noted in this case study, at GitHub's scale, all edge cases appear quickly.

When this code executes, end users always receive the correct result. If the `try` block returns a different value from `use`, it is logged, and the `use` value is returned. Thus, the worse case for end users is exactly what they would have gotten before the refactoring. After running the experiment for 4 days and experiencing no slow cases or mismatched results for 24 hours, they removed the old merge code and left the new code in place.

From our perspective, Scientist is a fitness function. This case study is an outstanding example of the strategic use of a holistic, continuous fitness function to allow developers to refactor a critical part of their infrastructure with confidence. They changed a key part of their architecture by running the new version alongside the existing one, essentially turning the legacy implementation into a consistency test.

Fidelity Fitness Functions

The Scientist tool implements a general type of verification called a *fidelity fitness function*: preserving the fidelity between a new system and an old one undergoing replacement. Many organizations build important functionality over long periods of time without enough testing or discipline, until eventually the time comes to replace the application with newer technology yet still retain the same behavior as the old one. The older and more poorly documented the old system is, the more difficult it is for teams to replicate the desired behavior.

A fidelity fitness function allows for a side-by-side comparison between *old* and *new*. During the replacement process, both systems run in parallel, and a proxy allows teams to call `old`, `new`, or `both` in a controlled way until the team has ported each bit of discrete functionality. Some teams resist building such a mechanism because they realize the complexity of partitioning the old behavior and exact replication, but eventually they succumb to the necessity to achieve confidence.

Fitness Functions as a Checklist, Not a Stick

We realize that we have provided architects a metaphorical sharp stick they can use to poke and torture developers; that is not the point at all. We want to discourage architects from retreating to an ivory tower and devising more and more complex and interlocking fitness functions that increase the burden on developers while not adding corresponding value to the project.

Instead, fitness functions provide a way to enforce architectural principles. Many professions such as surgeons and airline pilots use (sometimes by mandate) checklists as part of their job. It's not because they don't understand their job or tend toward absentmindedness—rather, it avoids the natural tendency that people have when performing complex tasks over and over to accidentally skip steps. For example, every developer knows they shouldn't deploy a container with debug ports enabled, but they may forget during a push including many other tasks.

Many architects state architecture and design principles in wikis or other shared knowledge portals, but principles without execution fall by the wayside in the presence of schedule pressure and other constraints. Encoding those design and governance rules as fitness functions ensures they aren't skipped in the face of external forces.

Architects often write fitness functions but should always collaborate with developers, who must understand them and fix them upon occasional breakage. While fitness functions add overhead, they prevent the gradual degradation of a codebase (*bit rot*), allowing it to continue to evolve into the future.

Documenting Fitness Functions

Tests make good documentation because readers never doubt their honesty—they can always execute the tests to check results. Trust but verify!

Architects can document fitness functions in a variety of ways, all appropriate with other documentation within their organization. Some architects view the fitness functions themselves as sufficient to document their intent. However, tests (no matter how fluent) are harder for nontechnologists to read.

Many architects like Architectural Decision Records (ADRs) (*https://adr.github.io*) to document architecture decisions. Teams that use fitness functions add a section in the ADR specifying how to govern the enclosed design decisions.

Another alternative is to use a behavior-driven development (BDD) (*https://oreil.ly/r6lKy*) framework such as Cucumber (*https://cucumber.io*). These tools are designed to map native language to verification code. For example, take a look at the Cucumber test stated in Example 4-13.

Example 4-13. Cucumber assumptions

```
Feature: Is it Friday yet?
  Everybody wants to know when it's Friday

  Scenario: Sunday isn't Friday
    Given today is Sunday
    When I ask whether it's Friday yet
    Then I should be told "Nope"
```

The `Feature` described in Example 4-13 maps to a programming language method; a Java mapping appears in Example 4-14.

Example 4-14. Cucumber methods that map to descriptions

```
@Given("today is Sunday")
public void today_is_sunday() {
    // Write code here that turns the phrase above into concrete actions
    throw new io.cucumber.java.PendingException();
}
@When("I ask whether it's Friday yet")
public void i_ask_whether_it_s_friday_yet() {
    // Write code here that turns the phrase above into concrete actions
    throw new io.cucumber.java.PendingException();
}
@Then("I should be told {string}")
public void i_should_be_told(String string) {
    // Write code here that turns the phrase above into concrete actions
    throw new io.cucumber.java.PendingException();
}
```

Architects can use the mapping between native language declarations in Example 4-13 and method definitions in Example 4-14 to define fitness functions in more or less plain native language and map the execution in the corresponding method. This provides architects a way to document their decisions that also executes them.

The downside of using a tool like Cucumber is the impedance mismatch between capturing requirements (its original job) and documenting fitness functions.

Literate programming (*https://oreil.ly/bnICD*) was an innovation by Donald Knuth that attempted to merge documentation and source code, the goal being to allow cleaner documentation. He built special compilers for the then-current languages but got little support.

However, in modern ecosystems, tools like Mathematica (*https://oreil.ly/5mJXr*) and Jupyter notebooks (*https://jupyter.org*) are popular in disciplines such as data science. Architects can use Jupyter notebooks in particular to document and execute fitness functions.

In one case study (*https://oreil.ly/P99wA*), a team created a notebook to check for architectural rules using the structural code analyzer jQAssistant (*https://jqassistant.org*) in combination with the graph database Neo4j (*https://neo4j.com*). jQAssistant scans several artifacts (Java bytecode, Git history, Maven dependencies, etc.) and stores the structural information into the Neo4j database, as shown in Figure 4-24.

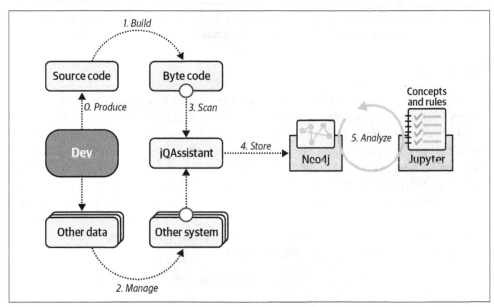

Figure 4-24. Governance workflow with Jupyter notebook

In Figure 4-24, the relationships between parts of the codebase are placed in the graph database, allowing the team to execute queries such as the following:

```
MATCH (e:Entity)<-[:CONTAINS]-(p:Package)
WHERE p.name <> "model"
RETURN e.fqn as MisplacedEntity, p.name as WrongPackage
```

When executed against a sample PetClinic application, the analysis creates the output shown in Figure 4-25.

Out[4]:	
MisplacedEntity	**WrongPackage**
org.springframework.samples.petclinic.repository.PetType	repository

Figure 4-25. The output of graph analysis

In Figure 4-25, the results indicate a governance violation, where all classes in the model package should implement an @Entity annotation.

Jupyter notebooks allow architects to define the text of the governance rules along with on-demand execution.

Documenting fitness functions is important because developers must understand why they exist so that fixing them isn't a nuisance. Finding a way to incorporate fitness function definitions within your organization's existing documentation framework allows for most consistent access. The execution of the fitness functions remains the top priority, but understandability is also important.

Summary

Fitness functions are to architecture governance as unit tests are to domain changes. However, the implementation of fitness functions varies depending on all the various factors that make up a particular architecture. There is no generic architecture—every one is a unique combination of decisions and subsequent technologies, often years, or decades, worth. Thus, architects must sometimes be clever in creating fitness functions. However, this isn't an example of needing to write an entire testing framework. Rather, architects often write these fitness functions in scripting languages such as Python or Ruby, writing 10 or 20 lines of "glue" code to combine the output of other tools. For example, consider Example 4-10, which harvests the output of logfiles and checks for particular string patterns.

One of our colleagues presented a great analogy for fitness functions, shown in Figure 4-26.

Figure 4-26. Fitness functions act as guardrails no matter what the road is made of

In Figure 4-26, the road can be made with a variety of material—asphalt, cobblestones, gravel, and so on. The guardrails exist to keep travelers on the road regardless of the type of vehicle or type of road. Fitness functions are architecture characteristics guardrails, created by architects to prevent system rot and support evolving systems over time.

PART II
Structure

Part I defined the *mechanics* of evolutionary architecture—how teams build fitness functions, deployment pipelines, and other mechanisms to govern and evolve software projects.

Part II concerns the *structure* of architecture. The topology of a software system has a huge impact on its evolvability. Structural design is a huge portion of the architect's job, and certain principles allow for cleaner evolution over time when designed correctly.

Modern systems have forced architects to consider the impact of data and its evolution alongside architecture, reflected in our chapters about that overlap.

CHAPTER 5

Evolutionary Architecture Topologies

Discussions about architecture frequently boil down to coupling: how the pieces of the architecture connect and rely on one another. Many architects decry coupling as a necessary evil, but it's difficult to build complex software without relying on (and coupling with) other components. Evolutionary architecture focuses on appropriate coupling—how to identify which dimensions of the architecture should be coupled to provide maximum benefit with minimal overhead and cost.

In this chapter, readers will garner a deeper understanding of architecture coupling, how that affects architectural structure, and how to evaluate the structure of software architectures to more effectively evolve them. We also provide some concrete terminology and advice on architecture topology from the component up through the system level.

Evolvable Architecture Structure

Different architecture styles have different evolution characteristics, but there is nothing inherent in the style that controls its ability to evolve. Rather, it boils down to the coupling characteristics supported by the architecture. It turns out that at least two different efforts from the past have identified the key enabler of evolution in software. Each of them provides a valuable perspective on coupling in architecture.

Connascence

In 1996, Meilir Page-Jones published *What Every Programmer Should Know About Object-Oriented Design* (Dorset House), which is a duplex book: one part covers an object-oriented design technique that did not prove to be popular. However, the lasting benefit from the book is a concept he named *connascence*. Here's how he defined the term:

Two components are connascent if a change in one would require the other to be modified in order to maintain the overall correctness of the system.

—Meilir Page-Jones

Essentially, connascence is an enhanced language to describe coupling. It's a great language for architects to teach tech leads and developers, because it gives them a more concise way to discuss coupling and (more importantly) how to improve it. Having a richer vocabulary takes advantage of the Sapir–Whorf hypothesis.

Sapir-Whorf Hypothesis

A principle suggesting that the structure of a language affects its speakers' worldview or cognition, meaning that people's perceptions are relative to their spoken language.

For example, many Far North cultures have more words for *snow* than those who live at the equator (who don't have to regularly distinguish between different types of snow). It could be argued that those people from the Far North have a deeper understanding of snow.

Page-Jones developed two types of connascence: *static* and *dynamic*.

Static connascence

Static connascence refers to source code–level coupling (as opposed to execution-time coupling, covered in "Dynamic connascence" on page 87); it is a refinement of the afferent and efferent couplings defined by *Structured Design*. In other words, architects view the following types of static connascence as the *degree* to which something is coupled, either afferently or efferently:

Connascence of Name (CoN)
Multiple components must agree on the name of an entity.

Names of methods represent the most common way that codebases are coupled and the most desirable, especially in light of modern refactoring tools that make system-wide name changes trivial.

Connascence of Type (CoT)
Multiple components must agree on the type of an entity.

This type of connascence refers to the common facility in many statically typed languages to limit variables and parameters to specific types. However, this capability isn't purely a language feature. Some dynamically typed languages offer selective typing, notably Clojure (*https://clojure.org*) and Clojure Spec (*https://clojure.org/about/spec*).

Connascence of Meaning (CoM) or Connascence of Convention (CoC)
> Multiple components must agree on the meaning of particular values.

The most common obvious case for this type of connascence in codebases is hardcoded numbers rather than constants. For example, it is common in some languages to consider defining int TRUE = 1; int FALSE = 0. Imagine the problems if someone flips those values.

Connascence of Position (CoP)
> Multiple components must agree on the order of values.

This is an issue with parameter values for method and function calls even in languages that feature static typing. For example, if a developer creates a method void updateSeat(String name, String seatLocation) and calls it with the values updateSeat("14D", "Ford, N"), the semantics aren't correct even if the types are.

Connascence of Algorithm (CoA)
> Multiple components must agree on a particular algorithm.

A common case for this type of connascence occurs when a developer defines a security hashing algorithm that must run on both the server and client and produce identical results to authenticate the user. Obviously, this represents a high form of coupling: if either algorithm changes any details, the handshake will no longer work.

Dynamic connascence

The other type of connascence Page-Jones defined is *dynamic connascence*, which analyzes calls at runtime. The following is a description of the different types of dynamic connascence:

Connascence of Execution (CoE)
> The order of execution of multiple components is important.

Consider this code:

```
email = new Email();
email.setRecipient("foo@example.com");
email.setSender("me@me.com");
email.send();
email.setSubject("whoops");
```

It won't work correctly because certain properties must be set in order.

Connascence of Timing (CoT)
The timing of the execution of multiple components is important.

The common case for this type of connascence is a race condition caused by two threads executing at the same time, affecting the outcome of the joint operation.

Connascence of Values (CoV)
This occurs when several values relate to one another and must change together.

Consider the case where a developer has defined a rectangle as four points, representing the corners. To maintain the integrity of the data structure, the developer cannot randomly change one of the points without considering the impact on the other points.

A more common and problematic case involves transactions, especially in distributed systems. When an architect designs a system with separate databases, yet needs to update a single value across all the databases, all the values must change together or not at all.

Connascence of Identity (CoI)
This occurs when multiple components must reference the same entity.

The common example of this type of connascence involves two independent components that must share and update a common data structure, such as a distributed queue.

Architects have a harder time determining dynamic connascence because we lack tools to analyze runtime calls as effectively as we can analyze the call graph.

Connascence properties

Connascence is an analysis tool for architects and developers, and some properties of connascence help developers use it wisely. The following is a description of each of these connascence properties:

Strength
Architects determine the *strength* of connascence by the ease with which a developer can refactor that type of coupling; different types of connascence are demonstrably more desirable, as shown in Figure 5-1. Architects and developers can improve the coupling characteristics of their codebase by refactoring toward better types of connascence.

Architects should prefer static connascence to dynamic connascence because developers can determine it through simple source code analysis, and modern tools make it trivial to improve static connascence. For example, consider the case of *Connascence of Meaning*, which developers can improve by refactoring to *Connascence of Name* by creating a named constant rather than a magic value.

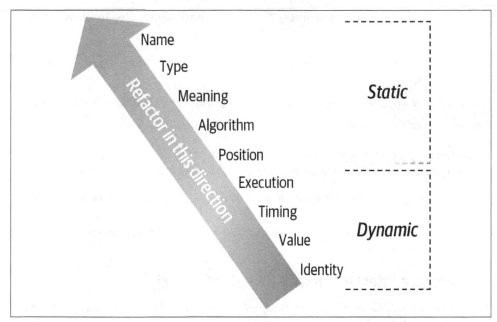

Figure 5-1. The strength of connascence provides a good refactoring guide

Locality

The *locality* of connascence measures the modules' proximal location to one another in the codebase. Proximal code (in the same module) typically has more and higher forms of connascence than more separated code (in separate modules or codebases). In other words, forms of connascence that indicate poor coupling when far apart are fine when closer together. For example, if two classes in the same component have connascence of meaning, it is less damaging to the codebase than if two components have the same form of connascence.

Developers must consider strength and locality together. Stronger forms of connascence found within the same module represent less code smell than the same connascence spread apart.

Degree

The *degree* of connascence relates to the size of its impact—does it impact a few classes or many? Lesser degrees of connascence damage codebases less. In other words, having high dynamic connascence isn't terrible if you have only a few modules. However, codebases tend to grow, making a small problem correspondingly bigger.

Page-Jones offers three guidelines for using connascence to improve systems modularity:

1. Minimize overall connascence by breaking the system into encapsulated elements.
2. Minimize any remaining connascence that crosses encapsulation boundaries.
3. Maximize the connascence within encapsulation boundaries.

The legendary software architecture innovator Jim Weirich repopularized the concept of connascence and offers two great pieces of advice (*https://oreil.ly/7TKTO*):

Rule of Degree: convert strong forms of connascence into weaker forms of connascence.

Rule of Locality: as the distance between software elements increases, use weaker forms of connascence.

Connascence Intersection with Bounded Context

Eric Evans's book *Domain-Driven Design* (*https://martinfowler.com/bliki/DomainDri venDesign.html*) has deeply influenced modern architectural thinking. *Domain-driven design* (DDD) is a modeling technique that allows for organized decomposition of complex problem domains. DDD defines the *bounded context*, where everything related to the domain is visible internally but opaque to other bounded contexts. The bounded context concept recognizes that each entity works best within a localized context. Thus, instead of creating a unified `Customer` class across the entire organization, each problem domain can create their own and reconcile differences at integration points. This isolation applies to other implementation details such as database schemas as well, leading to the degree of data isolation common in microservices, inspired by the concept of bounded context.

One goal of architects when designing systems based on DDD, including modular monoliths and microservices, is to prevent implementation details from "leaking" out of the bounded context. This doesn't prevent the ability for bounded contexts to communicate, but that communication is mediated via a contract (see "Contracts" on page 103 for more investigation of this topic).

Astute readers will notice commonality between the advice from 1993 about connascence *locality* and 2003's advice about *bounded context*: allowing coupling to spread to broader scopes creates *brittleness* in architecture. A brittle architecture is one where a small change in one place may cause unpredicted and nonlocalized breakages elsewhere.

For example, consider the extreme case that unfortunately appears in some architectures: exposing an application's database schema as an architecture integration point. The database schema for an application is part of what DDD calls the bounded context—an implementation detail. Exposing this detail to other applications means that a change in a single application's database may unpredictably break other applications. Thus, exposing implementation details to a broader scope harms the overall integrity of the architecture.

The common trend in architecture that we've known since at least 1993 (and likely even before) is to restrict implementation coupling to the tightest scope possible—we've just struggled with the best ways to express it. Whether we call it *bounded context* or *adhering to the locality principle of connascence*, architects have struggled, dealt, and reconciled with coupling for decades.

While bounded context is the latest attempt to express an effective coupling philosophy, it originates from and has ties to DDD, and thus refers to the abstract design aspects of a system. We need an architectural concept that reflects bounded context, yet expresses it in technical architecture terms and allows tighter alignment with architectural concerns (rather than abstract design concerns).

Architectural Quanta and Granularity

Software systems are bound together in a variety of ways. As software architects, we analyze software using many different perspectives. But component-level coupling isn't the only thing that binds software together. Many business concepts semantically bind parts of the system together, creating *functional cohesion*. To successfully evolve software, developers must consider *all* the coupling points that could break.

As defined in physics, the *quantum* is the minimum amount of any physical entity involved in an interaction. An *architectural quantum* is an independently deployable component with high functional cohesion, which includes all the structural elements required for the system to function properly. In a monolithic architecture, the quantum is the entire application; everything is highly coupled and therefore developers must deploy it en mass.

The term *quantum* is of course used heavily in the field of physics known as *quantum mechanics*. However, the authors chose the word for the same reasons physicists did. *Quantum* originated from the Latin word *quantus*, meaning "how great" or "how many." Before physics co-opted it, the legal profession used it to represent the "required or allowed amount"—for example, in damages paid. And the term also appears in the mathematics field of topology, concerning the properties of families of shapes. Because of its Latin roots, the singular is *quantum* and the plural is *quanta*, similar to the datum/data symmetry.

An architecture quantum measures several different aspects of both topology and behavior in software architecture related to how parts connect and communicate with one another.

Static coupling

Represents how static dependencies resolve within the architecture via contracts. These dependencies include operating system, frameworks and/or libraries delivered via transitive dependency management, and any other operational requirement to allow the quantum to operate.

Dynamic coupling

Represents how quanta communicate at runtime, either synchronously or asynchronously. Thus, fitness functions for this characteristic must be *continuous*, typically utilizing monitors.

The *static* and *dynamic* coupling defined here match the concepts from connascence. An easy way to think about the difference is that *static coupling* describes how services are *wired* together, whereas *dynamic coupling* describes how services *call* one another at runtime. For example, in a microservices architecture, a service must contain dependent components such as a database, representing static coupling—the service isn't operational without the necessary data. That service may *call* other services during the course of a workflow, which represents *dynamic* coupling. Neither service requires the other to be present to function, except for this runtime workflow. Thus, static coupling analyzes operational dependencies, and dynamic coupling analyzes communication dependencies.

Architecture quantum

An architecture quantum is an independently deployable artifact with high functional cohesion, high static coupling, and synchronous dynamic coupling.

A common example of an architecture quantum is a well-formed microservice within a workflow.

These definitions include important characteristics; let's cover each in detail as they inform most of the examples in the book.

Independently Deployable

Independently deployable implies several different aspects of an architecture quantum—each quantum represents a separate deployable unit within a particular architecture. Thus, a monolithic architecture—one that is deployed as a single unit—is by definition a single architecture quantum. Within a distributed architecture such as microservices, developers tend toward the ability to deploy services independently, often in a highly automated way. Thus, from an *independently deployable* standpoint, a service within a microservices architecture represents an architecture quantum (contingent on coupling—see below).

Making each architecture quantum represent a deployable asset within the architecture serves several useful purposes. First, the boundary represented by an architecture quantum serves as a useful common language among architects, developers, and operations—each understands the common scope under question: architects understand the coupling characteristics, developers understand the scope of behavior, and operations understands the deployable characteristics.

Second, it represents one of the forces (static coupling) architects must consider when striving for proper granularity of services within a distributed architecture. Often in microservices architectures, developers face the difficult question of what service granularity offers the optimum set of trade-offs. Some of those trade-offs revolve around deployability: what release cadence does this service require, what other services might be affected, what engineering practices are involved, and so on. Architects benefit from a firm understanding of exactly where deployment boundaries lie in distributed architectures.

Third, *independent deployability* forces the architecture quantum to include common coupling points such as databases. Most discussions about architecture conveniently ignore issues such as databases and user interfaces, but real-world systems must commonly deal with those problems. Thus, any system that uses a shared database fails the architecture quantum criterion for independent deployment unless the database deployment is in lockstep with the application. Many distributed systems that would otherwise qualify for multiple quanta fail the independently deployable part if they share a common database that has its own deployment cadence. Thus, merely considering the deployment boundaries doesn't solely provide a useful measure. Architects should also consider the second criterion for an architecture quantum, *high functional cohesion*, to limit the architecture quantum to a useful scope.

High Functional Cohesion

High functional cohesion refers structurally to the proximity of related elements: classes, components, services, and so on. Throughout history, computer scientists defined a variety of types of cohesion, scoped in this case to the generic *module*, which may be represented as *classes* or *components*, depending on platform. From a domain standpoint, the technical definition of *high functional cohesion* overlaps with the goals of the *bounded context* in domain-driven design: behavior and data that implement a particular domain workflow.

From a purely *independent deployability* standpoint, a giant monolithic architecture qualifies as an architecture quantum. However, it almost certainly isn't highly functionally cohesive but rather includes the functionality of the entire system. The larger the monolith, the less likely it is to be singularly functionally cohesive.

Ideally, in a microservices architecture, each service models a single domain or workflow and therefore exhibits high functional cohesion. Cohesion in this context isn't about how services interact to perform work but how independent and coupled one service is to another service.

High Static Coupling

High static coupling implies that the elements inside the architecture quantum are tightly wired together, which is really an aspect of contracts. Architects recognize things like REST and SOAP as contract formats, but method signatures and operational dependencies (via coupling points such as IP addresses and URLs) also represent contracts, which we cover in "Contracts" on page 103.

An architecture quantum is in part a measure of static coupling, and the measure is quite simple for most architecture topologies. For example, the following diagrams show the architecture styles featured in the book *Fundamentals of Software Architecture*, with the architecture quantum static coupling illustrated.

Any of the monolithic architecture styles will necessarily have a quantum of one, as illustrated in Figure 5-2.

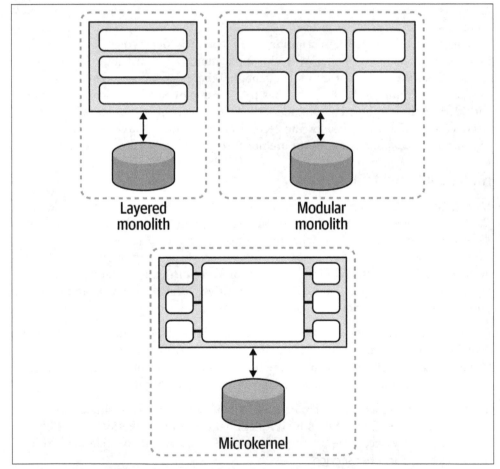

Figure 5-2. Monolithic architectures always have a quantum of one

As illustrated in Figure 5-2, any architecture that deploys as a single unit and utilizes a single database will always have a single quantum—the architecture quantum measure of static coupling includes the database, so a system that relies on a single database cannot have more than a single quantum. Thus, the static coupling measure of an architecture quantum helps identify coupling points in architecture, not just within the software components under development. Most domain architectures contain a single coupling point, typically a database, that makes their quantum measure one.

So far, the static coupling measurement of architecture quantum has evaluated all the topologies to *one*. However, distributed architectures create the possibility of multiple quanta but don't necessarily guarantee it. For example, the mediator style of event-driven architecture will always be evaluated to a single architecture quantum, as illustrated in Figure 5-3.

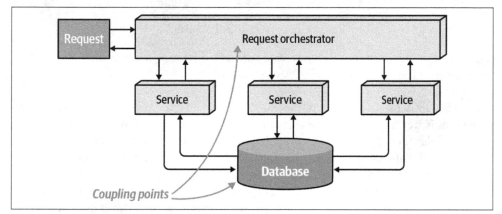

Figure 5-3. A mediated event-driven architecture has a single architecture quantum

In Figure 5-3, even though the style represents a distributed architecture, two coupling points push this architecture toward a single architecture quantum: the database, as is common with monolithic architectures above, but also the `Request Orchestrator` itself—any holistic coupling point necessary for the architecture to function forms an architecture quantum around it.

Broker event-driven architectures (those without a central mediator) are less coupled, but that doesn't guarantee complete decoupling. Consider the event-driven architecture illustrated in Figure 5-4.

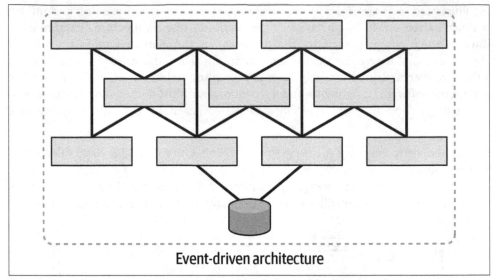

Event-driven architecture

Figure 5-4. Even a distributed architecture such as a broker-style event-driven architecture can be a single quantum

Figure 5-4 illustrates a broker-style event-driven architecture (without a central mediator) that is nevertheless a single architecture quantum because all the services utilize a single relational database, which acts as a common coupling point. The question answered by *static analysis* of an architecture quantum is whether it depends on the architecture necessary to bootstrap the service. Even in the case of an event-driven architecture where some of the services don't access the database, if they rely on services that *do* access the database, then they become part of the static coupling of the architecture quantum.

But what about situations in distributed architectures where common coupling points don't exist? Consider the event-driven architecture illustrated in Figure 5-5. The architects designed an event-driven system with two data stores and no static dependencies between the sets of services. Note that either architecture quantum can run in a production-like ecosystem. It may not be able to participate in all workflows required by the system, but it runs successfully and operates—sending requests and receiving them within the architecture.

The static coupling measure of an architecture quantum assesses the coupling dependencies between architectural and operational components. Thus, the operating system, data store, message broker, container orchestration, and all other operational dependencies form the static coupling points of an architecture quantum, using the strictest possible contracts (more about the role of contracts in architecture quanta in "Contracts" on page 103).

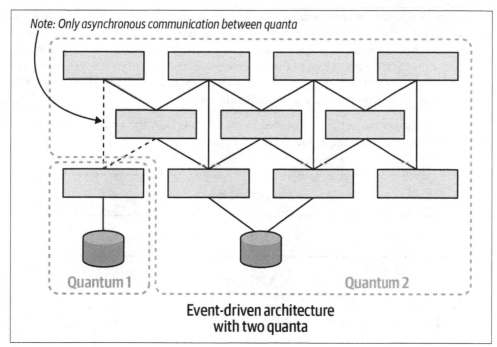

Figure 5-5. An event-driven architecture with two quanta

The microservices architecture style features highly decoupled services, including data dependencies. Architects in these architectures favor high degrees of decoupling and take care not to create coupling points between services, allowing the individual services to form their own quanta, as shown in Figure 5-6.

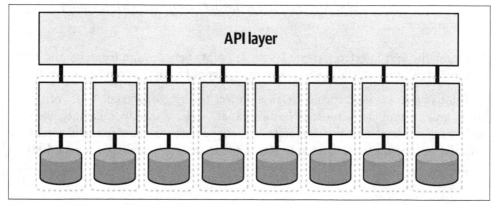

Figure 5-6. Microservices may form their own quanta

In Figure 5-6, each service (acting as a bounded context) may have its own set of architecture characteristics—one service might have higher levels of scalability or security than another. This granular level of architecture characteristics scoping represents one of the advantages of the microservices architecture style. High degrees of decoupling allow teams working on a service to move as quickly as possible, without worrying about breaking other dependencies.

However, if the system is tightly coupled to a user interface, the architecture forms a single architecture quantum, as illustrated in Figure 5-7.

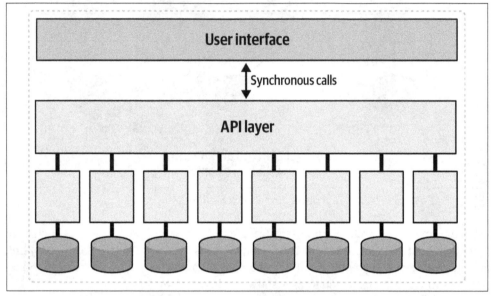

Figure 5-7. A tightly coupled user interface can reduce a microservices architecture quantum to one

Traditionally, user interfaces create coupling points between the frontend and backend, and most user interfaces won't operate if portions of the backend aren't available.

Additionally, it will be difficult for an architect to design different levels of operational architecture characteristics (performance, scale, elasticity, reliability, etc.) for each service if they all must cooperate in a single user interface (particularly in the case of synchronous calls, covered in "Dynamic Quantum Coupling" on page 100).

Architects design user interfaces utilizing asynchronicity that doesn't create coupling between front and back. A trend on many microservices projects is to use a *micro-frontend* framework for user interface elements in a microservices architecture. In such an architecture, the user interface elements that interact on behalf of the services are emitted from the services themselves. The user interface surface acts as a canvas where the user interface elements can appear and also facilitates loosely coupled communication between components, typically using events. Such an architecture is illustrated in Figure 5-8.

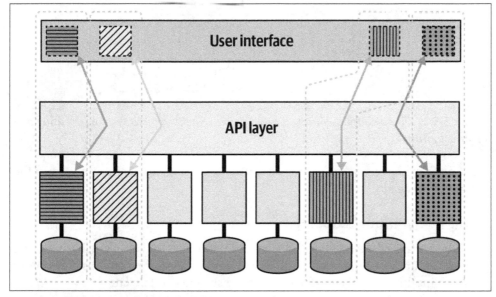

Figure 5-8. In a micro-frontend architecture, each service + user interface component forms an architecture quantum

In Figure 5-8, the four shaded services along with their corresponding micro-frontends form architecture quanta: each of these services may have different architecture characteristics.

Any coupling point in an architecture can create static coupling points from a quantum standpoint. Consider the impact of a database shared between two systems, as illustrated in Figure 5-9.

The static coupling of a system provides valuable insight, even in complex systems involving integration architecture. Increasingly, a common architecture technique for understanding legacy architecture involves creating a static quantum diagram of how things are "wired" together, which helps determine which systems will be impacted by change and offers a way of understanding (and potentially decoupling) the architecture.

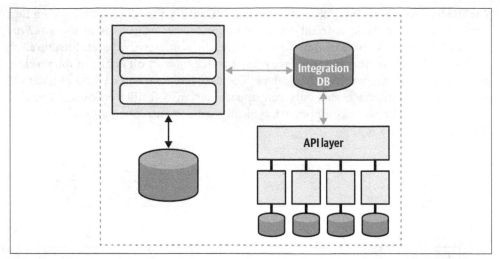

Figure 5-9. A shared database forms a coupling point between two systems, creating a single quantum

Static coupling is only one of the forces at play in distributed architectures—the other is *dynamic* coupling.

Dynamic Quantum Coupling

The last portion of the architecture quantum definition concerns synchronous coupling at runtime—in other words, the behavior of architecture quanta as they interact with one another to form workflows within a distributed architecture.

The nature of *how* services call one another creates difficult trade-off decisions because it represents a multidimensional decision space, influenced by three interlocking forces:

Communication
Refers to the type of connection synchronicity used: *synchronous* or *asynchronous*

Consistency
Describes whether the workflow communication requires atomicity or can utilize eventual consistency

Coordination
Describes whether the workflow utilizes an *orchestrator* or whether the services communicate via *choreography*

Communication

When two services communicate with each other, one of the fundamental questions for an architect is whether that communication should be *synchronous* or *asynchronous*.

Synchronous communication requires that the requestor wait for the response from the receiver, shown in Figure 5-10.

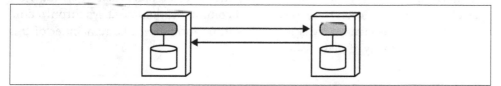

Figure 5-10. A synchronous call waits for a response from the receiver

In Figure 5-10, the calling service makes a call (using one of a number of protocols that support synchronous calls, such as gRPC) and *blocks* (does no further processing) until the receiver returns some value (or status indicating some state change or error condition).

Asynchronous communication occurs between two services when the caller posts a message to the receiver (usually via some mechanism such as a message queue), and once the caller gets acknowledgment that the message will be processed, it returns to work. If the request requires a response value, the receiver can use a reply queue to (asynchronously) notify the caller of the result, which is illustrated in Figure 5-11.

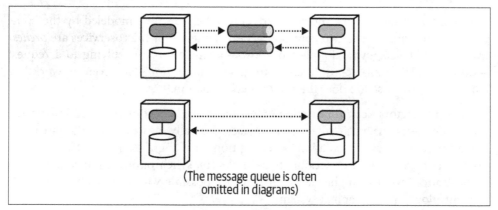

(The message queue is often omitted in diagrams)

Figure 5-11. Asynchronous communication allows parallel processing

In Figure 5-11, the caller posts a message to a message queue and continues processing until notified by the receiver that the requested information is available via return call. Generally, architects use message queues (illustrated by the metaphorical pipes which overlay the communication arrows) to implement asynchronous communication, but queues are common and create noise on diagrams, so many architects leave them off, as shown in the lower diagram. And, of course, architects can implement asynchronous communication without message queues using a variety of libraries or frameworks. Both diagrams in Figure 5-11 imply asynchronous messaging, but the bottom one provides visual shorthand and less implementation detail.

Architects must consider a number of significant trade-offs when choosing how services will communicate. Decisions around communication affect synchronization, error handling, transactionality, scalability, and performance. The remainder of this book delves into many of these issues.

Consistency

Consistency refers to the strictness of transactional integrity that communication calls must adhere to. Atomic transactions (all-or-nothing transactions requiring consistency *during* the processing of a request) lie on one side of the spectrum, and different degrees of eventual consistency lie on the other side.

Transactionality—having several different services participate in an all-or-nothing transaction—is one of the most difficult problems to model in distributed architectures, resulting in the general advice to try to avoid cross-service transactions. This complex subject is covered in the book *Software Architecture: The Hard Parts* (O'Reilly) and is beyond the scope of this book.

Coordination

Coordination refers to how much coordination the workflow modeled by the communication requires. The two common generic patterns for microservices are *orchestration* and *choreography*. Simple workflows—a single service replying to a request —don't require special consideration from this dimension. However, as workflow complexity grows, so too does the need for coordination.

These three factors—communication, consistency, and coordination—all inform the important decisions an architect must make. Critically, however, architects cannot make these choices in isolation—each option has a gravitational effect on the others. For example, transactionality is easier in synchronous architectures with orchestration, whereas higher levels of scale are possible with eventually consistent-asynchronous-choreographed systems.

Thinking about these forces as being related to each other forms a three-dimensional space, illustrated in Figure 5-12.

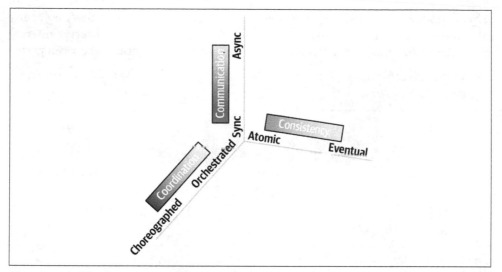

Figure 5-12. The dimensions of dynamic quantum coupling

In Figure 5-12, each force in play during service communication appears as a dimension. For a particular decision, an architect could graph the position in space representing the strength of these forces. From a practical standpoint, architects must create matrices to investigate the impact of changing any one of these conjoined forces.

Contracts

One constant factor in software architecture that cuts across and affects virtually every aspect of architect decision-making is *contracts*, broadly defined as how disparate parts of an architecture connect with one another. The dictionary definition (*https://oreil.ly/bJa12*) of a contract is:

Contract
A written or spoken agreement, especially one concerning employment, sales, or tenancy, that is intended to be enforceable by law.

In software, we use contracts broadly to describe things like integration points in architecture, and many contract formats are part of the design process of software development: SOAP, REST, gRPC, XML-RPC, and an alphabet soup of other acronyms. However, we broaden that definition and make it more consistent:

Contract
The format used by parts of an architecture to convey information or dependencies.

This definition of *contract* encompasses all techniques used to "wire together" parts of a system, including transitive dependencies for frameworks and libraries, internal and external integration points, caches, and any other communication between parts.

Contracts in software architecture range from strict to loose, as illustrated in Figure 5-13.

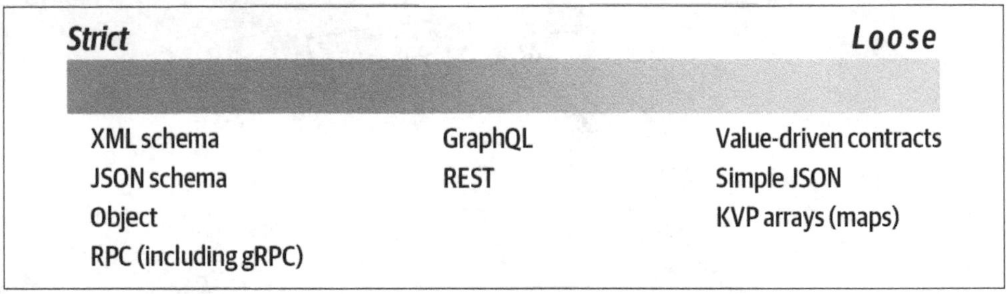

Strict		Loose
XML schema	GraphQL	Value-driven contracts
JSON schema	REST	Simple JSON
Object		KVP arrays (maps)
RPC (including gRPC)		

Figure 5-13. The spectrum of contract types from strict to loose

In Figure 5-13, where several exemplar contract types appear for illustration, a strict contract requires adherence to names, types, ordering, and all other details, leaving no ambiguity. An example of the strictest possible contract in software is a remote method call, using a platform mechanism such as RMI in Java. In that case, the remote call mimics an internal method call, matching name, parameters, types, and all other details.

Many strict contract formats mimic the semantics of method calls. For example, developers see a host of protocols that include some variation of the "RPC," traditionally an acronym for *Remote Procedure Call*. gRPC (*https://grpc.io*) is an example of a popular remote invocation framework that defaults to strict contracts.

Many architects like strict contracts because they model the semantic behavior of internal method calls. However, strict contracts create brittleness in integration architecture, something to avoid. As discussed in "Reuse Patterns" on page 112, something that is simultaneously frequently changing and used by several distinct architecture parts creates problems in architecture; contracts fit that description because they form the glue within a distributed architecture: the more frequently they must change, the more rippling problems they cause for other services. However, architects aren't forced to use strict contracts, and they should do so only when advantageous.

Even an ostensibly loose format such as JSON (*https://www.json.org/json-en.html*) offers ways to selectively add schema information to simple name/value pairs. Example 5-1 shows a strict JSON contract with schema information attached.

Example 5-1. Strict JSON contract

```
{
    "$schema": "http://json-schema.org/draft-04/schema#",
    "properties": {
      "acct": {"type": "number"},
      "cusip": {"type": "string"},
      "shares": {"type": "number", "minimum": 100}
  },
    "required": ["acct", "cusip", "shares"]
}
```

In Example 5-1, the first line references the schema definition we use and will validate against. We define three properties: `acct`, `cusip`, and `shares`, along with their types and, on the last line, which ones are required. This creates a strict contract, with required fields and types specified.

Examples of looser contracts include formats such as REST (*https://oreil.ly/3PFvE*) and GraphQL (*https://graphql.org*), which are very different formats but demonstrate looser coupling than RPC-based formats. For *REST*, the architect models resources rather than method or procedure endpoints, making for less brittle contracts. For example, if an architect builds a RESTful resource that describes parts of an airplane to support queries about seats, that query won't break in the future if someone adds details about engines to the resource—adding more information doesn't break what's there.

Similarly, *GraphQL* is used by distributed architectures to provide read-only aggregated data rather than perform costly orchestration calls across a wide variety of services. Consider the two examples of GraphQL representations appearing in Examples 5-2 and 5-3, providing two different but capable views of the `Profile` contract.

Example 5-2. Customer `Wishlist` `Profile` representation

```
type Profile {
    name: String
}
```

Example 5-3. Customer `Profile` representation

```
type Profile {
    name: String
    addr1: String
    addr2: String
    country: String
    . . .
}
```

The concept of *profile* appears in both Examples 5-2 and 5-3 but with different values. In this scenario, the Customer `Wishlist` doesn't have internal access to the customer's name, only a unique identifier. Thus, it needs access to a Customer `Profile` that maps the identifier to the customer name. The Customer `Profile` includes a large amount of information about the customer in addition to the name. As far as `Wishlist` is concerned, the only interesting thing in `Profile` is the name.

A common antipattern that some architects fall victim to is to assume that `Wishlist` might eventually need all the other parts, so they include them in the contract from the outset. This is an example of Stamp Coupling (*https://oreil.ly/Fk9tx*) and is an antipattern in most cases because it introduces breaking changes where they aren't needed, making the architecture fragile yet receiving little benefit. For example, if `Wishlist` cares only about the customer name from `Profile`, but the contract specifies every field in `Profile` (just in case), then a change in `Profile` that `Wishlist` doesn't care about causes a contract breakage and coordination to fix.

Keeping contracts at a "need to know" level strikes a balance between semantic coupling and necessary information without creating needless fragility in integration architecture.

At the far end of the spectrum of contract coupling lie extremely loose contracts, often expressed as name/value pairs in formats like YAML (*https://yaml.org*) and JSON, illustrated in Example 5-4.

Example 5-4. Name/value pairs in JSON

```
{
  "name": "Mark",
  "status": "active",
  "joined": "2003"
}
```

Nothing but the raw facts in Example 5-4! No additional metadata, type information, or anything else, just name/value pairs.

Using such loose contracts allows for extremely decoupled systems, often one of the goals in architectures such as microservices. However, the looseness of the contract comes with trade-offs, including lack of contract certainty, verification, and increased application logic. The formerly contractual concerns are often replaced with fitness functions.

Case Study: Microservices as an Evolutionary Architecture

A microservices architecture defines physical bounded contexts between architectural elements, encapsulating all the parts that might change. This type of architecture is designed to allow incremental change. In a microservices architecture, the bounded context serves as the quantum boundary and includes dependent components such as database servers. It may also include architecture components such as search engines and reporting tools—anything that contributes to the delivered functionality of the service, as shown in Figure 5-14.

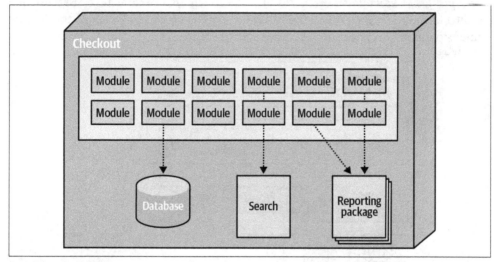

Figure 5-14. The architectural quantum in microservices encompasses the service and all its dependent parts

In Figure 5-14, the service includes code components, a database server, and a search engine component. Part of the bounded context philosophy of microservices operationalizes all the pieces of a service together, leaning heavily on modern DevOps practices. In the following section, we investigate some common architectural patterns and their typical quantum boundaries.

Traditionally isolated roles such as architect and operations must coordinate in an evolutionary architecture. Architecture is abstract until operationalized; developers must pay attention to how their components fit together in the real world. Regardless of which architecture pattern developers choose, architects should also explicitly define their quantum size. Small quanta imply faster change because of small scope. Generally, small parts are easier to work with than big ones. Quantum size determines the lower bound of the incremental change possible within an architecture.

Combining the engineering practices of Continuous Delivery with the physical partitioning of bounded context forms the philosophical basis for the microservice style of architecture, along with our architectural quantum concept.

In a layered architecture, the focus is on the *technical* dimension, or how the mechanics of the application work: persistence, UI, business rules, and so forth. Most software architectures focus primarily on these technical dimensions. However, an additional perspective exists. Suppose that one of the key bounded contexts in an application is *Checkout*. Where does it live in the layered architecture? Domain concepts like *Checkout* smear across the layers in this architecture. Because the architecture is segregated via technical layers, there is no clear concept of the *domain* dimension in this architecture, as can be seen in Figure 5-15.

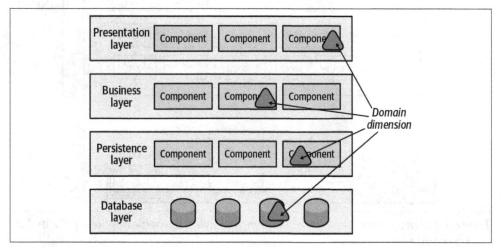

Figure 5-15. The domain dimension is embedded within technical architecture

In Figure 5-15, some portion of *Checkout* exists in the UI, another portion lives in the business rules, and persistence is handled by the bottom layers. Because layered architecture isn't designed to accommodate domain concepts, developers must modify each layer to make changes to domains. From a domain perspective, a layered architecture has zero evolvability. In highly coupled architectures, change is difficult because coupling between the parts developers want to change is high. Yet, in most projects, the common unit of change revolves around domain concepts. If a software development team is organized into silos resembling their role in the layered architecture, then changes to *Checkout* require coordination across many teams.

In contrast, consider an architecture where the *domain* dimension is the primary segregation of the architecture, as shown in Figure 5-16.

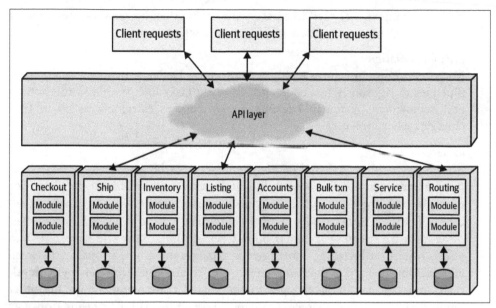

Figure 5-16. Microservices architectures partition across domain lines, embedding the technical architecture

As shown in Figure 5-16, each service is defined around the DDD concept, encapsulating the technical architecture and all other dependent components (like databases) into a bounded context and creating a highly decoupled architecture. Each service "owns" all parts of its bounded context and communicates with other bounded contexts via messaging (such as REST or message queues). Thus, no service is allowed to know the implementation details of another service (such as database schemas), preventing inappropriate coupling. The operational goal of this architecture is to replace one service with another without disrupting other services.

Microservices architectures generally follow seven principles, as discussed in *Building Microservices Architectures*:

Modeled around the business domain
> The emphasis in microservices design is on the business domain, not technical architecture. Thus, the quantum reflects the bounded context. Some developers make the mistaken association that a bounded context represents a single entity such as Customer; instead, it represents a business context and/or workflow such as CatalogCheckout. The goal in microservices isn't to see how small developers can make each services but rather to create a useful bounded context.

Hide implementation details
> The technical architecture in microservices is encapsulated within the service boundary, which is based on the business domain. Each domain forms a physical

bounded context. Services integrate with each other by passing messages or resources, not by exposing details like database schemas.

Culture of automation

Microservices architectures embrace Continuous Delivery, by using deployment pipelines to rigorously test code and automate tasks like machine provisioning and deployment. Automated testing in particular is extremely useful in fast-changing environments.

Highly decentralized

Microservices form a *shared nothing* architecture—the goal is to decrease coupling as much as possible. Generally, duplication is preferable to coupling. For example, both the `CatalogCheckout` and `ShipToCustomer` services have a concept called `Item`. Because both teams have the same name and similar properties, developers try to reuse it across both services, thinking it will save time and effort. Instead, it increases effort because changes must now propagate between all the teams that share the component. And whenever a service changes, developers must worry about changes to the shared component. If, on the other hand, each service has its own `Item` and passes information it needs from `CatalogCheckout` to `ShipToCustomer` without coupling to the component, it can change independently.

Deployed independently

Developers and operations expect that each service component will be deployed independently from other services (and other infrastructure), reflecting the physical manifestation of the bounded context. The ability for developers to deploy one service without affecting any other service is one of the defining benefits of this architectural style. Moreover, developers typically automate all deployment and operations tasks, including parallel testing and Continuous Delivery.

Isolate failure

Developers isolate failure both within the context of a microservice and in the coordination of services. Each service is expected to handle reasonable error scenarios and recover if possible. Many DevOps best practices (such as the Circuit Breaker pattern (*https://oreil.ly/l028d*), bulkheads, etc.) commonly appear in these architectures. Many microservices architectures adhere to the Reactive Manifesto (*http://www.reactivemanifesto.org*), a list of operational and coordination principles that lead to more robust systems.

Highly observable

Developers cannot hope to manually monitor hundreds or thousands of services (how many multicast SSH terminal sessions can one developer observe?). Thus, monitoring and logging become first-class concerns in this architecture. If operations cannot monitor one of these services, it might as well not exist.

The main goals of microservices are isolation of domains via physical bounded context and emphasis on understanding the problem domain. Therefore, the architectural quantum is the service, making this an excellent example of an evolutionary architecture. If one service needs to evolve to change its database, no other service is affected because no other service is allowed to know implementation details like schemas. Of course, the developers of the changing service will have to deliver the same information via the integration point between the services (hopefully protected by a fitness function like *consumer-driven contracts*), allowing the calling service developers the bliss of never knowing the change occurred.

Given that microservices is our exemplar for an evolutionary architecture, it is unsurprising that it scores well from an evolutionary standpoint.

Incremental change
> Both aspects of incremental change are easy in microservices architectures. Each service forms a bounded context around a domain concept, making it easy to make changes that only affect that context. Microservices architectures rely heavily on automation practices from *Continuous Delivery*, utilizing deployment pipelines and modern DevOps practices.

Guided change with fitness functions
> Developers can easily build both atomic and holistic fitness functions for microservices architectures. Each service has a well-defined boundary, allowing a variety of levels of testing within the service components. Services must coordinate via integration, which also requires testing. Fortunately, sophisticated testing techniques grew alongside the development of microservices.

If there are clear benefits, then why haven't developers embraced this style before? Years ago, automatic provisioning of machines wasn't possible. While we had virtual machine (VM) technology, they were often handcrafted with long lead times. Operating systems were commercial and licensed, with little support for automation. Real-world constraints like budgets impact architectures, which is one of the reasons developers build more and more elaborate shared resources architectures, segregated at the technical layers. If operations is expensive and cumbersome, architects build around it, as they did in enterprise service bus-driven service-oriented architectures.

The Continuous Delivery and DevOps movements added a new factor into the dynamic equilibrium. Now, machine definitions live in version control and support extreme automation. Deployment pipelines spin up multiple test environments in parallel to support safe continuous deployment. Because much of the software stack is open source, licensing and other concerns have less impact on architectures. The community reacted to the new capabilities emergent in the software development ecosystem to build more domain-centric architectural styles.

In microservices architecture, the domain encapsulates technical and other architectures, making evolution across domain dimensions easy. No one perspective on architecture is "correct" but rather a reflection of the goals developers build into their projects. If the focus is entirely on technical architecture, then making changes across that dimension is easier. However, if the domain perspective is ignored, then evolving across that dimension is no better than the Big Ball of Mud.

Reuse Patterns

As an industry, we have benefited greatly from reusable frameworks and libraries built by others, often open source and freely available. Clearly, the ability to reuse code is good. However, like all good ideas, many companies abuse this idea and create problems for themselves. Every corporation desires code reuse because software seems so modular, like electronics components. However, despite the promise that exists for truly modular software, it has consistently evaded us.

> Software reuse is more like an organ transplant than snapping together Lego blocks.
>
> —John D. Cook

While language designers have promised developers Lego blocks for a long time, we still seem to have organs. Software reuse is difficult and doesn't come automatically. Many optimistic managers assume any code that developers write is inherently reusable, but this is not always the case. Many companies have attempted and succeeded in writing truly reusable code, but it is intentional and difficult. Developers often spend a lot of time trying to build reusable modules that turn out to have little practical reuse.

In service-oriented architectures (SOAs), the common practice was to find commonalities and reuse as much as possible. For example, imagine that a company has two contexts: Checkout and Shipping. In an SOA, architects observe that both contexts include the concept of Customer. This, in turn, encourages them to consolidate both customers into a single Customer service, coupling both Checkout and Shipping to the shared service. Architects worked toward a goal of ultimate *canonicality* in SOA—every concept has a single (shared) home.

Ironically, the more effort developers put into making code reusable, the harder it is to use. Making code reusable involves adding options and decision points to accommodate the different uses. The more developers add hooks to enable reusability, the more they harm the basic *usability* of the code.

The more reusable code is, the less usable it is.

In other words, ease of code use is often inversely proportional to how reusable that code is. When developers build code to be reusable, they must add features to accommodate the myriad ways they and other developers will eventually use the code. All that future-proofing makes it more difficult for developers to use the code for a single purpose.

Microservices eschew code reuse, adopting the philosophy of *prefer duplication to coupling*: reuse implies coupling, and microservices architectures are extremely decoupled. However, the goal in microservices isn't to embrace duplication but rather to isolate entities within domains. Services that share a common class are no longer independent. In a microservices architecture, `Checkout` and `Shipping` would each have their own internal representation of `Customer`. If they need to collaborate on customer-related information, they send the pertinent information to each other. Architects don't try to reconcile and consolidate the disparate versions of `Customer` in their architecture. The benefits of reuse are illusory and the coupling it introduces comes with its disadvantages. Thus, while architects understand the downsides of duplication, they offset that localized damage to the architectural damage too much coupling introduces.

Code reuse can be an asset but also a potential liability. Make sure the coupling points introduced in your code don't conflict with other goals in the architecture. For example, microservices architectures typically use a service mesh to couple the parts of services together that help unify a particular architectural concern, such as monitoring or logging.

Effective Reuse = Abstraction + Low Volatility

A common problem faced by many architects today lies with reconciling two differing corporate objectives: holistic reuse versus isolation via bounded contexts, inspired by DDD. Large organizations understandably want to utilize as much reuse across their ecosystem as possible—the more they can reuse, the less they have to write from scratch. However, reuse creates coupling, which many architects try to avoid, especially coupling that extends too far.

Sidecars and Service Mesh: Orthogonal Operational Coupling

One of the design goals of microservices architectures is a high degree of decoupling, often manifested in the advice "Duplication is preferable to coupling." For example, let's say that two PenultimateWidgets services need to pass customer information, yet domain-driven design's bounded context insists that implementation details remain private to the service. A common solution allows each service its own internal representation of entities such as `Customer`, passing that information in loosely coupled ways such as name/value pairs in JSON. Notice that this allows each service to change its internal representation at will, including the technology stack, without breaking the integration. Architects generally frown on duplicating code because it causes synchronization issues, semantic drift, and a host of other issues, but sometimes forces exist that are worse than the problems of duplication, and coupling in microservices often fits that bill. Thus, in microservices architecture, the answer to the question of "should we duplicate or couple to some capability" is likely *duplicate*, whereas in another architecture style such as a service-based architecture, the correct answer is likely *couple*. It depends!

When designing microservices, architects have resigned themselves to the reality of implementation duplication to preserve decoupling. But what about the types of capabilities that *benefit* from high coupling, such as monitoring, logging, authentication and authorization, circuit breakers, and a host of other operational abilities that each service should have? Allowing each team to manage these dependencies often descends into chaos. For example, consider a company like PenultimateWidgets trying to standardize on a common monitoring solution, to make it easier to operationalize its various services. If each team is responsible for implementing monitoring for their service, how can the operations team be sure they did? Also, what about issues such as unified upgrades? If the monitoring tool needs to upgrade across the organization, how can teams coordinate that?

The common solution that has emerged in the microservices ecosystem over the past few years solves this problem in an elegant way using the *Sidecar pattern*, based on a much earlier architecture pattern defined by Alistair Cockburn known as the *Hexagonal architecture*, illustrated in Figure 5-17.

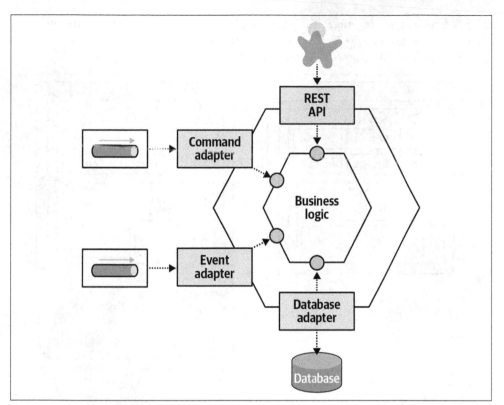

Figure 5-17. The Hexagonal Pattern separated domain logic from technical coupling

In Figure 5-17, what we would now call the domain logic resides in the center of the hexagon, which is surrounded by ports and adapters to other parts of the ecosystem (in fact, this pattern is alternately known as the *Ports and Adapters pattern*). While predating microservices by a number of years, this pattern has similarities to modern microservices, with one significant difference: data fidelity. The hexagonal architecture treated the database as just another adapter that can be plugged in, but one of the insights from DDD suggests that data schemas and transactionality should be inside the interior—like microservices.

The *Sidecar pattern* leverages the same concept as hexagonal architecture in that it decouples the domain logic from the technical (infrastructure) logic. For example, consider the two microservices shown in Figure 5-18.

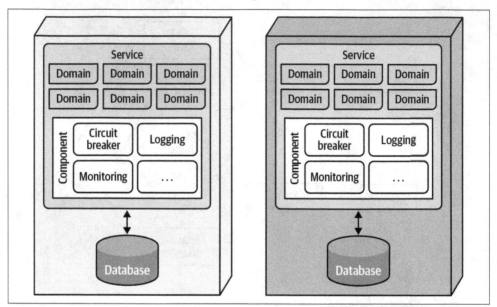

Figure 5-18. Two microservices that share the same operational capabilities

In Figure 5-18, each service includes a split between operational concerns (the larger components toward the bottom of the service) and domain concerns (pictured in the boxes toward the top of the service labeled "Domain"). If architects desire consistency in operational capabilities, the separable parts go into a sidecar component, metaphorically named for the sidecar that attaches to motorcycles (*https://oreil.ly/ YH5Uo*), whose implementation is either a shared responsibility across teams or managed by a centralized infrastructure group. If architects can assume that every service includes the sidecar, it forms a consistent operational interface across services, typically attached via a service plane, shown in Figure 5-19.

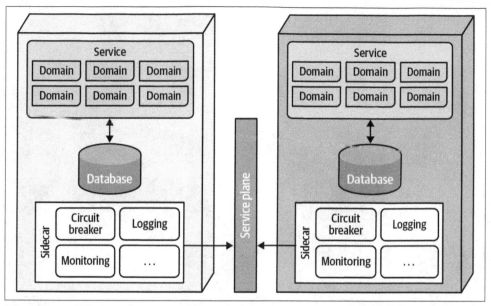

Figure 5-19. When each microservice includes a common component, architects can establish links between them for consistent control

If architects and operations can safely assume that every service includes the sidecar component (governed by fitness functions), it forms a service mesh, illustrated in Figure 5-20, where the boxes to the right of each service all interconnect, forming a "mesh."

Having a mesh allows architects and DevOps to create dashboards, control operational characteristics such as scale, and implement a host of other capabilities.

The Sidecar pattern allows governance groups like enterprise architects a reasonable restraint over too many polyglot environments: one of the advantages of microservices is a reliance on integration rather than a common platform, allowing teams to choose the correct level of complexity and capabilities on a service-by-service basis. However, as the number of platforms proliferates, unified governance becomes more difficult. Therefore, teams often use the consistency of the service mesh as a driver to support infrastructure and other cross-cutting concerns across multiple heterogeneous platforms. For example, without a service mesh, if enterprise architects want to unify around a common monitoring solution, then teams must build one sidecar per platform that supports that solution.

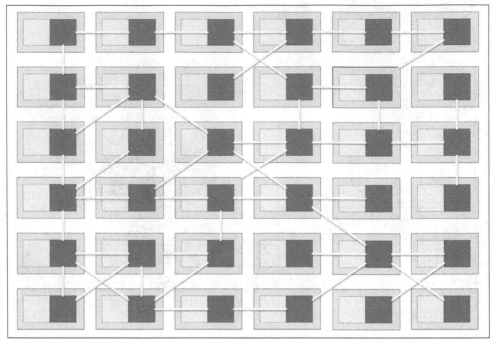

Figure 5-20. A service mesh is a set of operational links between services

The *Sidecar pattern* represents not only a way to decouple operational capabilities from domains, it's also an *orthogonal reuse* pattern to address orthogonal coupling (see "Orthogonal Coupling" on page 118). Often, architectural solutions require several different types of coupling, such as our current example of domain versus operational coupling. An orthogonal reuse pattern presents a way to reuse some aspect counter to one or more seams in the architecture. For example, microservices architectures are organized around domains, but operational coupling requires cutting across those domains. A sidecar allows an architect to isolate those concerns in a cross-cutting but consistent layer through the architecture.

Orthogonal Coupling

In mathematics, two lines are *orthogonal* if they intersect at right angles, which also implies independence. In software architecture, two parts of an architecture may be *orthogonally coupled*: two distinct purposes that must still intersect to form a complete solution. The obvious example from this chapter concerns operational concerns such as monitoring, which is necessary but independent from domain behavior like catalog checkout. Recognizing orthogonal coupling allows architects to find intersection points that cause the least entanglement between concerns.

The Sidecar pattern and service mesh offer a clean way to spread some sort of cross-cutting concern across a distributed architecture, and can be used by more than just operational coupling (see the next section). It offers an architectural equivalent to the Decorator pattern (*https://oreil.ly/BSM1F*) from the Gang of Four's book *Design Patterns*: it allows an architect to "decorate" behavior across a distributed architecture independent of the normal connectivity.

Data Mesh: Orthogonal Data Coupling

Observing the other trends in distributed architectures, Zhamak Dehghani and several other innovators derived the core idea from domain-oriented decoupling of microservices, the service mesh, and the Sidecar pattern and applied it to analytical data, with modifications. As we mentioned in the previous section, the *Sidecar pattern* provides a nonentangling way to organize orthogonal coupling; the separation between operational and analytical data is another excellent example of just such a coupling, but with more complexity than simple operational coupling.

Definition of Data Mesh

Data Mesh is an approach to sharing, accessing, and managing analytical data in a decentralized fashion. It satisfies a wide range of analytical use cases, such as reporting, training ML models, and generating insights. Contrary to the previous architecture, it does so by aligning the architecture and ownership of the data with the business domains and enabling a peer-to-peer consumption of data.

Data Mesh is founded on the following principles:

Domain ownership of data
> Data is owned and shared by the domains that are most intimately familiar with the data: those that either are originating the data or are the first-class consumers of the data. The architecture allows for the distributed sharing and access of the data from multiple domains and in a peer-to-peer fashion without the intermediate transformation steps required in data warehouses or the centralized storage of the Data Lake.

Data as a product
> To prevent siloing of data and to encourage domains to share their data, Data Mesh introduces the concept of data served as a product. It puts in place the organizational roles and success metrics necessary to ensure that domains provide their data in a way that provides a positive experience to data consumers across the organization. This principle leads to the introduction of a new architectural quantum, called a data product quantum, to maintain and serve discoverable, understandable, timely, secure, and high-quality data to consumers. This chapter introduces the architectural aspect of the data product quantum.

Self-serve data platform

> In order to empower the domain teams to build and maintain their data products, Data Mesh introduces a new set of self-serve platform capabilities. The capabilities focus on improving the experience of data product developers and consumers. It includes features such as declarative creation of data products, discoverability of data products across the mesh through search and browsing, and management of the emergence of other intelligent graphs such as lineage of data and knowledge graphs.

Computational federated governance

> This principle ensures that despite decentralized ownership of the data, organization-wide governance requirements such as compliance, security, privacy, quality of data, and interoperability of data products are met consistently across all domains. Data Mesh introduces a federated decision-making model composed of domain data product owners. The policies they formulate are automated and embedded as code in each and every data product. The architectural implication of this approach to governance is a platform-supplied embedded sidecar in each data product quantum to store and execute the policies at the point of access: data read or write.

Data Mesh is a wide-ranging topic, fully covered in the book *Data Mesh: Delivering Data-Driven Value at Scale* (O'Reilly). In this chapter, we focus on the core architectural element, the *data product quantum*.

Data product quantum

The core tenet of the Data Mesh lies atop modern distributed architectures such as microservices. Just as in the *service mesh*, teams build a *data product quantum* (DPQ) adjacent but coupled to their service, as illustrated in Figure 5-21.

The service *Alpha* contains both behavioral and transactional (operational) data. The domain also includes a *data product quantum*, which also contains code and data, which acts as an interface to the overall analytical and reporting portion of the system. The DPQ acts as an operationally independent but highly coupled set of behaviors and data.

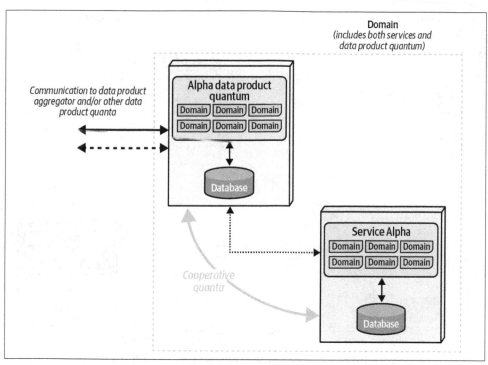

Figure 5-21. Structure of a data product quantum

Several types of DPQs commonly exist in modern architectures:

Source-aligned (native) DPQ
> Provides analytical data on behalf of the collaborating architecture quantum, typically a microservice, acting as a cooperative quantum.

Aggregate DQP
> Aggregates data from multiple inputs, either synchronously or asynchronously. For example, for some aggregations, an asynchronous request may be sufficient; for others, the aggregator DPQ may need to perform synchronous queries for a source-aligned DPQ.

Fit-for-purpose DPQ
> Custom-made DPQ to serve a particular requirement, which may encompass analytical reporting, business intelligence, machine learning, or some other supporting capability.

A particular domain may include multiple DPQs, depending on differing architecture characteristics for different types of analysis. For example, one DPQ may need different levels of performance than another.

Each domain that also contributes to analysis and business intelligence includes a DPQ, as illustrated in Figure 5-22.

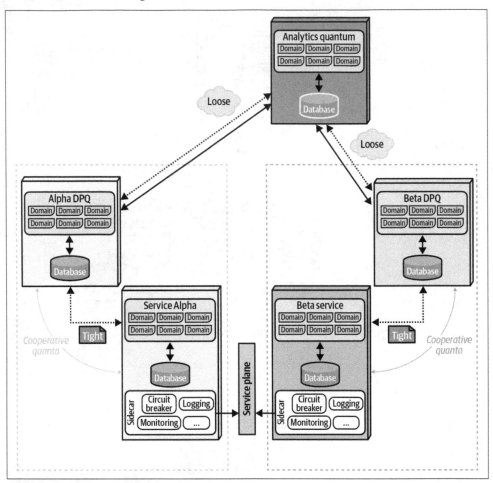

Figure 5-22. The data product quantum acts as a separate but highly coupled adjunct to a service

In Figure 5-22, the DPQ represents a component owned by the domain team responsible for implementing the service. It overlaps information stored in the database, and may have interactions with some of the domain behavior asynchronously. The data product quantum also likely has behavior as well as data for the purposes of analytics and business intelligence.

Each *data product quantum* acts as a *cooperative quantum* for the service itself:

Cooperative quantum
> An operationally separate quantum that communicates with its cooperator via asynchronous communication and eventual consistency yet features tight contract coupling with its cooperator and generally looser contract coupling to the analytics quantum, the service responsible for reports, analysis, business intelligence, and so on.

While the two cooperating quanta are operationally independent, they represent two sides of data: operational data in the service and analytical data in the data product quantum.

Some portion of the system will carry the responsibility for analytics and business intelligence, which will form its own domain and quantum. To operate, this analytical quantum has static quantum coupling to the individual data product quanta it needs for information. This service may make either synchronous or asynchronous calls to the DPQ, depending on the type of request. For example, some DPQs will feature a SQL interface to the analytical DPQ, allowing synchronous queries. Other requirements may aggregate information across a number of DPQs.

Data Mesh is an excellent example of the innovative mashup between microservices architectures and analytical data, and it is a road map for managing orthogonal coupling in distributed architectures. The concept of the *sidecar* and *cooperative quantum* allows architects to selectively "overlay" one architecture atop another. This allows preferred modeling of domains (such as DDD) while allowing separate concerns well-governed access to what they need.

Summary

Understanding the impact of structure on the ability to evolve a software system is key for architects. While a number of named architectural styles exist, the primary characteristic of those architectures that determines evolvability is controlled coupling. Whether inspired by the locality property of connascence or bounded context in DDD, controlling the extent of implementation coupling is the key to building evolvable architectures.

Contracts allow different architecture parts to communication without creating tight coupling points. Using loosely defined coupling points, flexible contracts, and contract fitness functions allows architects to define systems that meet requirements yet don't create impediments to governance or change.

CHAPTER 6

Evolutionary Data

Relational and other types of data stores are ubiquitous in modern software projects, a form of coupling that is often more problematic than architectural coupling. Data teams are generally not as accustomed to engineering practices such as unit testing and refactoring (which is gradually improving). Also, databases often become integration points, making data teams reluctant to make changes due to potential rippling side effects.

Data is an important dimension to consider when creating an evolvable architecture. Architectures like microservices require much more architectural consideration of data partitioning, dependencies, transactionality, and a host of other issues that were formerly only the realm of data teams. It is beyond the scope of this book to cover all the aspects of evolutionary database design. Fortunately, our co-author Pramod Sadalage, along with Scott Ambler, wrote *Refactoring Databases* (*http://data baserefactoring.com*), subtitled *Evolutionary Database Design*. We cover only the parts of database design that impact evolutionary architecture and encourage readers to read that book.

Evolutionary Database Design

Evolutionary design in databases occurs when developers can build and evolve the structure of the database as requirements change over time. Database schemas are abstractions, similar to class hierarchies. As the underlying real world changes, those changes must be reflected in the abstractions developers and data teams build. Otherwise, the abstractions gradually fall out of synchronization with the real world.

Evolving Schemas

How can architects build systems that support evolution but still use traditional tools like relational databases? The key to evolving database design lies in evolving schemas alongside code. Continuous Delivery addresses the problem of how to fit the traditional data silo into the continuous feedback loop of modern software projects. Developers must treat changes to database structure the same way they treat source code: tested, versioned, and incremental:

Tested
> The data team and developers should rigorously test changes to database schemas to ensure stability. If developers use a data mapping tool like an object-relational mapper (ORM), they should consider adding fitness functions to ensure the mappings stay in sync with the schemas.

Versioned
> Developers and the data team should version database schemas alongside the code that utilizes it. Source code and database schemas are symbiotic—neither functions without the other. Engineering practices that artificially separate these two necessarily coupled things cause needless inefficiencies.

Incremental
> Changes to the database schemas should accrue just as source code changes build up: incrementally as the system evolves. Modern engineering practices eschew manual updates of database schemas, preferring automated migration tools instead.

Database migration tools are utilities that allow developers (or the data team) to make small, incremental changes to a database that are automatically applied as part of a deployment pipeline. They exist along a wide spectrum of capabilities from simple command-line tools to sophisticated proto-IDEs. When developers need to make a change to a schema, they write small database migration (aka delta) scripts, as illustrated in Example 6-1.

Example 6-1. A simple database migration

```
CREATE TABLE customer (
    id BIGINT GENERATED BY DEFAULT AS IDENTITY (START WITH 1) PRIMARY KEY,
    firstname VARCHAR(60),
    lastname VARCHAR(60)
);
```

The migration tool takes the SQL snippet shown in Example 6-1 and automatically applies it to the developer's instance of the database. If the developer later realizes they want to add date of birth, rather than changing the original migration they can create a new one that modifies the original structure, as shown in Example 6-2.

Example 6-2. Adding date of birth to existing table using a migration

```
ALTER TABLE customer ADD COLUMN dateofbirth DATETIME;
```

Once developers have run migrations, the migrations are considered immutable—changes are modeled after double-entry bookkeeping. For example, suppose that Danielle the developer ran the migration in Example 6-2 as the 24th migration on a project. Later, she realizes `dateofbirth` isn't needed after all. She could just remove the 24th migration, and hence, the `dateofbirth` column. However, any code written after Danielle ran the migration will assume the presence of the `dateofbirth` column and will no longer work if the project needs to back up to an intermediate point (e.g., to fix a bug). Also, any other environment where this change was already applied will have the column and create a schema mismatch. Instead, she could remove the column by creating a new migration.

In Example 6-2, the developer modifies the existing schema to add a new column. Some migration tools support *undo* capabilities as well, as shown in Example 6-3. Supporting *undo* allows developers to easily move forward and backward through the schema versions. For example, suppose a project is on version 101 in the source code repository and needs to return to version 95. For the source code, developers merely check out version 95 from version control. But how can they ensure the database schema is correct for version 95 of the code? If they use migrations with *undo* capabilities, they can "undo" their way backward to version 95 of the schema, applying each migration in turn to regress to the desired version.

Example 6-3. Adding date of birth and undo migration to existing table

```
ALTER TABLE customer ADD COLUMN dateofbirth DATETIME;
--//@UNDO

ALTER TABLE customer DROP COLUMN dateofbirth;
```

However, most teams have moved away from building *undo* capabilities for three reasons. First, if all the migrations exist, developers can build the database just up to the point they need without backing up to a previous version. In our example, developers would build from 1 to 95 to restore version 95. Second, why maintain two versions of correctness, both forward and backward? To confidently support *undo*, developers must test the code, sometimes doubling the testing burden. Third, building comprehensive *undo* sometimes presents daunting challenges. For example, imagine that the migration dropped a table—how would the migration script preserve all data in the case of an *undo* operation? Prefix the table with *DROPPED_* and keep it around? This will quickly get complicated because of all the changes happening around the table, and soon the data in the *DROPPED* table will not be relevant anymore.

Database migrations allow both database admins and developers to manage changes to schema and code incrementally, by treating each as parts of a whole. By incorporating database changes into the deployment pipeline feedback loop, developers have more opportunities to incorporate automation and earlier verification into the project's build cadence.

Shared Database Integration

A common integration pattern highlighted here is Shared Database Integration (*https://oreil.ly/NxSsk*), which uses database as a sharing mechanism for data, as illustrated in Figure 6-1.

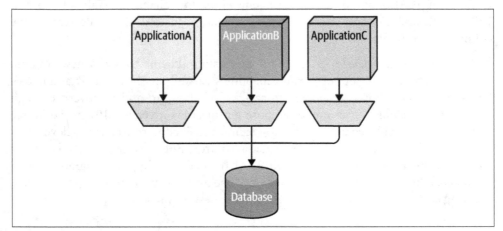

Figure 6-1. Using the database as an integration point

In Figure 6-1, the three applications share the same relational database. Projects frequently default to this integration style—every project is using the same relational database because of governance, so why not share data across projects? Architects quickly discover, however, that using the database as an integration point fossilizes the database schema across all sharing projects.

What happens when one of the coupled applications needs to evolve capabilities via a schema change? If ApplicationA makes changes to the schema, this could potentially break the other two applications. Fortunately, as discussed in the aforementioned *Refactoring Databases* book, a commonly utilized refactoring pattern is used to untangle this kind of coupling: the *Expand/Contract pattern*. Many database refactoring techniques avoid timing problems by building a transition phase into the refactoring, as illustrated in Figure 6-2.

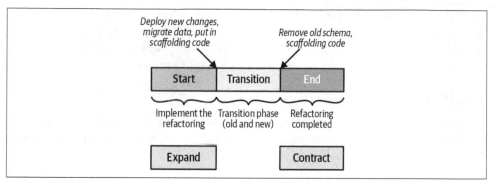

Figure 6-2. The Expand/Contract pattern for database refactoring

Using this pattern, developers have a starting state and an ending state, maintaining both the *old* and *new* states during the transition. This transition state allows for backward compatibility and also gives other systems in the enterprise enough time to catch up with the change. For some organizations, the transition state can last from a few days to months.

Here is an example of *Expand/Contract* in action. Consider the common evolutionary change of splitting a `name` column into `firstname` and `lastname`, which Penultimate-Widgets needs to do for marketing purposes. For this change, developers have the start state, the expand state, and the final state, as shown in Figure 6-3.

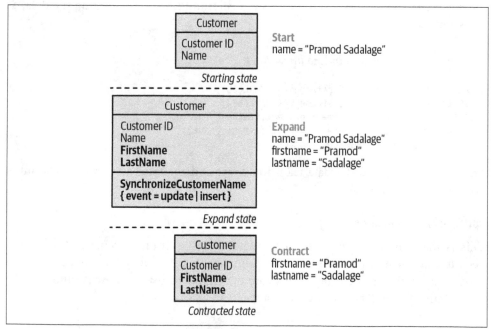

Figure 6-3. The three states of Expand/Contract refactoring

In Figure 6-3, the full name appears as a single column. During the transition, the PenultimateWidgets data team must maintain both versions to prevent breaking possible integration points in the database. They have several options for how we proceed to split the `name` column into `firstname` and `lastname`.

Option 1: No integration points, no legacy data

In this case, the developers have no other systems to think about and no existing data to manage, so they can add the new columns and drop the old column, as shown in Example 6-4.

Example 6-4. Simple case with no integration points and no legacy data

```
ALTER TABLE customer ADD firstname VARCHAR2(60);
ALTER TABLE customer ADD lastname VARCHAR2(60);
ALTER TABLE customer DROP COLUMN name;
```

For *Option 1*, the refactoring is straightforward: the data team can make the relevant change and get on with life.

Option 2: Legacy data, but no integration points

In this scenario, developers assume existing data to migrate to new columns but they have no external systems to worry about. They must create a function to extract the pertinent information from the existing column to handle migrating the data, as shown in Example 6-5.

Example 6-5. Legacy data but no integrators

```
ALTER TABLE Customer ADD firstname VARCHAR2(60);
ALTER TABLE Customer ADD lastname VARCHAR2(60);
UPDATE Customer set firstname = extractfirstname (name);
UPDATE Customer set lastname = extractlastname (name);
ALTER TABLE customer DROP COLUMN name;
```

This scenario requires the data team to extract and migrate the existing data but is otherwise straightforward.

Option 3: Existing data and integration points

This is the most complex and, unfortunately, most common scenario. Companies need to migrate existing data to new columns while external systems depend on the `name` column, which the other teams cannot migrate to use the new columns in the desired time frame. The required SQL appears in Example 6-6.

Example 6-6. Complex case with legacy data and integrators

```
ALTER TABLE Customer ADD firstname VARCHAR2(60);
ALTER TABLE Customer ADD lastname VARCHAR2(60);

UPDATE Customer set firstname = extractfirstname (name);
UPDATE Customer set lastname = extractlastname (name);

CREATE OR REPLACE TRIGGER SynchronizeName
BEFORE INSERT OR UPDATE
ON Customer
REFERENCING OLD AS OLD NEW AS NEW
FOR EACH ROW
BEGIN
  IF :NEW.Name IS NULL THEN
    :NEW.Name := :NEW.firstname||' '||:NEW.lastname;
  END IF;
  IF :NEW.name IS NOT NULL THEN
    :NEW.firstname := extractfirstname(:NEW.name);
    :NEW.lastname := extractlastname(:NEW.name);
  END IF;
END;
```

To build the transition phase in Example 6-6, the data team adds a trigger in the database that moves data from the old `name` column to the new `firstname` and `lastname` columns when the other systems are inserting data into the database, allowing the new system to access the same data. Similarly, developers or the data team concatenate the `firstname` and `lastname` columns into a `name` column when the new system inserts data so that the other systems have access to their properly formatted data.

Once the other systems modify their access to use the new structure (with separate first and last names), the *contraction* phase can be executed and the old column dropped:

```
ALTER TABLE Customer DROP COLUMN name;
```

If a lot of data exists and dropping the column will be time-consuming, the data team can sometimes set the column to "not used" (if the database supports this feature):

```
ALTER TABLE Customer SET UNUSED name;
```

After dropping the legacy column, if a read-only version of the previous schema is needed, the data team can add a functional column so that read access to the database is preserved:

```
ALTER TABLE CUSTOMER ADD (name AS
            (generatename (firstname,lastname)));
```

As illustrated in each scenario, the data team and developers can utilize the native facilities of databases to build evolvable systems.

Expand/Contract is a subset of a pattern called Parallel Change (*https://oreil.ly/ yd8FR*), a broad pattern used to safely implement backward-incompatible changes to an interface.

Inappropriate Data Entanglement

Data and databases form an integral part of most modern software architectures—developers who ignore this key aspect when trying to evolve their architecture suffer.

Databases and the data team form a particular challenge in many organizations because, for whatever reason, their tools and engineering practices are antiquated compared to the traditional development world. For example, the tools the data team uses daily are extremely primitive compared to any developer's IDE. Features that are common for developers don't exist for data teams: refactoring support, out-of-container testing, unit testing, dependency tracking, linting, mocking and stubbing, and so on.

The data structures in the databases are coupled with application code, and it's difficult for the data team to refactor the database without involvement of the users of the data structures, such as application developers; Extract, Transform, and Load developers; and report developers. Since involvement of different teams, resource coordination, and prioritization from the product team are necessary, the database refactoring becomes complex to execute and often gets deprioritized, leading to suboptimal database structures and abstractions.

Data Teams, Vendors, and Tool Choices

Why has the data world lagged so far behind the engineering practices of the software development world? The data team has many of the same needs as developers: testing, refactoring, and so on. Yet, while developer tools continue to advance, the same level of innovation hasn't penetrated the data world. It's not like tools aren't available—several third-party tools now exist to add better engineering support. But they don't sell well. Why?

Database vendors have created an interesting relationship between themselves and their consumers. For example, a data team for *DatabaseVendorX* has an almost irrational level of dedication to that vendor, because the data team's next job comes at least in part from the fact they are a certified *DatabaseVendorX* data team, not necessarily from their existing job. Thus, database vendors have secreted armies within enterprises all over the world, where loyalties lie with the vendor rather than the company. Data teams in this situation ignore tools and other development artifacts that don't come from the mother ship. The result is stagnation at the innovation level for engineering practices.

Data teams view their database vendors as the source of all heat and light in the universe and don't care what comes from other dark matter in their universe. The unfortunate side effect of this phenomenon is stagnation in tool advancement compared to developer tools. Consequently, the impedance mismatch between developers and data teams grows even bigger, as they don't share common engineering techniques. Convincing data teams to adopt Continuous Delivery practices forces them to use new tools, distancing them from the mother ship, which they try to avoid.

Fortunately, the popularity of open source and NoSQL databases has started breaking the hegemony of database vendors.

Two-Phase Commit Transactions

When architects discuss coupling, the conversation usually revolves around classes, libraries, and other aspects of the technical architecture. However, other avenues of coupling exist in most projects, including transactions; this is true in both monolithic and distributed architectures.

Transactions are a special form of coupling because transactional behavior doesn't appear in traditional technical architecture-centric tools. Architects can easily determine the afferent and efferent coupling between classes with a variety of tools. They have a much harder time determining the extent of transactional contexts. Just as coupling between schemas harms evolution, transactional coupling binds the constituent parts together in concrete ways, making evolution more difficult.

Transactions appear in business systems for a variety of reasons. First, business analysts love the idea of transactions—an operation that *stops the world* for some context briefly—regardless of the technical challenges. Global coordination in complex systems is difficult, and transactions represent a form of it. Second, transactional boundaries often tell how business concepts are really coupled together in their implementation. Third, the data team may own the transactional contexts, making it hard to coordinate breaking the data apart to resemble the coupling found in the technical architecture.

In Chapter 5, we discussed the architectural quantum boundary concept: the smallest architectural deployable unit, which differs from traditional thinking about cohesion by encompassing dependent components like databases. The binding created by databases is more imposing than traditional coupling because of transactional boundaries, which often define how business processes work. Architects sometimes err in trying to build an architecture with a smaller level of granularity than is natural for the business. For example, microservices architectures aren't particularly well suited for heavily transactional systems because the goal service quantum is so small.

Architects must consider all the coupling characteristics of their application: classes, package/namespace, library and framework, data schemas, and transactional contexts. Ignoring any of these dimensions (or their interactions) creates problems when trying to evolve an architecture. In physics, the *strong nuclear force* that binds atoms together is one of the strongest forces yet identified. Transactional contexts act like a strong nuclear force for architecture quanta.

 Database transactions act as a strong nuclear force, binding quanta together.

While systems often cannot avoid transactions, architects should try to limit transactional contexts as much as possible because they form a tight coupling knot, hampering the ability to change some components or services without affecting others. More importantly, architects should take aspects like transactional boundaries into account when thinking about architectural changes.

As we will discuss in Chapter 9, when migrating a monolithic architectural style to a more granular one, start with a small number of larger services first. When building a greenfield microservices architecture, developers should be diligent about restricting the size of service and data contexts. However, don't take the term *microservices* too literally—each service doesn't have to be small; rather, it should capture a useful bounded context.

When restructuring an existing database schema, it is often difficult to achieve appropriate granularity. Many data teams spend decades stitching a database schema together and have no interest in performing the reverse operation. Often, the necessary transactional contexts to support the business define the smallest granularity developers can make into services. While architects may aspire to create a smaller level of granularity, their efforts slip into inappropriate coupling if it creates a mismatch with data concerns. Building an architecture that structurally conflicts with the problem developers are trying to solve represents a damaging version of metawork, described in "Migrating Architectures" on page 154.

Age and Quality of Data

Another dysfunction that manifests in large companies is the fetishization of data and databases. We have heard more than one CTO say, "I don't really care that much about applications because they have a short lifespan, *but my data schemas are precious because they live forever!*" While it's true that schemas change less frequently than code, database schemas still represent an abstraction of the real world. While inconvenient, the real world has a habit of changing over time. The data team that believes that schemas never change is ignoring reality.

But if the data teams never refactor the database to make schema changes, how do they make changes to accommodate new abstractions? Unfortunately, *adding another join table* is a common process the data team uses to expand schema definitions. Rather than make a schema change and risk breaking existing systems, they just add a new table, joining it to the original using relational database primitives. While this works in the short term, it obfuscates the real underlying abstraction: in the real world, one entity is represented by multiple things. Over time, the *data teams* that rarely genuinely restructure schemas build an increasingly fossilized world, with byzantine grouping and bunching strategies. When the data team doesn't restructure the database, it's not preserving a precious enterprise resource; it's creating the concretized remains of every version of the schema, overlaid upon one another via join tables.

Legacy data quality presents another huge problem. Often, the data has survived many generations of software, each with its own persistence quirks, resulting in data that is inconsistent at best and garbage at worst. In many ways, trying to keep every scrap of data couples the architecture to the past, forcing elaborate workarounds to make things operate successfully.

Before trying to build an evolutionary architecture, make sure developers can evolve the data as well, both in terms of schema and quality. Poor structure requires refactoring, and data teams should perform whatever actions are necessary to baseline the quality of data. We prefer fixing these problems early rather than building elaborate, ongoing mechanisms to handle these problems in perpetuity.

Legacy schemas and data have value, but they also represent a tax on the ability to evolve. Architects, data teams, and business representatives need to have frank conversations about what represents *value* to the organization—keeping legacy data forever or the ability to make evolutionary change. Look at the data that has true value and preserve it, and make the older data available for reference but out of the mainstream of evolutionary development.

 Refusing to refactor schemas or eliminate old data couples your architecture to the past, which you cannot refactor.

Case Study: Evolving PenultimateWidgets' Routing

PenultimateWidgets has decided to implement a new routing scheme between pages, providing a navigational breadcrumb trail to users. Doing so means changing the way routing between pages has been done (using an in-house framework). Pages that implement the new routing mechanism require more context (origin page, workflow state, etc.), and thus require more data.

Within the routing service quantum, PenultimateWidgets currently has a single table to handle routes. For the new version, developers need more information, so the table structure will be more complex. Consider the starting point illustrated in Figure 6-4.

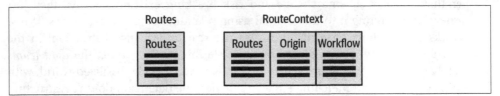

Figure 6-4. Starting point for new routing implementation

Not all pages at PenultimateWidgets will implement the new routing at the same time because different business units work at different speeds. Thus, the routing service must support both the old and new versions. We will see how that is handled via routing in Chapter 7. In this case, we must handle the same scenario at the data level.

Using the Expand/Contract pattern, a developer can create the new routing structure and make it available via the service call. Internally, both routing tables have a trigger associated with the route column so that changes to one are automatically replicated to the other, as shown in Figure 6-5.

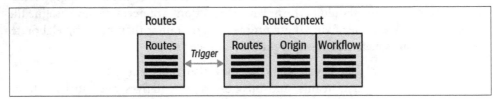

Figure 6-5. The transitional state, where the service supports both versions of routing

As seen in Figure 6-5, the service can support both APIs as long as developers need the old routing service. In essence, the application now supports two versions of routing information.

When the old service is no longer needed, the routing service developers can remove the old table and the trigger, as shown in Figure 6-6.

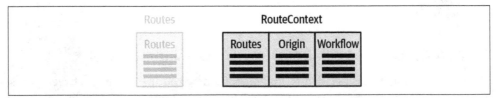

Figure 6-6. The ending state of the routing tables

In Figure 6-6, all services have migrated to the new routing capability, allowing the old service to be removed. This matches the workflow shown in Figure 6-2.

The database can evolve right alongside the architecture as long as developers apply proper engineering practices such as continuous integration, source control, and so on. This ability to easily change the database schema is critical: a database represents an abstraction based on the real world, which can change unexpectedly. While data abstractions resist change better than behavior, they must still evolve. Architects must treat data as a primary concern when building an evolutionary architecture.

Refactoring databases is an important skill and craft for the data team and developers to hone. Data is fundamental to many applications. To build evolvable systems, developers and the data team must embrace effective data practices alongside other modern engineering practices.

From Native to Fitness Function

Sometime choices in software architecture cause issues in other parts of the ecosystem. When architects embraced microservices architectures, which suggests one database per bounded context, it changed data teams' traditional perspective about databases: they are more accustomed to a single relational database, along with the conveniences those tools and model provide. For example, data teams pay close attention to referential integrity, to ensure the correctness of the connecting points of the data structure.

But what happens when architects want to break databases into a data-per-service architecture like microservices—how can they convince skeptical data teams that the advantages of microservices outweigh giving up some of their trusted mechanisms?

Because it is a form of governance, architects can reassure data teams by wiring continuous fitness functions into the build to ensure important pieces maintain integrity and address other issues.

Referential Integrity

Referential integrity is a form of governance, at the data schema level rather than architecture coupling. However, to an architect, both impact the ability to evolve the application by increasing coupling. For example, many cases exist where data teams are reluctant to break up tables into separate databases because of referential integrity, but that coupling prevents both services coupled to it from changing.

Referential integrity in databases refers to primary keys and their linkages. In distributed architectures, teams also have unique identifiers for entities, frequently expressed as GUIDs or some other random sequence. Thus, architects must write fitness functions to ensure that if, for example, a particular item is deleted by the owner of the information, that deletion is propagated to other services that might still reference the deleted entity. A number of patterns in event-driven architecture address these kinds of background tasks; one such example appears in Figure 6-7.

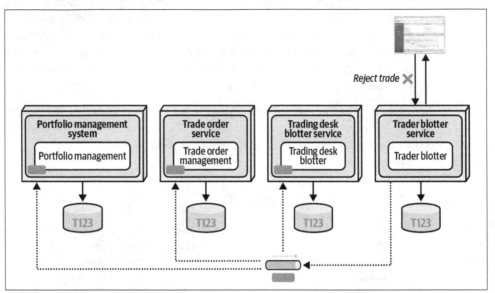

Figure 6-7. Using event-based data synchronization to handle referential integrity

In Figure 6-7, when the user interface rejects a trade via the `Trader Blotter` service, it propagates a message on a durable message queue that all interested services monitor, updating or deleting the changes as needed.

While referential integrity in databases is powerful, it sometimes creates undesirable coupling, which must be weighed against the benefits.

Data Duplication

When teams become accustomed to a single relational database, they don't often think of the two operations—*read* and *write*—as separate. However, microservices architectures force teams to think more carefully about which services can update information versus which services can just read it. Consider the common scenario faced by many teams new to microservices, illustrated in Figure 6-8.

A number of the services need access to several key parts of the system, for `Refer ence`, `Audit Tables`, `Configuration`, and `Customer`. How should the team handle this need? The solution shown in Figure 6-8 shares the tables with all the interested services, which is convenient but violates one of the tenets of microservices architectures to avoid coupling services to a common database. If the schema for any of these tables changes, it will ripple out to the coupled services, potentially requiring them to change.

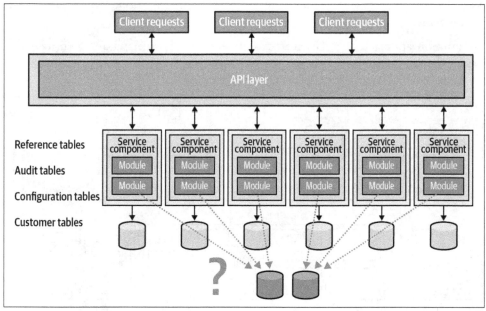

Reference tables

Audit tables

Configuration tables

Customer tables

Figure 6-8. Managing shared information in a distributed architecture

An alternative approach appears in Figure 6-9.

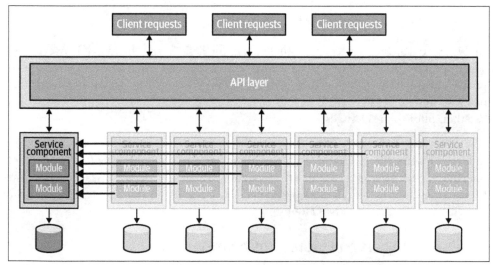

Figure 6-9. Modeling shared information as a service

In Figure 6-9, following the philosophy behind microservices, we model each shared bit of information as a distinct service. However, this exposes one of the problems in microservices—too much interservice communication, which can impact performance.

A common approach by many teams is to carefully consider who should *own* data (i.e., who can update it) versus who can *read* some version of it. The solution shown in Figure 6-10 uses in-process caching for read access.

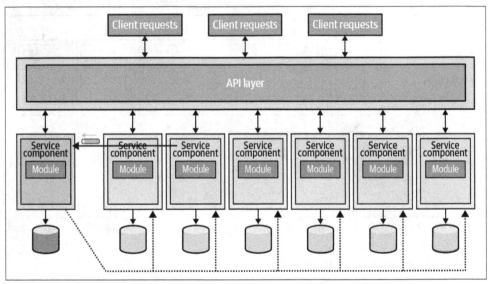

Figure 6-10. Using caching for read-only access

In Figure 6-10, the service components on the left "own" the data. However, on startup, each interested service reads and caches the data of interest, with an appropriate update frequency for cached information. If one of the righthand services needs to update the shared value, it does so via a request to the owning service, which can then publish the changes.

Architects use a variety of approaches to manage data access versus updates in modern architectures. Examples include change control, connection management scalability, fault tolerance, architectural quanta, database-type optimization, database transactions, and data relationships, which is covered in more detail in *Software Architecture: The Hard Parts* (O'Reilly).

Replacing Triggers and Stored Procedures

Another common mechanism data teams rely on are stored procedures, written in the native SQL for the database. While this is a powerful and performant option for manipulating data, it suffers from some challenges in modern software engineering practices. For example, stored procedures are hard to unit test, often have poor refactoring support, and separate behavior from the other behavior in source code.

Migrating to microservices often causes data teams to refactor stored procedures because the data in question no longer resides in a single database. In that case, the behavior must move to code, and teams must address issues such as data volume and transport. In modern NoSQL databases there may be triggers or serverless functions that trigger based on some data change. All of the database code has to be refactored.

Architects can use the same Expand/Contract pattern to extract behavior currently in stored procedures into application code, using the Migrate Method from Database pattern (*https://oreil.ly/afabK*) as shown Figure 6-11.

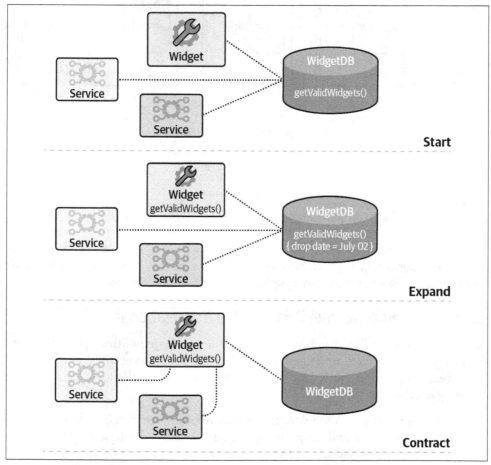

Figure 6-11. Extracting database code into services

During the expand phase, developers add the replacement method in the *Widgets Administration* service, and developers refactor other services to call the *Widgets*

Administration service. Initially, the new method acts as a pass-through to the stored procedure until the team can invisibly replace the functionality in well-tested code. During this period, the application supports calls to either the service or the stored procedure. In the *contract* phase, architects can use a fitness function to make sure all dependencies have migrated to calling the service and subsequently drop the stored procedure. This is the database version of the Strangler Fig pattern (*https://oreil.ly/BhDNV*).

Another option might be to avoid refactoring the stored procedure and build a broader data context instead, as illustrated in Figure 6-12.

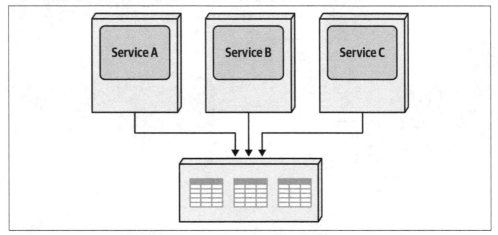

Figure 6-12. Building a broader data context to preserve stored procedures

In Figure 6-12, rather than replace the triggers and stored procedures in code, the team opted for a bigger granularity of service. No generic advice is possible here; teams must evaluate on a case-by-case basis the trade-offs of their decisions.

Case Study: Evolving from Relational to Nonrelational

Many organizations like PenultimateWidgets start with monolithic applications for good strategic reasons: time to market, simplicity, market uncertainty, and a host of other reasons. These applications typically include a single relational database, the industry standard for decades.

When breaking apart the monolith, teams may rethink their persistence as well. For example, for cataloging and categorizing analytics, a graph database might be better. For some problem domains, name/value pair databases provide better options. One of the beneficial features of highly distributed architectures such as microservices lies with architects' ability to choose different persistence mechanisms based on the problem rather than an arbitrary standard. A migration from a monolith to microservices might look like Figure 6-13.

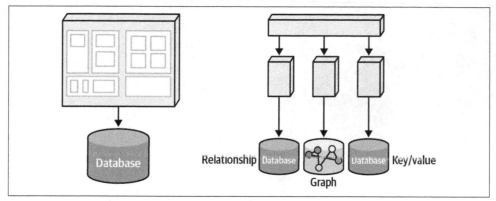

Figure 6-13. PenultimateWidgets' migration from a monolith to a microservices architecture

In Figure 6-13, catalog, analytics (used for market forecasting and other business intelligence), and operational data (such as sales status, transactions, etc.) all reside in a single database, sometimes bending the way a relational database is used to accommodate the various uses. However, when moving to microservices, the teams have the chance to break the monolithic data into different, more representative types. For example, some data might be better suited for key/value pairs rather than for strictly relational databases. Similarly, some problems that data teams can solve in seconds with a graph database can take hours or days in a relational one.

However, moving from a single type of database to multiple databases (even of the same type) can cause issues; everything in software architecture is a trade-off. Architects may struggle convincing data teams of the architectural requirement from microservices to break persistence into multiple data stores, so architects should highlight the trade-offs inherent in each approach.

Summary

The last part of our definition of an evolutionary architecture includes *across multiple dimensions*, and data is the most common extra-architecture concern that impacts the evolution of software systems. The advent of modern distributed architectures such as microservices forced architects to take on problems that used to belong solely to data teams. Restructuring architectures around bounded contexts means partitioning data as well, which comes with its own set of trade-offs.

Architects must both think more diligently about the impacts of data on architecture and collaborate with data teams just as with developers.

Impact

While we introduce *mechanics* and *structure* individually, in real systems they freely interact. Part III of this book covers the intersection of the engineering practices in Part I and the structural considerations from Part II.

CHAPTER 7

Building Evolvable Architectures

Until now, we've addressed the two primary aspects of evolutionary architecture—mechanics and structure—separately. Now we have enough context to tie them together.

Many of the concepts we discussed aren't new ideas but rather old ideas viewed through a new lens. For example, testing has existed for years, but not with the fitness function emphasis on architectural verification. *Continuous Delivery* defined the idea of deployment pipelines. Evolutionary architecture shows architects how to add governance to that automation.

Many organizations pursue Continuous Delivery practices as a way to increase engineering efficiency for software development, a worthy goal in itself. However, we're taking the next step, using those capabilities to create something more sophisticated—architectures that evolve with the real world.

So how can developers take advantage of these techniques on projects, both existing and new?

Principles of Evolutionary Architecture

Overarching both mechanics and structure in evolutionary architecture are five general principles. Let's look at them now.

Last Responsible Moment

The agile development world has long extolled the virtues of *last responsible moment*: delaying decisions as long as you can, but no longer. Making decisions too early tends toward overengineering, and too late leads to failure to meet architectural goals.

The goal isn't to unnecessarily delay. Rather, if an architect can find the correct inflection point in decision-making, they maximize the amount of information available. This helps because, ultimately, the architect's job lies with trade-off analysis, and the more information they have, the more trade-off criteria are available.

When making decisions too early, architects naturally want to keep options open, tending toward picking more general solutions. However, this can overcomplicate specific implementations without providing teams the benefits of generality.

Decide early what the objective drivers are and prioritize decisions accordingly.

Architect and Develop for Evolvability

Architects should treat *evolvability* as a first-class concern in architecture. That implies thinking about objective measures when analyzing architecture characteristics. It also implies thinking about appropriate coupling and how to avoid brittleness in your architecture.

As we discussed in Chapter 6, architects must think of data and other external integration points (static coupling for the architecture quantum) as first-class design considerations. For example, data teams should integrate database changes continuously just like code, and architects should consider data dependencies as equal to code dependencies.

Like many holistic parts of architecture, this principle applies to software development process and tooling as well. Choose both to support the least friction and highest degree of feedback.

Postel's Law

> Be conservative in what you do, be liberal in what you accept from others.
>
> —Jon Postel

An important principle we can add to the discussion around contracts in "Contracts" on page 103 is *Postel's Law*, a general principle that tries to soften coupling points as much as possible. When applied to contracts and communication, it offers a useful guideline for enabling evolution:

Be conservative in what you send
Don't send more information than necessary—if a collaborating service needs only a phone number, don't send a larger data structure. The more information in a contract, the more often other coupling points will take advantage of it, tightening a contract that could otherwise be looser.

Be liberal in what you accept from others
> You can accept more information than you consume. You don't need to consume more information than necessary, even if there is additional data available. If you only want a phone number, don't build a protocol for the entire address, only validate the phone number. This decouples a service from information/coupling points that it doesn't need.

Use versioning when breaking a contract
> Architects must honor contracts in integration architecture (automated via consumer-driven contracts), which means paying attention to the evolution of service functionality.

Much has been written in the architecture space about Postel's Law, for good reason—it offers good advice for decoupling, which in turn favors evolutionary architecture.

Architect for Testability

Many architects complain that their architecture has difficult areas to test, which isn't surprising when testability often isn't a priority when designing the architecture. Conversely, if architects design their architecture with testing in mind, they build easier ways to test parts of the architecture in isolation. For example, a lot of research and tools exist in the microservices ecosystem to facilitate testing, contributing to its general evolvability. In general, a correlation exists between a hard-to-test system and one that is hard to maintain and enhance.

A good example of architecture for testability also illustrates the *single responsibility principle*: every part of a system should have a single responsibility. For example, consider the formerly common antipattern of mixing business logic with messaging infrastructure via tools like Enterprise Service Bus. We realized that mixing concerns makes it difficult to test either behavior in isolation.

Conway's Law

Surprising coupling points happen in sometimes surprising parts of software development. Paying attention to team structure and what impact it has on architecture is a key to evolutionary architecture; we cover Conway's Law in "Don't Fight Conway's Law" on page 193).

Mechanics

Architects can operationalize the techniques for building an evolutionary architecture in three steps.

Step 1: Identify Dimensions Affected by Evolution

First, architects must identify which dimensions of the architecture they want to protect as it evolves. This always includes technical architecture, and usually things like data design, security, scalability, and the other "-ilities" architects have deemed important. This must involve other interested teams within the organization, including business, operations, security, and other affected parties. The *Inverse Conway Maneuver* (described in "Don't Fight Conway's Law" on page 193) is helpful here because it encourages multirole teams. Basically, this is the common behavior of architects at the onset of projects when identifying the architectural characteristics they want to support.

Step 2: Define Fitness Function(s) for Each Dimension

A single dimension often contains numerous fitness functions. For example, architects commonly wire a collection of code metrics into the deployment pipeline to ensure architectural characteristics of the codebase, such as preventing component dependency cycles. Architects document decisions about which dimensions deserve ongoing attention in a lightweight format such as a wiki. Then, for each dimension, they decide what parts may exhibit undesirable behavior when evolving, eventually defining fitness functions. Fitness functions may be automated or manual, and ingenuity will be necessary in some cases.

Step 3: Use Deployment Pipelines to Automate Fitness Functions

Lastly, architects must encourage incremental change on the project, defining stages in a deployment pipeline to apply fitness functions and managing deployment practices like machine provisioning, testing, and other DevOps concerns. Incremental change is the engine of evolutionary architecture, allowing aggressive verification of fitness functions via deployment pipelines and a high degree of automation to make mundane tasks like deployment invisible. Cycle time is the Continuous Delivery measure of engineering efficiency. Part of the responsibility of developers on projects that support evolutionary architecture is to maintain good cycle time. Cycle time is an important aspect of incremental change because many other metrics derive from it. For example, the velocity of new generations appearing in an architecture is proportional to its cycle time. In other words, if a project's cycle time lengthens, it slows down how fast the project can deliver new generations, which affects evolvability.

While the identification of dimensions and fitness functions occurs at the beginning of a new project, it is also an ongoing activity for both new and existing projects. Software suffers from the *unknown unknowns* problem: developers cannot anticipate everything. During construction, some part of the architecture often shows troubling signs, and building fitness functions can prevent this dysfunction from growing. While some fitness functions will naturally come to light at the beginning of a project, many won't reveal themselves until an architectural stress point appears. Architects must vigilantly watch for situations where nonfunctional requirements break and retrofit the architecture with fitness functions to prevent future problems.

Greenfield Projects

Building evolvability into new projects is much easier than retrofitting existing ones. First, developers have the opportunity to utilize incremental change right away, building a deployment pipeline at project inception. Fitness functions are easier to identify and plan before any code exists, making it easier to accommodate complex fitness functions because scaffolding has existed since inception. Second, architects don't have to untangle any undesirable coupling points that creep into existing projects. The architect can also put metrics and other verifications in place to ensure architectural integrity as the project changes.

Building new projects that handle unexpected change is easier if a developer chooses the correct architectural patterns and engineering practices to facilitate evolutionary architecture. For example, microservices architectures offer extremely low coupling and a high degree of incremental change, making that style an obvious candidate (and another contributing factor to its popularity).

Retrofitting Existing Architectures

Adding evolvability to existing architectures depends on three factors: component coupling, engineering practice maturity, and developer ease in crafting fitness functions.

Appropriate Coupling and Cohesion

Component coupling largely determines the evolvability of the technical architecture. Yet the best possible evolvable technical architecture is doomed if the data schema is rigid and fossilized. Cleanly decoupled systems make evolution easy; nests of exuberant coupling harm it. To build truly evolvable systems, architects must consider all affected dimensions of an architecture.

Beyond the technical aspects of coupling, architects must also consider and defend the functional cohesion of the components of their system. When migrating from one architecture to another, the functional cohesion determines the ultimate granularity of restructured components. That doesn't mean architects can't decompose components to a ridiculous level, but rather that components should have an appropriate size based on the problem context. For example, some business problems are more coupled than others, such as in the case of heavily transactional systems. Trying to build an extremely decoupled architecture that is counter to the problem is unproductive.

Engineering practices matter when defining how evolvable an architecture can be. While Continuous Delivery practices don't guarantee evolutionary architecture, it is almost impossible without them. Many teams embark on improved engineering practices for the sake of efficiency. However, once those practices cement, they become building blocks for advanced capabilities such as evolutionary architecture. Thus, the ability to build an evolutionary architecture is an incentive to improving efficiency.

Many companies reside in the transition zone between older practices and new. They may have solved low-hanging fruit like continuous integration but still have largely manual testing. While it slows cycle time, it is important to include manual stages in deployment pipelines. First, it treats each stage of an application's build the same—as a stage in the pipeline. Second, as teams slowly automate more pieces of deployment, manual stages may become automated ones with no disruption. Third, elucidating each stage brings awareness about the mechanical parts of the build, creating a better feedback loop and encouraging improvements.

The biggest single common impediment to building evolutionary architecture is intractable operations. If developers cannot easily deploy changes, all parts of the feedback cycle are hampered.

We encourage architects to start thinking of all kinds of architectural verification mechanisms as fitness functions, including things they have previously considered in an ad hoc manner. For example, many architectures have a service-level agreement around scalability and corresponding tests. They also have rules around security requirements, with accompanying verification mechanisms. Architects often think of these as separate categories, but both intents are the same: verify some feature of the architecture. By thinking of all architectural verification as fitness functions, there is more consistency when automation and other beneficial synergistic interactions are defined.

Refactoring Versus Restructuring

Developers sometimes co-opt terms that sound cool and make them into broader synonyms, as is the case for *refactoring*. As defined by Martin Fowler, refactoring is the process of restructuring existing computer code without changing its external behavior. For many developers, *refactoring* has become synonymous with *change*, but there are key differences.

It is very rare that a team refactors an architecture; rather, they *restructure* it, making substantive changes to both structure and behavior. Architecture patterns exist in part to make certain architectural characteristics primary in an application. Switching patterns entails switching priorities, which isn't refactoring. For example, architects might choose an event-driven architecture for scalability. If the team switches to a different architectural pattern, it likely won't support the same level of scalability.

COTS Implications

In many organizations, developers don't own all the parts that make up their ecosystem. COTS (commercial off-the-shelf) and package software is prevalent in large companies, creating challenges for architects building evolvable systems.

COTS systems must evolve alongside other applications within an enterprise. Unfortunately, these systems don't support evolution well. Here are aspects of evolutionary architecture that are generally poorly supported by COTS systems:

Incremental change

Most commercial software falls woefully short of industry standards for automation and testing. Architects and developers must often build logical barriers between integration points and build whatever testing is possible, frequently treating the entire system as a black box. Enforcing agility in terms of deployment pipelines, DevOps, and other modern practices offers challenges to development teams.

Appropriate coupling

Package software often commits the worst sins in terms of coupling. Generally, the system is opaque, with a defined API developers use to integrate. Inevitably, that API suffers from the problem described in "Antipattern: Last 10% Trap and Low Code/No Code" on page 177, allowing almost (but not quite) enough flexibility for developers to get useful work done.

Fitness functions

Adding fitness functions to package software is perhaps the biggest hurdle to enable evolvability. Generally, tools of this ilk don't expose enough internals to allow unit or component testing, making behavioral integration testing the last resort. These tests are less desirable because they are necessarily coarse grained, must run in a complex environment, and must test a large swath of behavior of the system.

Work diligently to hold integration points to your level of maturity. If that isn't possible, realize that some parts of the system will be easier for developers to evolve than others.

Another worrisome coupling point introduced by many package software vendors is opaque database ecosystems. In the best-case scenarios, the package software manages the state of the database entirely, exposing selected appropriate values via integration points. In the worst case, the vendor database *is* the integration point to the rest of the system, vastly complicating changes on either side of the API. In this case, architects and DBAs must wrestle control of the database away from the package software for any hope of evolvability.

If trapped with necessary package software, architects should build as robust a set of fitness functions as possible and automate their running at every possible opportunity. Lack of access to internals relegates testing to less desirable techniques.

Migrating Architectures

Many companies end up migrating from one architectural style to another. For example, architects choose simple-to-understand architecture patterns at the beginning of a company's IT history, often layered architecture monoliths. As the company grows, the architecture comes under stress. One of the most common paths of migration is from monolith to some kind of service-based architecture, for reasons of the general domain-centric shift in architectural thinking, covered in "Case Study: Microservices as an Evolutionary Architecture" on page 107. Many architects are tempted by the highly evolutionary microservices architecture as a target for migration, but this is often quite difficult, primarily because of existing coupling.

When architects think of migrating architecture, they typically think of the coupling characteristics of classes and components, but they ignore many other dimensions affected by evolution, such as data. Transactional coupling is as real as coupling between classes and just as insidious to eliminate when restructuring architecture. These extra-class coupling points become a huge burden when trying to break the existing modules into too-small pieces.

Many senior developers build the same types of applications year after year and become bored with the monotony. Most developers would rather *write* a framework than *use* a framework to create something useful: *Metawork is more interesting than work*. Work is boring, mundane, and repetitive, whereas building new stuff is exciting.

This manifests in two ways. First, many senior developers start writing the infrastructure that other developers use, rather than using existing (often open source) software. We once worked with a client who had been on the cutting edge of technology. They built their own application server, web framework in Java, and just about every other bit of infrastructure. At one point, we asked if they had built their own operating system too, and when they said, "No," we asked, "Why not?!? You built everything else from scratch!"

Upon reflection, the company needed capabilities that weren't available. However, when open source tools became available, they already owned their lovingly hand-crafted infrastructure. Rather than cut over to the more standard stack, they opted to keep their own because of minor differences in approach. A decade later, their best developers worked in full-time maintenance mode, fixing their application server, adding features to their web framework, and performing other mundane chores. Rather than applying innovation on building better applications, they permanently slaved away on plumbing.

Architects aren't immune to building things just because it sounds like fun or will improve their resume. In general, building *important* things like frameworks and libraries is more enjoyable than slogging through a mundane business problem—but that's the job!

 Metawork is more interesting than work.

Don't fall into the trap of implementing something just for the sake of implementing it. Make sure you have considered and measured all the trade-offs before committing to an irrevocable path.

Migration Steps

Many architects find themselves faced with the challenge of migrating an outdated monolithic application to a more modern service-based approach. Experienced architects realize that a host of coupling points exist in applications, and one of the first tasks when untangling a codebase is understanding how things are joined. When decomposing a monolith, the architect must take coupling and cohesion into account to find the appropriate balance. For example, one of the most stringent constraints of the microservices architectural style is the insistence that the database reside inside the service's bounded context. When decomposing a monolith, even if it is possible to break the classes into small enough pieces, breaking the transactional contexts into similar pieces may present an insurmountable hurdle.

Many architects end up migrating from monolithic applications to service-based architectures. Consider the starting point architecture shown in Figure 7-1.

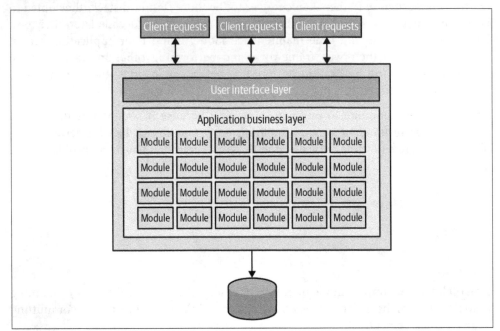

Figure 7-1. A monolith architecture as the starting point for migration, a "share every-thing" architecture

Building extremely granular services is easier in new projects but difficult in existing migrations. So how can we migrate the architecture in Figure 7-1 to the service-based architecture shown in Figure 7-2?

Performing the kind of migration shown in Figures 7-1 and 7-2 comes with a host of challenges: service granularity, transactional boundaries, database issues, and issues like how to handle shared libraries. Architects must understand why they want to perform this migration, and it must be a better reason than "it's the current trend." Splitting the architecture into domains, along with better team structure and operational isolation, allows for easier incremental change, one of the building blocks of evolutionary architecture, because the focus of work matches the physical work artifacts.

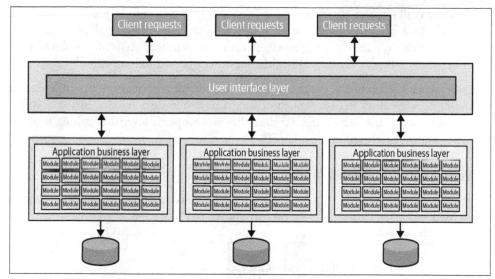

Figure 7-2. The service-based, "share as little as possible" end result of the migration

When decomposing a monolithic architecture, finding the correct service granularity is key. Creating large services alleviates problems like transactional contexts and orchestration but does little to break the monolith into smaller pieces. Too-fine-grained components lead to too much orchestration, communication overhead, and interdependency between components.

For the first step in migrating architecture, developers identify new service boundaries. Teams may decide to break monoliths into services via a variety of partitions as follows:

Business functionality groups

A business may have clear partitions that mirror IT capabilities directly. Building software that mimics the existing business communication hierarchy falls distinctly into an applicable use of Conway's Law (see "Don't Fight Conway's Law" on page 193).

Transactional boundaries

Many businesses have extensive transactional boundaries they must adhere to. When decomposing a monolith, architects often find that transactional coupling is the hardest to break apart, as discussed in "Two-Phase Commit Transactions" on page 133.

Deployment goals

Incremental change allows developers to selectively release code on different schedules. For example, the marketing department might want a much higher cadence of updates than inventory. Partitioning services around operational concerns like speed to release makes sense if that criterion is highly important. Similarly, a portion of the system may have extreme operational characteristics (like scalability). Partitioning services around operational goals allows developers to track (via fitness functions) health and other operational metrics of the service.

Coarser service granularity means many of the coordination problems inherent in microservices go away because more of the business context resides inside a single service. However, the larger the service, the more operational difficulties tend to escalate (another architectural trade-off).

Evolving Module Interactions

Migrating shared modules (including components) is another common challenge faced by developers. Consider the structure shown in Figure 7-3.

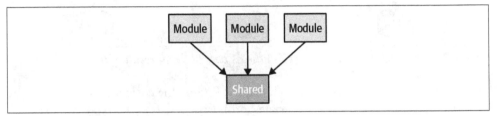

Figure 7-3. Modules with efferent and afferent coupling

In Figure 7-3, all three modules share the same library. However, the architect needs to split these modules into separate services. How can she maintain this dependency?

Sometimes the library may be split cleanly, preserving the separate functionality each module needs. Consider the situation shown in Figure 7-4.

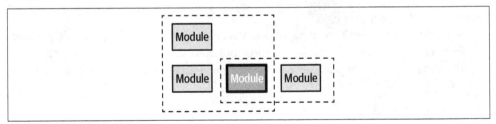

Figure 7-4. Modules with a common dependency

In Figure 7-4, both modules need the conflicting one shown in red (bold border). If developers are lucky, the functionality may be cleanly split down the middle, partitioning the shared library into the relevant parts needed by each dependent, as shown in Figure 7-5.

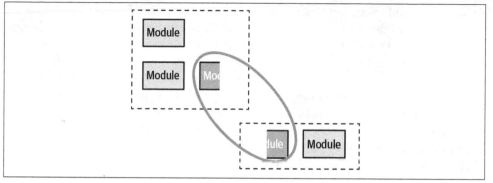

Figure 7-5. Splitting the shared dependency

Architects don't have many useful code-level metrics, but here is a rare handy one. The Chidamber & Kemerer metrics suite (*https://oreil.ly/Gklqp*) includes useful metrics for determining whether a module is a good candidate to split or whether architects should use an approach called LCOM (*https://oreil.ly/EvhWN*) (Lack of Cohesion in Methods). LCOM measures structural cohesion in classes or components and exists in several different variants (LCOM1, LCOM2, etc.) to measure slightly different things. However, at its core, this metric measures *lack* of cohesion. Consider the three cases in Figure 7-6.

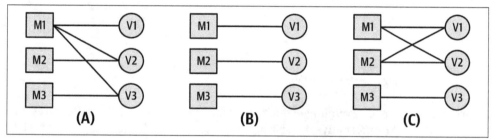

Figure 7-6. Three classes with differing cohesion levels

In Figure 7-6, *M* represents a method and *V* represents a field within the class. In this example, *A* represents a class with higher cohesion—more of the methods use fields—than *B*, which lacks cohesion. In fact, *B* could be split into three separate classes without difficulty.

LCOM measures the failed opportunities to take advantage of coupling points—in the example, *B* would score higher in LCOM than *A* or *C*, both of which have mixed cohesion.

This metric is available for any platform that supports the CK metrics suite; for example, a common open source Java implementation is ckjm (*https://oreil.ly/dPKf8*).

LCOM is useful to an architect performing an architectural migration because a common part of that process deals with shared classes or components. When decomposing a monolith, architects can pretty easily determine how to partition the major parts of the problem domain. However, what about ancillary classes and other components—just how coupled are they? For example, when building a monolith, if a need arises in several places for some concept like Address, the team will share a single Address class, which makes sense. However, when it comes time to break up the monolith, what should they do with the Address class? The LCOM metric helps architects determine whether the class never should have been a single class in the first place—if this metric scores high, it isn't cohesive. However, if LCOM scores low, architects must choose a different approach.

Two options remain: first, developers can extract the module into a shared library (such as a JAR, DLL, gem, or some other component mechanism) and use it from both locations, as shown in Figure 7-7.

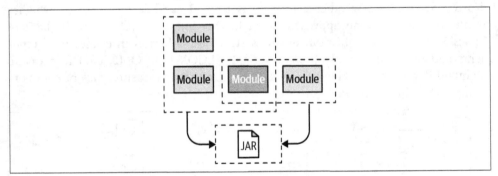

Figure 7-7. Sharing a dependency via a JAR file

Sharing is a form of coupling, which is highly discouraged in architectures like microservices. An alternative to sharing a library is replication, as illustrated in Figure 7-8.

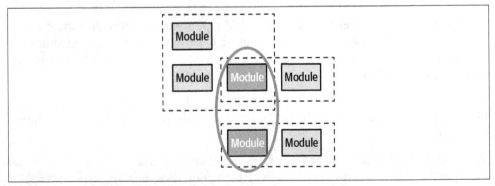

Figure 7-8. Duplicating a shared library to eliminate a coupling point

In a distributed environment, developers may achieve the same kind of sharing using messaging or service invocation.

When developers have identified the correct service partitioning, the next step is *separation* of the business layers from the UI. Even in microservices architectures, the UIs often resolve back to a monolith—after all, developers must show a unified UI at some point. Thus, developers commonly separate the UIs early in the migration, creating a mapping proxy layer between UI components and the backend services they call. Separating the UI also creates an anticorruption layer, insulating UI changes from architecture changes.

The next step is *service discovery*, allowing services to find and call one another. Eventually, the architecture will consist of services that must coordinate. By building the discovery mechanism early, developers can slowly migrate parts of the system that are ready to change. Developers often implement service discovery as a simple proxy layer: each component calls the proxy, which in turn maps to the specific implementation.

> All problems in computer science can be solved by another level of indirection, except of course for the problem of too many indirections.
>
> —Dave Wheeler and Kevlin Henney

Of course, the more levels of indirection developers add, the more confusing navigating the services becomes.

When migrating an application from a monolithic application architecture to a more services-based one, the architect must pay close attention to how modules are connected in the existing application. Naïve partitioning introduces serious performance problems. The connection points in the application become integration architecture connections, with the attendant latency, availability, and other concerns. Rather than tackle the entire migration at once, a more pragmatic approach is to gradually decompose the monolithic architecture into services, looking at factors like transaction boundaries, structural coupling, and other inherent characteristics to create several restructuring iterations. First, break the monolith into a few large "portions of the application" chunks, fix up the integration points, and rinse and repeat. Gradual migration is preferred in the microservices world.

> When migrating from a monolith, build a small number of larger services first.
>
> —Sam Newman, *Building Microservices*

Next, developers choose and detach the service from the monolith, fixing any calling points. Fitness functions play a critical role here—developers should build fitness functions, make sure the newly introduced integration points don't change, and add consumer-driven contracts.

Guidelines for Building Evolutionary Architectures

We've used a few biology metaphors throughout the course of the book, and here is another. Our brains did not evolve in a nice, pristine environment where each capability was carefully built. Instead, each layer is based on primeval layers beneath. Much of our core autonomic behavior (like breathing, eating, etc.) resides in parts of our brain not very different from reptilian brains. Instead of wholesale replacement of core mechanisms, evolution builds new layers on top.

Software architecture in large enterprises follows a similar pattern. Rather than rebuild each capability anew, most companies try to adapt whatever is present. As much as we like to talk about architecture in pristine, idealized settings, the real world often exhibits a contrary mess of technical debt, conflicting priorities, and limited budgets. Architecture in large companies is built like the human brain: lower-level systems still handle critical plumbing details but have some old baggage. Companies hate to decommission something that works, leading to escalating integration architecture challenges.

Retrofitting evolvability into an existing architecture is challenging. If developers never built easy change into the architecture, it is unlikely to appear spontaneously. No architect, now matter how talented, can transform a Big Ball of Mud into a modern microservices architecture without immense effort. Fortunately, projects can receive benefits without changing their entire architecture by building some flexibility points into the existing one.

Remove Needless Variability

One of the goals of Continuous Delivery is stability—building on known good parts. A common manifestation of this goal is the modern DevOps perspective on building immutable infrastructure. We discussed the dynamic equilibrium of the software development ecosystem in Chapter 1—nowhere is that more apparent in how much the foundation shifts around software dependencies. Software systems undergo constant change, as developers update capabilities, issue service packs, and generally tweak their software. Operating systems are a great example, as they endure constant change.

Modern DevOps has solved the dynamic equilibrium problem locally by replacing *snowflakes* with *immutable infrastructure*. *Snowflake infrastructure* represents assets manually crafted by an operations person, and all future maintenance is done by hand. Chad Fowler coined the term *immutable infrastructure* (*https://oreil.ly/5f7rT*) in his blog post, "Trash Your Servers and Burn Your Code: Immutable Infrastructure and Disposable Components". Immutable infastructure refers to systems defined entirely programmatically. All changes to the system must occur via the source code, not by modifying the running operating system. Thus, the entire system is immutable from an operational standpoint—once the system is bootstrapped, no other changes occur.

While immutability may sound like the opposite of evolvability, quite the opposite is true. Software systems are composed of thousands of moving parts, all interlocking in tight dependencies. Unfortunately, developers still struggle with unanticipated side effects of changes to one of those parts. By locking down the possibility of unanticipated change, we control more of the factors that make systems fragile. Developers strive to replace variables in code with constants to reduce vectors of change. DevOps introduced this concept to operations, making it more declarative.

Immutable infrastructure follows our advice to *remove needless variables*. Building software systems that evolve means controlling as many unknown factors as possible. It is virtually impossible to build fitness functions that can anticipate how the latest service pack of the operating system might affect the application. Instead, developers build the infrastructure anew each time the deployment pipeline executes, catching breaking changes as aggressively as possible. If developers can remove known foundational, changeable parts such as the operating system as a possibility, they have less ongoing testing burden to carry.

Architects can find all sorts of avenues to convert changeable things to constants. Many teams extend the immutable infrastructure advice to the development environment as well. How many times has some team member exclaimed, "But it works on my machine!"? By ensuring every developer has the exact same image, a host of needless variables disappear. For example, most development teams automate the update of development libraries through repositories, but what about updates to tools like IDEs? By capturing the development environment as immutable infrastructure, developers always work on the same foundation.

Building an immutable development environment also allows useful tools to spread throughout projects. Pair programming is a common practice in many agile engineering–focused development teams, including pair rotation, where each team member changes regularly, from every few hours to every few days. However, it's frustrating when a tool appears on the computer a developer used yesterday that isn't present today. Building a single source for developer systems makes it easy to add useful tools to all systems at once.

The Hazards of Snowflakes

A story in a popular blog called, "Knightmare: A DevOps Cautionary Tale" (*https:// oreil.ly/vjZxI*) serves as a warning about snowflake servers. A financial services company previously had an algorithm called PowerPeg that handled trading details, but that code hadn't been used in a number of years. However, the developers never removed the code. It resided underneath a feature toggle that remained off. Because of regulatory changes, developers implemented a new trading algorithm

---

called SMARS. Because they were lazy, they decided to reuse the old PowerPeg feature flag to implement the new SMARS code. On August 1, 2012, developers deployed the new code to seven servers. Unfortunately, their system ran on eight servers and one of them wasn't updated. When they enabled the PowerPeg feature toggle, seven servers started selling—and the other started buying! Developers had accidentally set up the worst market scenario—they had automated selling low and buying high. Convinced that the new code was the culprit, developers rolled back the new code on the seven servers but left the feature toggle on, meaning the PowerPeg code now ran on all servers. It took them 45 minutes to rein in the chaos, with a loss of over $400 million. Luckily, an angel investor saved them, as that was more than the company was worth.

This story highlights the problems with unknown variability. Reusing an old feature flag is reckless—the best practice for feature flags is removing them aggressively as soon as their purpose is fulfilled. Not automating deploying critical software to servers is also considered reckless in modern DevOps environments.

Make Decisions Reversible

Inevitably, systems that aggressively evolve will fail in unanticipated ways. When these failures occur, developers need to craft new fitness functions to prevent future occurrences. But how do you recover from a failure?

Many DevOps practices exist to allow *reversible decisions*—decisions that need to be undone. For example *blue/green deployments*, where operations have two identical (probably virtual) ecosystems—*blue* ones and *green* ones—are common in DevOps. If the current production system is running on *blue*, *green* is the staging area for the next release. When the *green* release is ready, it becomes the production system and *blue* temporarily shifts to backup status. If something goes awry with *green*, operations can go back to *blue* without too much pain. If *green* is fine, *blue* becomes the staging area for the next release.

Feature toggles are another common way developers make decisions reversible. By deploying changes underneath feature toggles, developers can release them to a small subset of users (called canary releasing (*https://oreil.ly/oXXK4*)) to vet the change. If a feature behaves unexpectedly, developers can switch the toggle back to the original and correct the fault before trying again. Make sure you remove the outdated ones!

Using feature toggles greatly reduces risk in these scenarios. Service routing—routing to a particular instance of a service based on request context—is another common method to canary-release in microservices ecosystems.

Prefer Evolvable over Predictable

> …because as we know, there are known knowns; there are things we know we know. We also know there are known unknowns; that is to say we know there are some things we do not know. But there are also unknown unknowns—the ones we don't know we don't know.
>
> —Donald Rumsfeld, former US Secretary of Defense

Unknown unknowns are the nemesis of software systems. Many projects start with a list of *known unknowns*: things developers know they must learn about the domain and technology. However, projects also fall victim to *unknown unknowns*: things no one knew were going to crop up yet have appeared unexpectedly. This is why all Big Design Up Front software efforts suffer—architects cannot design for unknown unknowns.

> All architectures become iterative because of *unknown unknowns*; agile just recognizes this and does it sooner.
>
> —Mark Richards

While no architecture can survive the unknown, we know that dynamic equilibrium renders predictability useless in software. Instead, we prefer to build *evolvability* into software: if projects can easily incorporate changes, architects don't need a crystal ball. Architecture is not a solely up-front activity—projects constantly change in both explicit and unexpected ways throughout their life. One safeguard commonly used by developers to insulate themselves from change is an *anticorruption layer*.

Build Anticorruption Layers

Projects often need to couple themselves to libraries that provide incidental plumbing: message queues, search engines, and so on. The *Abstraction Distraction antipattern* describes the scenario where a project "wires" itself too much to an external library, either commercial or open source. Once it becomes time for developers to upgrade or switch the library, much of the application code utilizing the library has baked-in assumptions based on the previous library abstractions. Domain-driven design includes a safeguard against this phenomenon called an *anticorruption layer*. Here is an example.

Agile architects prize the *last responsible moment* principle when making decisions, which is used to counter the common hazard in projects of buying complexity too early. We worked intermittently on a Ruby on Rails project for a client who managed wholesale car sales. After the application went live, an unexpected workflow arose. It turned out that used-car dealers tended to upload new cars to the auction site in large batches, both in number of cars and number of pictures per car. We realized that, as much as the general public doesn't trust used-car dealers, dealers *really* don't trust one another; thus, each car must include a photo covering essentially every molecule of the car. Users wanted a way to begin an upload, then either get progress via some UI mechanism like a progress bar, or check back later to see if the batch was done. Translated to technical terms, they wanted asynchronous upload.

A message queue is one traditional architectural solution to this problem, and the team discussed whether to add an open source queue to the architecture. A common trap at this juncture for many projects is the attitude of "We know we'll need a message queue for lots of stuff eventually, so let's get the fanciest one we can now and grow into it later." The problem with this approach is *technical debt*: stuff that's part of your project that isn't supposed to be there and is in the way of stuff that is supposed to be there. Most developers treat crufty old code as the only form of technical debt, but projects can inadvertently *buy* technical debt as well via premature complexity.

For the project, the architect encouraged developers to find a simpler way. One developer discovered BackgrounDRb (*https://oreil.ly/kwV4y*), an extraordinarily simple open source library that simulates a single message queue backed by a relational database. The architect knew this simple tool would probably never scale to other future problems, but she didn't have other objections. Rather than try to predict future usage, she instead made it relatively easy to replace by placing it behind an API. In the *last responsible moment*, answer questions such as "Do I have to make this decision now?", "Is there a way to safely defer this decision without slowing any work?", and "What can I put in place now that will suffice but I can easily change later if needed?"

Around the one-year anniversary, a second request for asynchronicity appeared in the form of timed events around sales. The architect evaluated the situation and decided that a second instance of BackgrounDRb would suffice, put it in place, and moved on. At around the two-year anniversary, a third request appeared for constantly updating values like caches and summaries. The team realized that the current solution couldn't handle the new workload. However, they now had a good idea about what kind of asynchronous behavior the application needed. At that point, the project switched over to Starling (*https://oreil.ly/Ub25x*), a simple but more traditional message queue. Because the original solution was isolated behind an interface, it took one pair of developers less than one iteration (one week on that project) to complete the transition—without disrupting other developers' work on the project.

Because the architect put an anticorruption layer in place with an interface, replacing one piece of functionality became a mechanical exercise. Building an anticorruption layer encourages the architect to think about the *semantics* of what they need from the library, not the *syntax* of the particular API. But this is not an excuse to *abstract all the things!* Some development communities love preemptive layers of abstraction to a distracting degree, but understanding suffers when you must call a `Factory` to get a `proxy` to a remote interface to a `Thing`. Fortunately, most modern languages and IDEs allow developers to be *just in time* when extracting interfaces. If a project finds itself bound to an out-of-date library in need of change, the IDE can *extract an interface* on behalf of the developer, making a Just In Time (JIT) anticorruption layer.

 Build Just In Time anticorruption layers to insulate against library changes.

Controlling the coupling points in an application, especially to external resources, is one of an architect's key responsibilities. Try to find the pragmatic time to add dependencies. As an architect, remember that dependencies provide benefits but also impose constraints. Make sure the benefits outweigh the cost in updates, dependency management, and so on.

> Developers understand the benefits of everything and the trade-offs of nothing!
>
> —Rich Hickey, creator of Clojure

Architects must understand both benefits and trade-offs and build engineering practices accordingly.

Using anticorruption layers encourages evolvability. While architects can't predict the future, we can at least lower the cost of change so that it doesn't impact us so negatively.

Build Sacrificial Architectures

In his book *Mythical Man Month*, Fred Brooks says to "Plan to Throw One Away" (*https://oreil.ly/cCgfe*) when building a new software system.

> The management question, therefore, is not whether to build a pilot system and throw it away. You will do that. [...] Hence plan to throw one away; you will, anyhow.
>
> —Fred Brooks

His point was that once a team has built a system, they know all the unknown unknowns and proper architecture decisions that are never clear from the outset—the next version will profit from all those lessons. At an architectural level, developers struggle to anticipate radically changing requirements and characteristics. One way to learn enough to choose a correct architecture is to build a proof of concept. Martin Fowler defines a sacrificial architecture (*https://oreil.ly/sNPtz*) as an architecture designed to be thrown away if the concept proves successful. For example, eBay started as a set of Perl scripts in 1995, migrated to C++ in 1997, and then to Java in 2002. Obviously, eBay has been a resounding success in spite of rearchitecting the system several times. Twitter is another good example of successful utilization of this approach. When Twitter released, it was written in Ruby on Rails to achieve fast time to market. However, as Twitter became popular, the platform couldn't support the scale, resulting in frequent crashes and limited availability. Many early users became all too familiar with Twitter's failure beacon, shown in Figure 7-9.

Figure 7-9. Twitter's famous Fail Whale

Thus, Twitter restructured its architecture to replace the backend with something more robust. However, it could be argued that this tactic is the reason the company survived. If the Twitter engineers had built the final, robust platform from the beginning, it would have delayed their entry into the market long enough for *Snitter* or some alternative short-form messaging service to beat them to market. Despite the growing pains, starting with a sacrificial architecture eventually paid off.

Cloud environments make sacrificial architecture more attractive. If developers have a project they want to test, building the initial version in the cloud greatly reduces the resources required to release the software. If the project is successful, architects can take the time to build a more suitable architecture. If developers are careful about anticorruption layers and other evolutionary architecture practices, they can mitigate some of the pains of the migration.

Many companies build a sacrificial architecture to achieve a minimum viable product (*https://oreil.ly/SgSj8*) to prove a market exists. While this is a good strategy, the team must eventually allocate time and resources to build a more robust architecture, hopefully less visibly than Twitter.

One other aspect of technical debt impacts many initially successful projects, elucidated again by Fred Brooks, when he refers to the *second system syndrome*—the tendency of small, elegant, and successful systems to evolve into giant, feature-laden monstrosities due to inflated expectations. Business people hate to throw away functioning code, so architecture tends toward always adding, never removing, or decommissioning.

Technical debt works effectively as a metaphor because it resonates with project experience and represents faults in design, regardless of the driving forces behind them. Technical debt aggravates inappropriate coupling on projects—poor design frequently manifests as pathological coupling and other antipatterns that make restructuring code difficult. As developers restructure architecture, their first step should be to remove the historical design compromises that manifest as technical debt.

Mitigate External Change

A common feature of every development platform is *external dependencies*: tools, frameworks, libraries, and other assets provided by and (more importantly) updated via the internet. Software development sits on a towering stack of abstractions, each built on the abstractions before. For example, operating systems are an external dependency outside the developer's control. Unless companies want to write their own operating system and all other supporting code, they must rely on external dependencies.

Most projects rely on a dizzying array of third-party components, applied via build tools. Developers like dependencies because they provide benefits, but many developers ignore the fact that they come with a cost as well. When relying on code from a third party, developers must create their own safeguards against unexpected occurrences: breaking changes, unannounced removal, and so on. Managing these external parts of projects is critical to creating evolutionary architecture.

The 11 Lines of Code That Broke the Internet

In early 2016, JavaScript developers learned a harsh lesson about the hazards of depending on trivial things. A developer who had created a large number of small utilities became disgruntled because one of his modules clashed with the name of a commercial software project, which asked him to rename his module. Rather than comply, he removed more than 250 of his modules, including one library called `left pad.io`, 11 lines of code to pad strings with zeros or spaces (if 11 lines of code can be called a "library"). Unfortunately, many major JavaScript projects (including `node.js`) relied on this dependency. When it disappeared, everyone's JavaScript deployments broke.

The repository administrator for JavaScript packages took the unprecedented move of restoring the code to restore the ecosystem, but it spawned a deeper conversation in the community about the wisdom of the trends around dependency management.

This story contains two valuable lessons for architects. First, remember that external libraries provide *both* benefits and cost. Make sure the benefits justify the cost. Second, don't allow external forces to affect the stability of your builds. If an upstream required dependency suddenly disappears, you should reject that change.

In "Go To Statement Considered Harmful," Edsger Dijkstra's March 1968 letter to the Editor of *Communications of the ACM*, the legendary figure in computer science famously punctured the existing best practice of unstructured coding, leading eventually to the structured programming revolution. Since that time, "considered harmful" has become a trope in software development.

> Transitive dependency management is our "considered harmful" moment.
>
> —Chris Ford (no relation to Neal)

Chris's point is that, until we recognize the severity of the problem, we cannot determine a solution. While we're not offering a solution to the problem, we need to highlight it because it critically affects evolutionary architecture. Stability is one of the foundations of both Continuous Delivery and evolutionary architecture. Developers cannot build repeatable engineering practices atop uncertainty. Allowing third parties to make changes to core dependencies defies this principle.

We recommend that developers take a more proactive approach to dependency management. A good start on dependency management models external dependencies using a *pull* model. For example, set up an internal version-control repository to act as a third-party component store, and treat changes from the outside world as pull requests to that repository. If a beneficial change occurs, allow it into the ecosystem. However, if a core dependency disappears suddenly, reject that pull request as a destabilizing force.

Using a Continuous Delivery mindset, the third-party component repository utilizes its own deployment pipeline. When an update occurs, the deployment pipeline incorporates the change, then performs a build and smoke test on the affected applications. If successful, the change is allowed into the ecosystem. Thus, third-party dependencies use the same engineering practices and mechanisms of internal development, usefully blurring the lines across this often unimportant distinction between in-house written code and dependencies from third parties—at the end of the day, it's all code in a project.

Updating Libraries Versus Frameworks

Architects make a common distinction between *libraries* and *frameworks*, with the colloquial definition of "a developer's code calls a library whereas the framework calls a developer's code." Generally, developers subclass from frameworks (which in turn call those derived classes), thus the distinction that the framework calls code. Conversely, library code generally comes as a collection of related classes and/or functions developers call as needed. Because the framework calls the developer's code, it creates a high degree of coupling to the framework. Contrast that with library code, which is generally more utilitarian code (like XML parsers, network libraries, etc.) and has a lower degree of coupling.

We prefer libraries because they introduce less coupling to your application, making them easier to swap out when the technical architecture needs to evolve.

 Prefer libraries over frameworks where possible.

One reason to treat libraries and frameworks differently comes down to engineering practices. Frameworks include capabilities such as UI, object-relational mapper, scaffolding like model-view-controller, and so on. Because the framework forms the scaffolding for the remainder of the application, all the code in the application is subject to impact by changes to the framework. Many of us have felt this pain viscerally—any time a team allows a fundamental framework to become outdated by more than two major versions, the effort (and pain) to finally update it is excruciating.

Because frameworks are a fundamental part of applications, teams must be aggressive about pursuing updates. Libraries generally form less brittle coupling points than frameworks do, allowing teams to be more casual about upgrades. One informal governance model treats framework updates as *push* updates and library updates as *pull* updates. When a fundamental framework (one whose afferent/efferent coupling numbers are above a certain threshold) updates, teams should apply the update as soon as the new version is stable and they can allocate time for the change. Even though it will take time and effort, the time spent early is a fraction of the cost if the team perpetually procrastinates on the update.

Because most libraries provide utilitarian functionality, teams can afford to update them only when new desired functionality appears, using more of an "update when needed" model.

 Update framework dependencies aggressively; update libraries passively.

Version Services Internally

In any integration architecture, developers inevitably must version service endpoints as the behavior evolves. Developers use two common patterns to version endpoints, *Version Numbering* or *Internal Resolution*. For version numbering, developers create a new endpoint name, often including the version number, when a breaking change occurs. This allows older integration points to call the legacy version while newer ones call the newer version. The alternative is internal resolution, where callers never change the endpoint—instead, developers build logic into the endpoint to determine the context of the caller, returning the correct version. The advantage of retaining the name forever is less coupling to specific version numbers in calling applications.

In either case, severely limit the number of supported versions. The more versions there are, the more testing and other engineering burdens there will be. Strive to support only two versions at a time, and only temporarily.

 When versioning services, prefer internal versioning to numbering; support only two versions at a time.

Case Study: Evolving PenultimateWidgets' Ratings

PenultimateWidgets has a microservices architecture so the developers can make small changes. Let's look more closely at the details of one of those changes, switching star ratings, as outlined in Chapter 3. Currently, PenultimateWidgets has a star rating service, whose parts are shown in Figure 7-10.

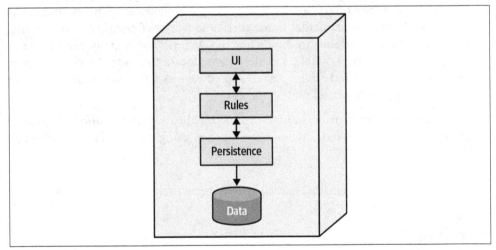

Figure 7-10. The internals of PenultimateWidgets' StarRating service

As shown in Figure 7-10, the star rating service consists of a database and a layered architecture, with persistence, business rules, and a UI. Not all of PenultimateWidgets' microservices include the UI. Some services are primarily informational, whereas others have UIs tightly coupled to the service's behavior, as is the case with star ratings. The database is a traditional relational database that includes a column to track ratings for a particular item ID.

When the team decided to update the service to support half-star ratings, they modified the original service as shown in Figure 7-11.

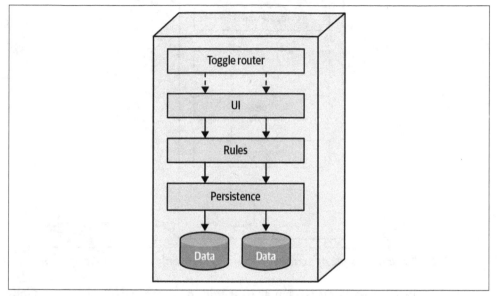

Figure 7-11. The transitional phase, where StarRating *supports both types*

In Figure 7-11, they added a new column to the database to handle the additional data—whether a rating has an additional half-star. The architects also added a proxy component to the service to resolve the return differences at the service boundary. Rather than force calling services to "understand" the version numbers of this service, the star rating service resolves the request type, sending back whichever format is requested. This is an example of using *routing* as an evolutionary mechanism. The star rating service can exist in this state as long as some services still want star ratings.

Once the last dependent service has evolved away from whole-star ratings, developers can remove the old code path, as shown in Figure 7-12.

Developers can remove the old code path and perhaps remove the proxy layer to handle version differences (or perhaps leave it to support future evolution).

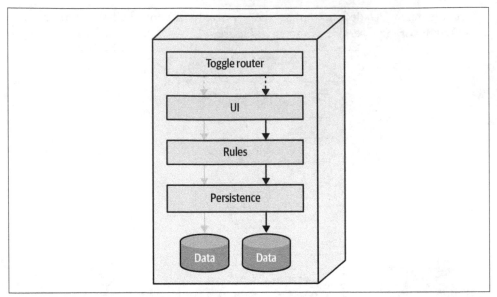

Figure 7-12. The ending state of StarRating, supporting only the new type of rating

In this case, PenultimateWidgets' change wasn't difficult from a data evolution standpoint because the developers were able to make an additive change, meaning they can add to the database schema rather than change it. What about the case where the database must change as well because of a new feature? Refer to the discussion on evolutionary data design in Chapter 6.

Fitness Function-Driven Architecture

A common practice in agile software development is *test-driven development*, where developers write unit tests before writing the corresponding functionality. A similar process can be used in architecture, particularly when the success of the application depends on meeting some stringent capabilities. Building a fitness function that governs that capability to help drive design ensures that it stays top of mind as the architect designs other parts.

The creators of the LMAX architecture (*https://oreil.ly/8YJ92*) famously utilized this approach. Because of changes to laws governing markets in a particular country, regular citizens could participate in the market online (buying and selling) without needing a special license. However, for this application to be successful, they had to be able to manage millions of transactions per second. For various reasons, the technology platform of choice was Java, which wasn't known for scale at this level by default. Thus, the first thing they built was a fitness function that measured transaction speed, and they started experimenting with designs to achieve this high goal. They started with threads but couldn't get even close to the desired goal. Next, they tried various implementations of the actor model (*https://oreil.ly/6g2mk*) but also couldn't get near their goal. In measuring every part of the system, they realized that the business logic they were running was a tiny percentage of computation time—everything else was a context switch.

Armed with this knowledge, they designed an architecture approach known as input and output disruptors (*https://oreil.ly/HLVIo*), which used a single thread and ring buffers to eventually achieve over six million transactions per second on a single thread. The architecture is described in detail at *https://martinfowler.com/articles/lmax.html* (and many parts are open source).

During this process, the team popularized the term *mechanical sympathy* in relation to hardware and software, based on one of the architects being a fan of Formula One racing. In that sport, commentators note that really great drivers have "mechanical sympathy" for their car—they understand how each part works and can "feel" when things are good or bad. In software, mechanical sympathy refers to understanding the layers underneath abstractions to fully understand what drives each piece of, for example, performance. When a request/response sequence occurs, exactly what takes time during that call, all the way down to the network layer, and how might a team optimize it?

Mechanical sympathy requires fitness functions both to define aspirational goals and to govern those strict requirements as changes occur. Once the LMAX team achieved their initial goal, they left the fitness functions in place as they built out the remainder of the solution, changing directions several time as approaches came into conflict with their fitness functions.

A number of software development teams have started adopting this approach of Fitness Function–Driven Architecture, particularly in situations like the above where meeting some aspirational architecture characteristic's goal determines success. Just as in test-driven development, fitness function–driven architecture ensures that changes don't impact success criteria.

Summary

Like all things in software architecture, the aspects of evolutionary architecture cannot be separated—fitness function and structure collaborate to help architects build evolvability.

It took many years for practices such as continuous integration and test-driven development to become standard parts of software engineering practices. Many architects use pieces of evolutionary architecture with monitors, ad hoc metrics, and other occasionally applied verifications but still use outdated governance such as architecture review boards, code reviews, and other proven ineffective practices.

Architects who want to build systems that can survive many changes in both domain and technology can build fitness functions and control coupling via contracts to build systems that provide high degrees of feedback about important things. As a few of the thousand things that make up our software change, architects need confidence that everything still works correctly, provided by the practices of evolutionary architecture.

CHAPTER 8

Evolutionary Architecture Pitfalls and Antipatterns

We've spent a lot of time discussing appropriate levels of coupling in architectures. However, we also live in the real world, and see lots of coupling that *harms* a project's ability to evolve.

We identify two kinds of bad engineering practices that manifest in software projects —*pitfalls* and *antipatterns*. Many developers use the word *antipattern* as jargon for "bad," but the real meaning is more subtle. A software antipattern has two parts. First, an antipattern is a practice that initially looks like a good idea but turns out to be a mistake. Second, better alternatives exist for most antipatterns. Architects notice many antipatterns only in hindsight, so they are hard to avoid. A *pitfall* looks superficially like a good idea but immediately reveals itself to be a bad path. We cover both pitfalls and antipatterns in this chapter.

Technical Architecture

In this section, we focus on common practices in the industry that specifically harm a team's ability to evolve the architecture.

Antipattern: Last 10% Trap and Low Code/No Code

Neal once was the CTO of a consulting firm that built projects for clients in a variety of 4GLs, including Microsoft Access. He assisted in the decision to eliminate Access and eventually all the 4GLs from the business after observing that every Access project started as a booming success but ended in failure, and he wanted to understand why. He and a colleague observed that, in Access and other 4GLs popular at the time, 80% of what the client wanted was quick and easy to build.

These environments were modeled as rapid application development tools, with drag-and-drop support for UIs and other niceties. However, the next 10% of what the client wanted was, while possible, extremely difficult—because that functionality wasn't built into the tool, framework, or language. So clever developers figured out a way to hack tools to make things work: adding a script to execute where static things were expected, chaining methods, and other hacks. The hack only gets you from 80% to 90%. Ultimately the tool can't solve the problem completely—a phrase we coined as the *Last 10% Trap*—leaving every project a disappointment. While 4GLs made it easy to build simple things fast, they didn't scale to meet the demands of the real world. Developers returned to general-purpose languages.

The Last 10% Trap manifests periodically in waves of tools meant to remove the complexity of software development while (allegedly) allowing full-featured development, with predictable results. The current manifestation of this trend lies with *low-code/no-code* development environments, ranging from full-stack development to specialized tools like orchestrators.

While there is nothing wrong with low-code environments, they are almost universally oversold as a panacea for software development, one that business stakeholders are eager to embrace for perceived speed of delivery. Architects should consider them for specialized tasks but realize up front that limitations exist and try to determine what impacts those limitations will have in their ecosystem.

Generally, when experimenting with a new tool or framework, developers create the simplest "Hello, World" project possible. With low-code environments, easy things should be incredibly easy. Instead, what the architect needs to know is what the tool *cannot* do. Thus, instead of simple things, try to find the limits early, to allow building alternatives for what the tool cannot handle.

 For low-code/no-code tools, evaluate the *hardest* problems first, not the easiest ones.

Case Study: Reuse at PenultimateWidgets

PenultimateWidgets has highly specific requirements for data input in a specialized grid for its administration functionality. Because the application required this view in multiple places, PenultimateWidgets decided to build a reusable component, including UI, validation, and other useful default behaviors. By using this component, developers can build new, rich administration interfaces easily.

However, virtually no architecture decision comes without some trade-off baggage. Over time, the component team has become their own silo within the organization, tying up several of PenultimateWidgets' best developers. Teams that use the component must request new features through the component team, which is swamped with bug fixes and feature requests. Worse, the underlying code hasn't kept up with modern web standards, making new functionality hard or impossible.

While the PenultimateWidgets architects achieved reuse, it eventually resulted in a bottleneck effect. One advantage of reuse is that developers can build new things quickly. Yet, unless the component team can keep up with the innovation pace of the dynamic equilibrium, technical architecture component reuse is doomed to eventually become an antipattern.

We're not suggesting teams avoid building reusable assets, but rather that they evaluate them continually to ensure they still deliver value. In the case of PenultimateWidgets, once architects realized that the component was a bottleneck, they broke the coupling point. Any team that wants to fork the component code to add their own new features is allowed to do so (as long as the application development team supports the changes), and any team that wants to opt out to use a new approach is unshackled from the old code entirely.

Two pieces of advice emerge from PenultimateWidgets' experience. First, when coupling points impede evolution or other important architectural characteristics, break the coupling by forking or duplication.

In PenultimateWidgets' case, they broke the coupling by allowing teams to take ownership of the shared code themselves. While adding to their burden, it released the drag on their ability to deliver new features. In other cases, perhaps some shared code can be abstracted from the larger piece, allowing more selective coupling and gradual decoupling.

Second, architects must continually evaluate the fitness of the "-ilities" of the architecture to ensure they still add value and haven't become antipatterns.

All too often architects make a decision that is the correct decision at the time but becomes a bad decision over time because of changing conditions like dynamic equilibrium. For example, architects design a system as a desktop application, yet the industry herds them toward a web application as users' habits change. The original decision wasn't incorrect, but the ecosystem shifted in unexpected ways.

Antipattern: Vendor King

Some large enterprises buy enterprise resource planning (ERP) software to handle common business tasks like accounting, inventory management, and other common chores. This works if companies are willing to bend their business processes and other decisions to accommodate the tool, and it can be used strategically when architects understand limitations as well as benefits.

However, many organizations become overambitious with this category of software, leading to the *Vendor King antipattern*, an architecture built entirely around a vendor's product that pathologically couples the organization to a tool. Companies that buy vendor software plan to augment the package via its plug-ins to flesh out the core functionality to match their business. However, a lot of the time ERP tools can't be customized enough to fully implement what is needed, and developers find themselves hamstrung by the limitations of the tool *and* the fact that they have centered the architectural universe on it. In other words, architects have made the vendor the king of the architecture, dictating future decisions.

To escape this antipattern, treat all software as just another integration point, even if it initially has broad responsibilities. By assuming integration at the outset, developers can more easily replace behavior that isn't useful with other integration points, dethroning the king.

By placing an external tool or framework at the heart of the architecture, developers severely restrict their ability to evolve in two key ways, both technically and from a business process standpoint. Developers are technically constrained by choices the vendor makes in terms of persistence, supported infrastructure, and a host of other constraints. From a business standpoint, large encapsulating tools ultimately suffer from the problems discussed in "Antipattern: Last 10% Trap and Low Code/No Code" on page 177. From a business process standpoint, the tool simply can't support the optimal workflow; this is a side effect of the Last 10% Trap. Most companies end up knuckling under the framework, modifying their processes rather than trying to customize the tool. The more companies do that, the fewer differentiators exist between companies, which is fine as long as that differentiation isn't a competitive advantage. Companies often choose the alternative, discussed in "Pitfall: Product Customization" on page 188, which is another trap.

The *Let's Stop Working and Call It a Success* principle is one developers commonly encounter when dealing with ERP packages in the real world. Because they require huge investments of both time and money, companies are reluctant to admit when they don't work. No CTO wants to admit they wasted millions of dollars, and the tool vendor doesn't want to admit to a bad multiyear implementation. Thus, each side agrees to stop working and call it a success, with much of the promised functionality unimplemented.

 Don't couple your architecture to a vendor king.

Rather than fall victim to the Vendor King antipattern, treat vendor products as just another integration point. Developers can insulate vendor tool changes from impacting their architecture by building anticorruption layers between integration points.

Pitfall: Leaky Abstractions

> All nontrivial abstractions, to some degree, are leaky.
> —Joel Spolsky

Modern software resides in a tower of abstractions: operating systems, frameworks, dependencies, and a host of other pieces. As developers, we build abstractions so that we don't have to perpetually think at the lowest levels. If developers were required to translate the binary digits that come from hard drives into text to program, they would never get anything done! One of the triumphs of modern software is how well we can build effective abstractions.

But abstractions come at a cost because no abstraction is perfect—if it were, it wouldn't be an abstraction; it would be the real thing. As Joel Spolsky put it, all nontrivial abstractions leak. This is a problem for developers because we come to trust that abstractions are always accurate, but they often break in surprising ways.

Increased tech stack complexity has made the abstraction distraction problem worse recently. Consider the typical technology stack, circa 2005, shown in Figure 8-1.

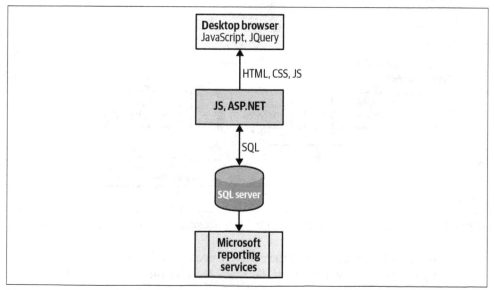

Figure 8-1. A typical technology stack in 2005

In the software stack depicted in Figure 8-1, the vendor names on the boxes change depending on local conditions. Over time, as software has become increasingly specialized, our technology stack has become more complex, as illustrated in Figure 8-2.

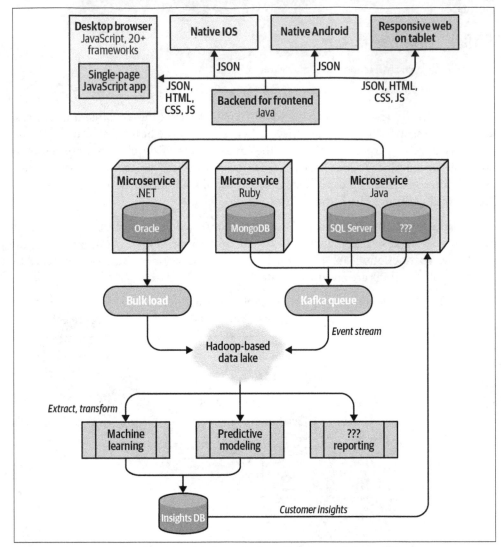

Figure 8-2. A typical software stack from the last decade, with lots of moving parts

As seen in Figure 8-2, every part of the software ecosystem has expanded and become more complex. As the problems developers face have become more complex, so have their solutions.

Primordial abstraction ooze, where a breaking abstraction at a low level causes unexpected havoc, is one of the side effects of increasing complexity in the technology stack. What if one of the abstractions at the lowest level exhibits a fault—for example, some unexpected side effect from a seemingly harmless call to the database? Because so many layers exist, the fault will wind its way to the top of the stack, perhaps metastasizing along the way, manifesting in a deeply embedded error message at the UI. Debugging and forensic analysis become more difficult as the complexity of the technology stack increases.

> Always fully understand at least one abstraction layer below the one you normally work in.
>
> —Many software sages

While understanding the layer below is good advice, this becomes more difficult as the software becomes more specialized and therefore more complex.

Increased technology stack complexity is an example of the dynamic equilibrium problem. Not only does the ecosystem change, but the constituent parts become more complex and intertwined over time as well. Our mechanism for protecting evolutionary change—fitness functions—can protect the fragile join points of architecture. Architects define invariants at key integration points as fitness functions, which run as part of a deployment pipeline, ensuring abstractions don't start to leak in undesirable ways.

Understand the fragile places within your complex technology stack and automate protections via fitness functions.

Pitfall: Resume-Driven Development

Architects become enamored of exciting new developments in the software development ecosystem and want to play with the newest toys. However, to choose an effective architecture, they must look closely at the problem domain and choose the most suitable architecture that delivers the most desired capabilities with the fewest damaging constraints. Unless, of course, the goal of the architecture is the *resume-driven development* pitfall—utilizing every framework and library possible to tout that knowledge on a resume.

Don't build architecture for the sake of architecture—you are trying to solve a problem.

Always understand the problem domain before choosing an architecture rather than the other way around.

Incremental Change

Many factors in software development make incremental change difficult. For many decades, software wasn't written with the goal of agility in mind but rather around goals like cost reduction, shared resources, and other external constraints. Consequently, many organizations don't have the building blocks in place to support evolutionary architectures.

As discussed in the book *Continuous Delivery* (Addison-Wesley) (*http://continuousdelivery.com*), many modern engineering practices support evolutionary architecture.

Antipattern: Inappropriate Governance

Software architecture never exists in a vacuum; it is often a reflection of the environment in which it was designed. A decade ago, operating systems were expensive, commercial offerings. Similarly, database servers, application servers, and the entire infrastructure for hosting applications was commercial and expensive. Architects responded to these real-world pressures by designing architectures to maximize shared resources. Many architecture patterns like SOA flourished in that era. A common governance model evolved in that environment to maximize shared resources as a cost-saving measure. Many of the commercial motivations for tools like application servers grew from this tendency. However, packing multiple resources on machines is undesirable from a development standpoint because of inadvertent coupling. No matter how effective the isolation is between shared resources, resource contention eventually rears its head.

Over the past decade, changes have occurred to the dynamic equilibrium of the development ecosystem. Now developers can build architectures where components have a high degree of isolation (like microservices), eliminating the accidental coupling exacerbated by shared environments. But many companies still adhere to the old governance playbook. A governance model that values shared resources and homogenized environments makes less sense because of recent improvements such as the DevOps movement.

> Every company is now a software company.
>
> —*Forbes Magazine*, Nov. 30, 2011

What *Forbes* means in that famous quote is that if an airline company's iPad application is terrible, it will eventually impact the company's bottom line. Software competency is required for any cutting-edge company, and increasingly for any company that wishes to remain competitive. Part of that competency includes how it manages development assets like environments.

When developers can create resources like virtual machines and containers for no cost (either monetary or time), a governance model that values a single solution becomes *innappropriate governance*. A better approach appears in many microservices environments. One common characteristic of microservices architectures is the embrace of polyglot environments, where each service team can choose a suitable technology stack to implement their service rather than try to homogenize on a corporate standard. Traditional enterprise architects cringe when they hear that advice, which is the polar opposite of the traditional approach. However, the goal in most microservices projects isn't to pick different technologies cavalierly to right-size the technology choice for the size of the problem.

In modern environments, it is inappropriate governance to homogenize on a single technology stack. This leads to the inadvertent overcomplication problem, where governance decisions add useless multipliers to the effort required to implement a solution. For example, standardizing on a single vendor's relational database is a common practice in large enterprises, for obvious reasons: consistency across projects, easily fungible staff, and so on. However, a side effect of that approach is that most projects suffer from overengineering. When developers build monolithic architectures, governance choices affect everyone. Thus, when choosing a database, the architect must look at the requirements of every project that will use this capability and make a choice that will serve the most complex case. Unfortunately, many projects won't have the most complex case or anything like it. A small project may have simple persistence needs yet must take on the full complexity of an industrial-strength database server for consistency.

With microservices, because none of the services are coupled via technical or data architecture, different teams can choose the right level of complexity and sophistication required to implement their service. The ultimate goal is simplification, to align service stack complexity to technical requirements. This partitioning tends to work best when the team wholly owns their service, including the operational aspects.

Forced Decoupling

One of the goals of the microservices architecture style is extreme decoupling of the technical architecture, allowing services to be replaced with no side effects. However, if developers all share the same codebase or even platform, *not* coupling requires some degree of developer discipline (because the temptation to reuse existing code is strong) and safeguards to make sure coupling doesn't happen by accident. Building services in different technology stacks is one way to achieve technical architecture decoupling. Many companies try to avoid this approach because they fear it hurts the ability to move employees across projects. However, Chad Fowler

---

(*http://chadfowler.com*), an architect at the former company Wunderlist, took the opposite approach: he *insisted* that teams use different technology stacks to avoid inadvertent coupling. His philosophy is that accidental coupling is a bigger problem than developer portability.

Many companies are encapsulating distinct functionality into a platform as a service (*https://oreil.ly/fl3h7*) for use internally, hiding technology choices (and therefore coupling opportunities) behind well-defined interfaces.

From a practical governance standpoint in large organizations, we find the *"just enough" governance* model works well: pick three technology stacks for standardization—simple, intermediate, and complex—and allow individual service requirements to drive stack requirements. This gives teams the flexibility to choose a suitable technology stack while still providing the company some benefits of standards.

Case Study: "Just Enough" Governance at PenultimateWidgets

For years, architects at PenultimateWidgets tried to standardize all development on Java and Oracle. However, as they built more granular services, they realized that this stack imposed a great deal of complexity on small services. But they didn't want to fully embrace the "every project chooses their own technology stack" approach of microservices because they still wanted some portability of knowledge and skills across projects. In the end, they chose the "just enough" governance route with three technology stacks:

Small
    For very simple projects without stringent scalability or performance requirements, they chose Ruby on Rails and MySQL.

Medium
    For medium projects, they chose GoLang and either Cassandra, MongoDB, or MySQL as the backend, depending on the data requirements.

Large
    For large projects, they stayed with Java and Oracle, as they work well with variable architecture concerns.

Pitfall: Lack of Speed to Release

The engineering practices in Continuous Delivery (*http://continuousdelivery.com*) address the factors that slow down software releases, and those practices should be considered axiomatic for evolutionary architecture to be successful. While the extreme version of Continuous Delivery, continuous deployment, isn't required for an evolutionary architecture, a strong correlation exists between the ability to release software and the ability to evolve that software design.

If companies build an engineering culture around continuous deployment, expecting that all changes will make their way to production only if they pass the gauntlet laid out by the deployment pipeline, developers become accustomed to constant change. On the other hand, if releases are a formal process that require a lot of specialized work, the chances of being able to leverage evolutionary architecture diminish.

Continuous Delivery strives for data-driven results, employing metrics to learn how to optimize projects. Developers must be able to measure things to understand how to make them better. One of the key metrics Continuous Delivery tracks is *cycle time*, a metric related to *lead time*: the time between the initiation of an idea and that idea manifesting in working software. However, lead time includes many subjective activities, such as estimation, prioritization, and others, making it a poor engineering metric. Instead, Continuous Delivery tracks *cycle time*: the elapsed time between the initiation and completion of a unit of work, which in this case is software development. The cycle time clock starts when a developer starts working on a new feature and expires when that feature is running in a production environment. The goal of cycle time is to measure engineering efficiency; the reduction of cycle time is one of the key goals of Continuous Delivery.

Cycle time is critical for evolutionary architecture as well. In biology, fruit flies are commonly used in experiments to illustrate genetic characteristics partially because they have a rapid life cycle—new generations appear fast enough to see tangible results. The same is true in evolutionary architecture—faster cycle time means the architecture can evolve more quickly. Thus, a project's cycle time determines how fast the architecture can evolve. In other words, evolution speed is proportional to cycle time, as expressed by

$$v \propto c$$

where v represents velocity of change and c is cycle time. Developers cannot evolve the system faster than the project's cycle time. In other words, the faster that teams can release software, the faster they can evolve parts of their system.

Cycle time is therefore a critical metric in evolutionary architecture projects—faster cycle time implies a faster ability to evolve. In fact, cycle time is an excellent candidate for an atomic, process-based fitness function. For example, developers set up a project with a deployment pipeline with automation, achieving a cycle time of three hours. Over time, the cycle time gradually increases as developers add more verifications and integration points to the deployment pipeline. Because time to market is an important metric on this project, they establish a fitness function to raise an alarm if the cycle time creeps beyond four hours. Once it has hit the threshold, developers may decide to restructure how their deployment pipeline works or decide that a four-hour cycle time is acceptable. Fitness functions can map to any behavior developers want to monitor on projects, including project metrics. Unifying project concerns as fitness functions allows developers to set up future decision points, also known as the *last responsible moment*, to reevaluate decisions. In the previous example, developers now must decide which is more important: a three-hour cycle time or the set of tests they have in place. On most projects, developers make this decision implicitly by never noticing a gradually rising cycle time and thus never prioritizing conflicting goals. With fitness functions, they can install thresholds around anticipated future decision points.

 Speed of evolution is a function of cycle time; faster cycle time allows faster evolution.

Good engineering, deployment, and release practices are critical to success with an evolutionary architecture, which in turn allows new capabilities for the business via hypothesis-driven development.

Business Concerns

Finally, we talk about inappropriate coupling driven by business concerns. Most of the time, business people aren't nefarious characters trying to make things difficult for developers; rather, they have priorities that drive inappropriate decisions from an architectural standpoint, which inadvertently constrain future options. We cover a handful of business pitfalls and antipatterns.

Pitfall: Product Customization

Salespeople want options to sell. The caricature of salespeople has them selling any requested feature before determining whether their product actually contains that feature. Thus, salespeople want infinitely customizable software to sell. However, that capability comes at a cost along a spectrum of implementation techniques:

Unique build for each customer
> In this scenario, salespeople promise unique versions of features on a tight time scale, forcing developers to use techniques like version control branches and tagging to track versions.

Permanent feature toggles
> Feature toggles, which we introduced in Chapter 3, are sometimes used strategically to create permanent customizations. Developers can use feature toggles to either build different versions for different clients or create a "freemium" version of a product—a free version that allows users to unlock premium features for a cost.

Product-driven customization

    Some products go so far as to add customization via the UI. Features in this case are permanent parts of the application and require the same care as all other product features.

With both feature toggles and customization, the testing burden increases significantly because the product contains many permutations of possible pathways. Along with testing scenarios, the number of fitness functions developers need to develop likely increases as well, to protect possible permutations.

Customization also impedes evolvability, but this shouldn't discourage companies from building customizable software; rather, they should realistically assess the associated costs.

Antipattern: Reporting Atop the System of Record

Most applications have different uses depending on the business function. For example, some users need order entry, while others require reports for analysis. Organizations struggle to provide all the possible perspectives (e.g., order entry versus monthly reporting) required by businesses, especially if everything must come from the same monolithic architecture and/or database structure. Architects struggled in the service-oriented architecture era trying to support every business concern via the same set of "reusable" services. They found that the more generic the service was, the more developers needed to customize it to be of use.

Reporting is a good example of inadvertent coupling in monolithic architectures. Architects and DBAs want to use the same database schema for both system of record and reporting, but they encounter problems because a design to support both is optimized for neither. A common pitfall developers and report designers conspire to create in layered architecture illustrates the tension between concerns. Architects build layered architecture to cut down on incidental coupling, creating layers of isolation and separation of concerns. However, reporting doesn't need separate layers to support its function, just data. Additionally, routing requests through layers adds latency. Thus, many organizations with good layered architectures allow report designers to couple reports directly to database schemas, destroying the ability to make changes to the schema without wrecking reports. This is a good example of conflicting business goals subverting the work of architects and making evolutionary change extremely difficult. While no one set out to make the system hard to evolve, it was the cumulative effect of decisions.

Many microservices architectures solve the reporting problem by separating behavior, where the isolation of services benefits separation but not consolidation. Architects commonly build these architectures using event streaming or message queues to populate domain "system of record" databases, each embedded within the architectural quantum of the service, using eventual consistency rather than transactional behavior. A set of reporting services also listens to the event stream, populating a denormalized reporting database optimized for reporting. Using eventual consistency frees architects from coordination—a form of coupling from an architectural stand-point—allowing different abstractions for different uses of the application.

For a more modern approach to reporting specifically and analytical data more broadly, see "Data Mesh: Orthogonal Data Coupling" on page 119.

Pitfall: Excessively Long Planning Horizons

Budgeting and planning processes often drive the need for assumptions and early decisions as the basis for those assumptions. However, the larger the planning horizon is without an opportunity to revisit the plan means many decisions (or assumptions) are made with the least amount of information. In the early planning phases, developers spend significant effort on activities like research, often in the form of reading, to validate their assumptions. Based on their studies, what is "best practice" or "best in class" at that time forms part of the basic fundamental assumptions before developers write any code or release software to end users. More and more effort put into the assumptions, even if they turn out to be false in six months, leads to a strong attachment to them. The sunk cost fallacy (*https://en.wikipedia.org/wiki/Sunk_costs*) describes decisions affected by emotional investment. Put simply, the more someone invests time or effort into something, the harder it becomes to abandon it. In software, this is seen in the form of the *irrational artifact attachment*—the more time and effort you invest in planning or a document, the more likely you will protect what's contained in the plan or document even in the face of evidence that it is inaccurate or outdated.

Don't become irrationally attached to handcrafted artifacts.

Beware of long planning cycles that force architects into irreversible decisions and find ways to keep options open. Breaking large programs of work into smaller, early deliverables tests the feasibility of both the architectural choices and the development infrastructure. Architects should avoid following technologies that require a significant up-front investment before software is actually built (e.g., large licenses and support contracts) and before they have validated through end-user feedback that the technology actually fits the problem they are trying to solve.

Summary

As in any architecture practice, evolutionary architecture embraces many trade-offs: technical, business, operational, data, integration, and many more. Patterns (and antipatterns) appear so much in architecture because they provide not only advice but—critically—the *context* where that advice makes sense. Reusing software assets is an obvious organizational goal, but architects must evaluate what trade-offs that might entail: often, too much coupling is more harmful than duplication.

We discuss patterns but not *best practices*, which are virtually nonexistent in software architecture. *Best practice* implies that an architect can turn their brain off whenever they encounter a particular situation—after all, this is the *best* way to handle this practice. However, everything in software architecture is a trade-off, meaning that architects must evaluate trade-offs anew for virtually every decision. Patterns and antipatterns can help identify contextualized advice and which antipatterns to avoid.

CHAPTER 9

Putting Evolutionary Architecture into Practice

Finally, we look at the steps required to implement the ideas around evolutionary architecture. This includes both technical and business concerns, including organization and team impacts. We also suggest where to start and how to sell these ideas to your business.

Organizational Factors

The impact of software architecture has a surprisingly wide breadth on a variety of factors not normally associated with software, including team impacts, budgeting, and a host of others. Let's look at a common set of factors that impact your ability to put evolutionary architecture into practice.

Don't Fight Conway's Law

In April 1968, Melvin Conway submitted a paper to *Harvard Business Review* titled "How Do Committees Invent?" (*https://oreil.ly/bIOG5*). In this paper, Conway introduced the notion that the social structures, particularly the communication paths between people, inevitably influence final product design.

As Conway describes, in the very early stage of the design, a high-level understanding of the system is made to understand how to break down areas of responsibility into different patterns. The way that a group breaks down a problem affects choices that they can make later.

He codified what has become known as *Conway's Law*:

> Organizations which design systems … are constrained to produce designs which are copies of the communication structures of these organizations.
>
> —Melvin Conway

As Conway notes, when technologists break down problems into smaller chunks to delegate, they introduce coordination problems. In many organizations, formal communication structures or rigid hierarchy appears to solve this coordination problem but often leads to inflexible solutions. For example, in a layered architecture where the team is separated by technical function (user interface, business logic, etc.), solving common problems that cut vertically across layers increases coordination overhead. People who have worked in startups and then have joined large multinational corporations have likely experienced the contrast between the nimble, adaptable culture of the former and the inflexible communication structures of the latter. A good example of Conway's Law in action might be trying to change the contract between two services, which could be difficult if the successful change of a service owned by one team requires the coordinated and agreed-upon effort of another.

In his paper, Conway was effectively warning software architects to pay attention not only to the architecture and design of the software, but also to the delegation, assignment, and coordination of the work between teams.

In many organizations, teams are divided according to their functional skills. Some common examples include:

Frontend developers
  A team with specialized skills in a particular UI technology (e.g., HTML, mobile, desktop)

Backend developers
  A team with unique skills in building backend services, sometimes API tiers

Database developers
  A team with unique skills in building storage and logic services

Consider the common structure/team alignment illustrated in Figure 9-1.

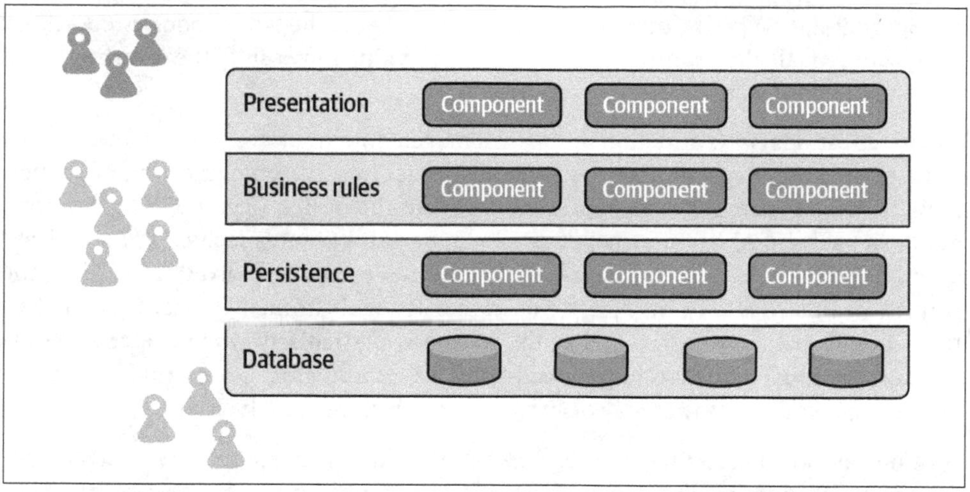

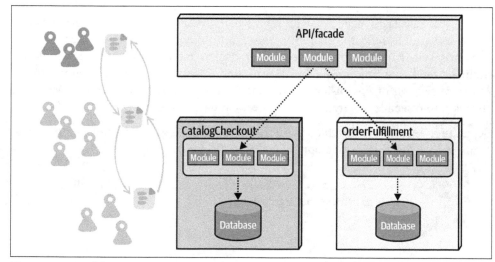

Figure 9-1. Layered architectures facilitate separating team members by technical capabilities

This team organization works relatively well if companies utilize a layered architecture based on similar technical layers, modeled after observations in "Don't Fight Conway's Law" on page 193. However, if a team switches to a distributed architecture such as microservices yet keeps the same organization, the side effect is increased messaging between layers, as illustrated in Figure 9-2.

Figure 9-2. Building microservices yet maintaining layers increases communication overhead

In Figure 9-2, changes to domain concepts like `CatalogCheckout` requires coordination between all the technical parts of the domain, increasing the overhead and slowing development.

In organizations with functional silos, management divides teams to make their human resources department happy without much regard to engineering efficiency. Although each team may be good at their part of the design (e.g., building a screen, adding a backend API or service, or developing a new storage mechanism), to release a new business capability or feature all three teams must be involved in building the feature. Teams typically optimize for efficiency for their immediate tasks rather than the more abstract, strategic goals of the business, particularly when under schedule pressure. Instead of delivering an end-to-end feature value, teams often focus on delivering components that may or may not work well with each other.

As Conway noted in his paper, *every time a delegation is made and somebody's scope of inquiry is narrowed, the class of design alternatives which can be effectively pursued is also narrowed.* Stated another way, it's hard for someone to change something if the thing she wants to change is owned by someone else. Software architects should pay attention to how work is divided and delegated to align architectural goals with team structure.

Many companies that build architectures such as microservices structure their teams around service boundaries rather than siloed technical architecture partitions. In the ThoughtWorks Technology Radar (*https://oreil.ly/MAQoN*), we call this the Inverse Conway Maneuver (*https://oreil.ly/usLhg*). Organization of teams in such a manner is ideal because team structure will impact myriad dimensions of software development and should reflect the problem size and scope. For example, when building a microservices architecture, companies typically structure teams that resemble the architecture by cutting across functional silos and including team members who cover every angle of the business and technical aspects of the architecture. Modeling the team to resemble the architecture appears in Figure 9-3.

Separating teams to resemble architecture is becoming increasingly common as teams realize the benefits of mapping teams to architecture.

Structure teams to look like your target architecture, and it will be easier to achieve that architecture.

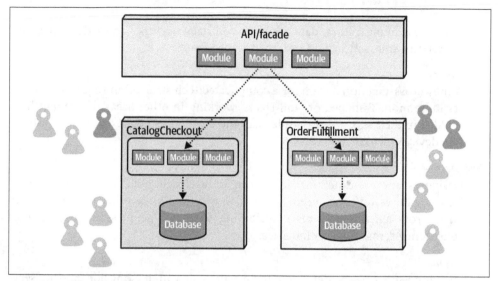

Figure 9-3. Using the Inverse Conway Maneuver to simplify communication

Teams structured around domains rather than technical capabilities have several advantages when it comes to evolutionary architecture and exhibit some common characteristics.

Default to cross-functional teams

Domain-centric teams tend to be *cross-functional*, meaning every product role is covered by someone on the team. The goal of a domain-centric team is to eliminate operational friction. In other words, the team has all the roles needed to design, implement, and deploy their service, including traditionally separate roles like operations. But these roles must change to accommodate this new structure, which includes the following roles:

Architecture
    Design architecture to eliminate inappropriate coupling that complicates incremental change. Notice that this doesn't require an exotic architecture like microservices. A well-designed modular monolithic application may display the same ability to accommodate incremental change (although architects must design the application explicitly to support this level of change).

Business analysts
    In products with high areas of domain complexity, due to complex rules, configuration, or product history, business analysts (BAs) support the rest of the team with expertise. In cross-functional teams, BAs are now co-located with the team to provide fast feedback on proposed changes.

Data

Database administrators, data analysts, and data scientists must deal with new granularity, transaction, and system of record issues.

Developers

A fully cross-functional team for a complicated tech stack often requires developers to be more T-shaped or "full-stack," working in other areas they might have avoided in their silos. For example, backend developers might do some mobile or web development or vice versa.

Designers

Designers in cross-functional teams can work closely with their team on user-facing features but may need to spend more time with other designers from other cross-functional teams contributing to the same product to guarantee consistency across the user interface.

Operations

Slicing up services and deploying them separately (often alongside existing services and deployed continuously) is a daunting challenge for many organizations with traditional IT structures. Naïve old-school architects believe that component and operational modularity are the same thing, but this is often not the case in the real world. Automating DevOps tasks like machine provisioning and deployment is critical to success.

Product managers

Often described as the "CEO" for a product, most product managers (PMs) prioritize customer needs and business outcomes for a certain product area such as the "Growth" or Customer Registration area, Payment area, or Customer Support. In a cross-functional setup, a PM no longer needs to coordinate with many technical teams as they should have all the skills necessary to deliver on their product area. Working in cross-functional teams gives the PM more time to coordinate with others PMs or internal stakeholders to deliver a seamless end-to-end product.

Testing

Testers must become accustomed to the challenges of integration testing across domains, such as building integration environments, creating and maintaining contracts, and so on.

One goal of cross-functional teams is to eliminate coordination friction. On traditional siloed teams, developers often must wait on a DBA to make changes or wait for someone in operations to provide resources. Making all the roles local eliminates the incidental friction of coordination across silos.

While it would be luxurious to have every role filled by qualified engineers on every project, most companies aren't that lucky. Key skill areas are always constrained by external forces like market demand. So, many companies aspire to create cross-functional teams but cannot because of resources. In those cases, constrained resources may be shared across projects. For example, rather than have one operations engineer per service, perhaps they rotate across several different teams.

By modeling architecture and teams around the domain, the common unit of change is now handled within the same team, reducing artificial friction. A domain-centric architecture may still use layered architecture for its other benefits, such as separation of concerns. For example, the implementation of a particular microservice might depend on a framework that implements the layered architecture, allowing that team to easily swap out a technical layer. Microservices encapsulate the technical architecture inside the domain, inverting the traditional relationship.

Amazon's "Two Pizza" Teams

Amazon became famous for its product team approach, which it called *two-pizza teams*. Its philosophy is that no team shall be larger than can be fed with two large pizzas. The motivation behind this partitioning is more about communication than team size—the larger the team, the more people each team member must communicate with. Each team is cross-functional, and they also embrace the philosophy of "you build it, you run it," meaning each team has complete ownership of their service, including operationalizing it.

Having small, cross-functional teams also takes advantage of human nature. Amazon's "two-pizza team" mimics small-group primate behavior. Most sports teams have around 10 players, and anthropologists believe that preverbal hunting parties were also around this size. Building highly responsible teams leverages innate social behavior, making team members more responsible. For example, suppose a developer in a traditional project structure wrote some code two years ago that blew up in the middle of the night, forcing someone in operations to respond to a pager in the night and fix it. The next morning, our careless developer may not even realize they accidentally caused a panic in the middle of the night. On a cross-functional team, if the developer wrote code that blew up in the night and someone from his team had to respond to it, the next morning our hapless developer would have to look across the table at the sad, tired eyes of the team member they inadvertently affected. It should make our errant developer want to be a better teammate.

Creating cross-functional teams prevents finger pointing across silos and engenders a feeling of ownership in the team, encouraging team members to do their best work.

Finding New Resources via Automating DevOps

Neal once consulted for a company that offered a hosted service. They had a dozen development teams, all with well-defined modules. However, they had an operations group who managed all maintenance, provisioning, monitoring, and other common tasks. The manager commonly received complaints from developers who wanted faster turnaround on needed resources like database and web servers. To alleviate some of the pressure, he started assigning an operations person one day a week to each project. During that day, the developers were happy as could be—no waiting around for resources! Alas, the manager didn't have enough resources to do that regularly.

Or so he thought. We discerned that much of the manual work performed by operations was accidental complexity: misconfigured machines, a hodgepodge of manufacturers and brands, and many other repairable offenses. Once everything was well cataloged, we helped them automate the provisioning of new machines using Puppet (*http://puppetlabs.com*). After this work, the operations team had enough members to permanently embed an operations engineer on each project and still have enough people to manage the automated infrastructure.

They didn't hire new engineers, nor did they significantly change their job roles. Instead, they applied modern engineering practices to automate things that humans shouldn't deal with regularly, freeing them to be better partners in development efforts.

Organize teams around business capabilities

Organizing teams around domains implicitly means organizing them around business capabilities. Many organizations expect their technical architecture to represent its own complex abstraction, loosely related to business behavior because architects' traditional emphasis has been around purely technical architecture, that is typically segregated by functionality. A layered architecture is designed to make swapping technical architecture layers easier, not make working on a domain entity like Customer easier. Most of this emphasis was driven by external factors. For example, many architectural styles of the past decade focused heavily on maximizing shared resources because of expense.

Architects have gradually detangled themselves from commercial restrictions via the embrace of open source in all corners of most organizations. Shared resource architecture has inherent problems around inadvertent interference between parts. Now that developers have the option of creating custom-made environments and functionality, it is easier for them to shift emphasis away from technical architectures and focus more on domain-centric ones to better match the common unit of change in most software projects.

Organize teams around business capabilities, not job functions.

Balance cognitive load with business capabilities

Since we wrote the first edition of this book, our industry has uncovered better approaches for team design optimized for the continuous flow of value. In their book, *Team Topologies: Organizing Business and Technology Teams for Fast Flow*, Manuel Pais and Matthew Skelton refer to four different team patterns:

Stream-aligned teams
>are aligned to a flow of work from (usually a segment of) the business domain.

Enabling teams
>help stream-aligned teams overcome obstacles and detect missing capabilities such as learning new skills/technologies.

Complicated subsystem teams
>own a part of the business domain that demands significant mathematics/calculation/technical expertise.

Platform teams
>are a grouping of other team types that provide a compelling internal product to accelerate delivery by stream-aligned teams.

In their model, using stream-aligned teams maps to our recommendation of aligning teams around "Business Capabilities" with a small caveat: team design must also account for *cognitive load*. A team with an excessive cognitive load, either from a complex domain area or from a complex set of technologies, will struggle to deliver. As an example, if you have ever worked with processing payments, there is a high domain cognitive load caused by payment scheme–specific rules and exceptions. Dealing with one payment scheme might be manageable for a single team, but if that team has to maintain five or six concurrent payment schemes, they are likely to exceed their team cognitive load even without considering additional technical complexity.

The response to this might be to try to have multiple stream-aligned teams or, where needed, a complicated subsystem team. For example, you might have a single stream-aligned team taking care of the end-to-end user journey for processing a payment, and then additionally have a complicated system team for a specific payment scheme (e.g., Mastercard or Visa).

The book *Team Topologies* reinforces the idea we should arrange teams around the domain's business capabilities but also need to take into account cognitive load.

Think product over project

One mechanism many companies use to shift their team emphasis is to model their work around *products* rather than *projects*. Software projects have a common workflow in most organizations. A problem is identified, a development team is formed, and they work on the problem until "completion," at which time they turn the software over to operations for care, feeding, and maintenance for the rest of its life. Then the project team moves on to the next problem.

This causes a slew of common problems. First, because the team has moved on to other concerns, bug fixes and other maintenance work is often difficult to manage. Second, because the developers are isolated from the operational aspects of their code, they care less about things like quality. In general, the more layers of indirection between a developer and their running code, the less connection they have to that code. This sometimes leads to an "us versus them" mentality between operational silos, which isn't surprising, as many organizations have incentivized workers to exist in conflict. Third, the concept of "project" has a temporal connotation: projects end, which affects the decision process of those who work on it.

Thinking of software as a *product* shifts the company's perspective in three ways. First, products live forever, unlike the lifespan of projects. Cross-functional teams (frequently based on the Inverse Conway Maneuver) stay associated with their product. Second, each product has an owner who advocates for its use within the ecosystem and manages things like requirements. Third, because the team is cross-functional, each role needed by the product is represented: PMs, BAs, designers, developers, QA, DBA, operations, and any other required roles.

The real goal of shifting from a *project* to a *product* mentality concerns long-term company buy-in. Product teams take ownership responsibility for the long-term quality of their product. Thus, developers take ownership of quality metrics and pay more attention to defects. This perspective also helps provide a long-term vision to the team. The book *Project to Product: How to Survive and Thrive in the Age of Digital Disruption with the Flow Framework* by Mik Kersten (IT Revolution Press) covers the organizational changes and a framework for guiding an organization through this cultural and structural change.

Avoid excessively large teams

Many companies have found anecdotally that large development teams don't work well, and J. Richard Hackman, a famous expert on team dynamics, offers an explanation as to why. It's not the number of people but the number of connections they must maintain. He uses the formula shown in Equation 9-1 to determine how many connections exist between people, where *n* is the number of people.

Equation 9-1. Number of connections between people

$$\frac{n(n-1)}{2}$$

In Equation 9-1, as the number of people grows, the number of connections grows rapidly, as shown in Figure 9-4.

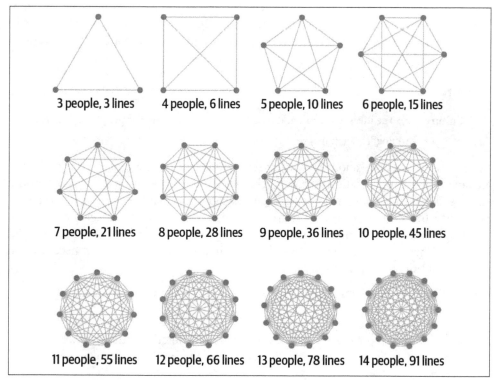

Figure 9-4. As the number of people grows, the connections grow rapidly

In Figure 9-4, when the number of people on a team reaches 14, they must manage 91 links; when it reaches 50 team members, the number of links is a daunting 1,225. Thus, the motivation to create small teams revolves around the desire to cut down on communication links. And these small teams should be cross-functional to eliminate artificial friction imposed by coordinating across silos, which often accidentally drives up the number of collaborators on a project.

Each team shouldn't have to know what other teams are doing, unless integration points exist between the teams. Even then, fitness functions should be used to ensure integrity of integration points.

Strive for a low number of connections between development teams.

Team coupling characteristics

The way firms organize and govern their own structures significantly influences the way software is built and architected. In this section, we explore the different organizational and team aspects that make building evolutionary architectures easier or harder. Most architects don't think about how team structure affects the coupling characteristics of the architecture, but it has a huge impact.

Culture

> **Culture**, (n.): The ideas, customs, and social behavior of a particular people or society.
>
> —Oxford English Dictionary

Architects should care about how engineers build their system and watch out for the behaviors their organization rewards. The activities and decision-making processes architects use to choose tools and create designs can have a big impact on how well software endures evolution. Well-functioning architects take on leadership roles, creating the technical culture and designing approaches for how developers build systems. They teach and encourage in individual engineers the skills necessary to build evolutionary architecture.

An architect can seek to understand a team's engineering culture by asking questions like:

- Does everyone on the team know what fitness functions are and consider the impact of new tool or product choices on the ability to evolve new fitness functions?
- Are teams measuring how well their system meets their defined fitness functions?
- Do engineers understand cohesion and coupling? What about connascence?
- Are there conversations about what domain and technical concepts belong together?
- Do teams choose solutions not based on what technology they want to learn but based on its ability to make changes?
- How are teams responding to business changes? Do they struggle to incorporate small business changes, or are they spending too much time on them?

Adjusting the behavior of the team often involves adjusting the process around the team, as people respond to what is asked of them to do.

> Tell me how you measure me, and I will tell you how I will behave.
>
> —Dr. Eliyahu M. Goldratt (The Haystack Syndrome)

If a team is unaccustomed to change, an architect can introduce practices that start making that a priority. For example, when a team considers a new library or framework, the architect can ask the team to explicitly evaluate, through a short experiment, how much extra coupling the new library or framework will add. Will engineers be able to easily write and test code outside of the given library or framework, or will the new library and framework require additional runtime setup that may slow down the development loop?

In addition to the selection of new libraries or frameworks, code reviews are a natural place to consider how well newly changed code supports future changes. If there is another place in the system that will suddenly use another external integration point, and that integration point will change, how many places would need to be updated? Of course, developers must watch out for overengineering, prematurely adding additional complexity or abstractions for change. The *Refactoring* book (*https://refactoring.com*) contains relevant advice:

> The first time you do something, you just do it. The second time you do something similar, you wince at the duplication, but you do the duplicate thing anyway. The third time you do something similar, you refactor.

Many teams are driven and rewarded most often for delivering new functionality, with code quality and the evolvable aspect considered only if teams make it a priority. An architect who cares about evolutionary architecture needs to watch out for team actions that prioritize design decisions that help with evolvability or find ways to encourage it.

Culture of Experimentation

Successful evolution demands experimentation, but some companies fail to experiment because they are too busy delivering to plans. Successful experimentation is about regularly running small activities to try out new ideas (both from a technical and product perspective) and to integrate successful experiments into existing systems.

> The real measure of success is the number of experiments that can be crowded into 24 hours.
>
> —Thomas Alva Edison

Organizations can encourage experimentation in a variety of ways:

Bringing ideas from outside

Many companies send their employees to conferences and encourage them to find new technologies, tools, and approaches that might solve a problem better. Other companies bring in external advice or consultants as sources of new ideas.

Encouraging explicit improvement

Toyota is most famous for its culture of kaizen, or continuous improvement. Everyone is expected to continually seek constant improvements, particularly those closest to the problems and empowered to solve them.

Implementing spike and stabilize

A spike solution is an extreme programming practice where teams generate a throwaway solution to quickly learn a tough technical problem, explore an unfamiliar domain, or increase confidence in estimates. Using spike solutions increases learning speed at the cost of software quality; no one would want to put a spike solution straight into production because it would lack the necessary thought and time to make it operational. It was created for learning, not as the well-engineered solution.

Creating innovation time

Google is well known for its 20% time, where employees can work on any project for 20% of their time. Other companies organize Hackathons (*https://oreil.ly/ 4EXZx*) and allow teams to find new products or improvements to existing products. Atlassian holds regular 24-hour sessions called ShipIt (*https://oreil.ly/ GdsjU*) days.

Following set-based development

Set-based development focuses on exploring multiple approaches. At first glance, multiple options appear costly because of extra work, but in exploring several options simultaneously, teams end up with a better understanding of the problem at hand and discover real constraints with tooling or approach. The key to effective set-based development is to prototype several approaches in a short period (i.e., less than a few days) to build more concrete data and experience. A more robust solution often appears after taking into account several competing solutions.

Connecting engineers with end users

Experimentation is successful only when teams understand the impact of their work. In many firms with an experimentation mindset, teams and product people see firsthand the impact of decisions on customers and are encouraged to experiment to explore this impact. A/B testing (*https://oreil.ly/BrOHR*) is one such practice companies use with this experimentation mindset. Another practice companies implement is sending teams and engineers to observe how users interact with their software to achieve a certain task. This practice, taken from the pages of the usability community, builds empathy with end users, and engineers often return with a better understanding of user needs, and with new ideas to better fulfill them.

CFO and Budgeting

Many traditional functions of enterprise architecture, such as budgeting, must reflect changing priorities in an evolutionary architecture. In the past, budgeting was based on the ability to predict long-term trends in a software development ecosystem. However, as we've suggested throughout this book, the fundamental nature of dynamic equilibrium destroys predictability.

In fact, an interesting relationship exists between architectural quanta and the cost of architecture. As the number of quanta rises, the cost per quantum goes down, until architects reach a sweet spot, as illustrated in Figure 9-5.

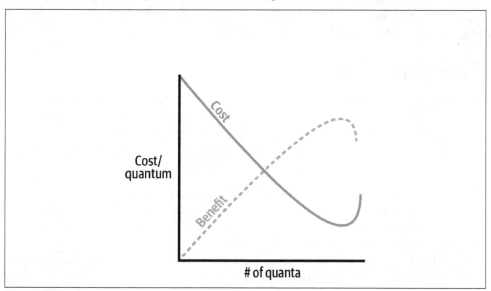

Figure 9-5. The relationship between architectural quanta and cost

In Figure 9-5, as the number of architectural quanta rises, the cost of each diminishes because of several factors. First, because the architecture consists of smaller parts, the separation of concerns should be more discrete and defined. Second, rising numbers of physical quanta require automation of their operational aspects because, beyond a certain point, it is no longer practical for people to handle chores manually.

However, it is possible to make quanta so small that the sheer numbers become more costly. For example, in a microservices architecture, it is possible to build services at the granularity of a single field on a form. At that level, the coordination cost between each small part starts dominating other factors in the architecture. Thus, at the extremes of the graph, the sheer number of quanta drives benefit per quantum down.

In an evolutionary architecture, architects strive to find the sweet spot between the proper quantum size and the corresponding costs. Every company is different. For example, a company in an aggressive market may need to move faster and therefore desire a smaller quantum size. Remember, the speed at which new generations appear is proportional to cycle time, and smaller quanta tend to have shorter cycle times. Another company may find it pragmatic to build a monolithic architecture for simplicity.

As we face an ecosystem that defies planning, many factors determine the best match between architecture and cost. This reflects our observation that the role of architects has expanded: Architectural choices have more impact than ever.

Rather than adhere to decades-old "best practice" guidelines about enterprise architecture, modern architects must understand the benefits of evolvable systems along with the inherent uncertainty that goes with them.

The Business Case

We cover a lot of technical details throughout this book, but unless you can show business value from this approach, it appears to nontechnologists as metawork. Thus, architects should be able to make the case that evolutionary architecture can improve both confidence in change and automated governance. However, more direct benefits exist in the kinds of capabilities this architectural approach enables.

Architects can sell the idea of evolutionary architecture by talking to business stakeholders in terms they understand and appreciate (rather than the nuances of architectural plumbing): talk to them about A/B testing and the ability to learn from customers. Underlying these advanced interaction techniques are the supporting mechanics and structure of evolutionary architecture, including the ability to perform hypothesis-, and data-driven development.

Hypothesis- and Data-Driven Development

The GitHub example in "Case Study: Architectural Restructuring While Deploying 60 Times per Day" on page 76 using the Scientist framework is an example of *data-driven development*—allow data to drive changes and focus efforts on technical change. A similar approach that incorporates business rather than technical concerns is *hypothesis-driven development*.

In the week between Christmas 2013 and New Year's Day 2014, Facebook encountered a problem (*https://oreil.ly/xd432*): more photos were uploaded to Facebook in that week than all the photos on Flickr, and more than a million of them were flagged as offensive. Facebook allows users to flag photos they believe are potentially offensive and then reviews them to determine objectively if they are. But this dramatic increase in photos created a problem: there was not enough staff to review the photos.

Fortunately, Facebook has modern DevOps and the ability to perform experiments on its users. When asked about the chances a typical Facebook user has been involved in an experiment, one Facebook engineer claimed, "Oh, 100%—we routinely have more than 20 experiments running at a time." Engineers used this experimental capability to ask users follow-up questions about *why* photos were deemed offensive and discovered many delightful quirks of human behavior. For example, people don't like to admit that they look bad in a photo but will freely admit that the photographer did a poor job. By experimenting with different phrasing and questions, the engineers could query their actual users to determine why they flagged a photo as offensive. In a relatively short amount of time, Facebook shaved off enough false positives to restore offensive photos to a manageable problem by building a platform that allowed for experimentation.

In the book *Lean Enterprise* (O'Reilly), the authors describe the modern process of *hypothesis-driven development*. Under this process, rather than gathering formal requirements and spending time and resources building features into applications, teams should leverage the scientific method instead. Once teams have created the minimal viable product version of an application (whether as a new product or by performing maintenance work on an existing application), they can build hypotheses during new feature ideation rather than requirements. Hypothesis-driven development hypotheses are couched in terms of the hypothesis to test, what experiments can determine the results, and what validating the hypothesis means to future application development.

For example, rather than change the image size for sales items on a catalog page because a business analyst thought it was a good idea, state it as a hypothesis instead: if we make the sales images bigger, we hypothesize that it will lead to a 5% increase in sales for those items. Once the hypothesis is in place, run experiments via A/B testing—one group with bigger sales images and one without—and tally the results.

Even agile projects with engaged business users incrementally build themselves into a bad spot. An individual decision by a business analyst may make sense in isolation, but when combined with other features may ultimately degrade the overall experience. In an excellent case study (*https://oreil.ly/28dst*), the mobile.de team followed a logical path of accruing new features haphazardly to the point where sales were diminishing, at least in part because their UI had become so convoluted, as is often the result of development continuing on mature software products. Different philosophical approaches included more listings, better prioritization, and better grouping.

To help them make this decision, they built three versions of the UI and allowed their users to decide.

The engine that drives agile software methodologies is the nested feedback loop: testing, continuous integration, iterations, and so on. And yet, the part of the feedback loop that incorporates the ultimate users of the application has eluded teams. Using hypothesis-driven development, we can incorporate users in an unprecedented way, learning from behavior and building what users really find valuable.

Hypothesis-driven development requires the coordination of many moving parts: evolutionary architecture, modern DevOps, modified requirements gathering, and the ability to run multiple versions of an application simultaneously. Service-based architectures (like microservices) usually achieve side-by-side versions by intelligent routing of services. For example, one user may execute the application using a particular constellation of services while another request may use an entirely different set of instances of the same services. If most services include many running instances (for scalability, for example), it becomes trivial to make some of those instances slightly different with enhanced functionality and to route some users to those features.

Experiments should run long enough to yield significant results. Generally, it is preferable to find a measurable way to determine better outcomes rather than annoy users with things like pop-up surveys. For example, does one hypothesized workflow allow the user to complete a task with fewer keystrokes and clicks? By silently incorporating users into the development and design feedback loop, you can build much more functional software.

Fitness Functions as Experimental Media

One common use of fitness functions by architects is to answer hypotheses. Architects have many decisions that have never existed here or anywhere in this particular manifestation, leading to educated guesses about architecture concerns. However, once teams have implemented a solution, the architect can use fitness functions to validate hypotheses. Here are several examples derived from real-world projects.

Case study: UDP communications

PenultimateWidgets has an ecosystem with a large number of ETL (Extract, Transform, and Load) jobs and batch processes. The team created a custom monitoring tool to ensure the execution of tasks, such as `Send Reports`, `Consolidate Information`, and so on, as shown in Figure 9-6.

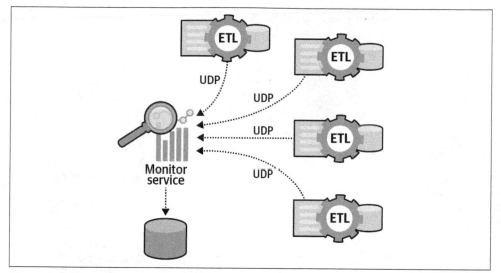

Figure 9-6. Custom monitoring tool for ETL communication

Architects designed the system in Figure 9-6 to use a UDP protocol between the ETL jobs and the monitoring service. Sometimes the completion messages would get lost, leading the team to raise an alert that the task was unfinished, which then led them to assign a person to manage that false positive. The architects decided to build a fitness function to answer the question: what percentage of messages are not being covered by the custom monitoring tool? If the number is greater than 10%, the decision is to replace the monitoring tool with a more standard implementation.

To test the hypothesis that the custom tool wasn't as reliable as the creators assumed, the team built a fitness function to:

- Calculate the estimated number of messages from all the applications and the frequency of the messages in a controlled environment (like PreProd or UAT) via monitoring

- Create a Mock Service to simulate that number of requests

- Use the Mock Service to read the processed messages from the Monitor Service database, to get a metric about the percentage of lost messages and maximum number of messages the application can handle without crashing, and store that information in a JSON file

- Process the JSON file with an analytics tool such as Pandas (*https://pan das.pydata.org*) to create results

The fitness function solution appears in Figure 9-7.

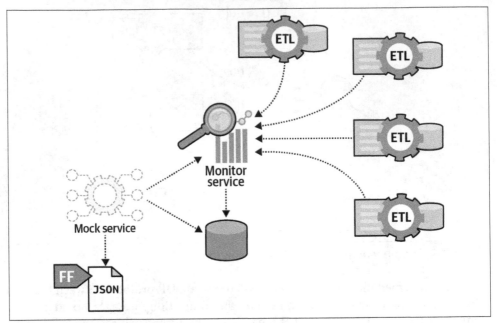

Figure 9-7. Fitness function to test hypothesis

After processing, the team concluded that fully 40% of messages were lost at high scale, calling the reliability of the custom solution into question and leading the team to decide to change the implementation.

Case study: Security dependencies

PenultimateWidgets has a dreaded security breach in some of its library dependencies, leading the team to implement a lengthly manual process upon application change to validate the software supply chain. However, this review process harmed the team's ability to move as quickly as their market demands.

To improve the feedback time on security checks, the team built a stage in their continuous integration pipeline to scan the library dependency list, validating each version against a real-time updated block list, and raising an alert if any project uses an affected library, as shown in Figure 9-8.

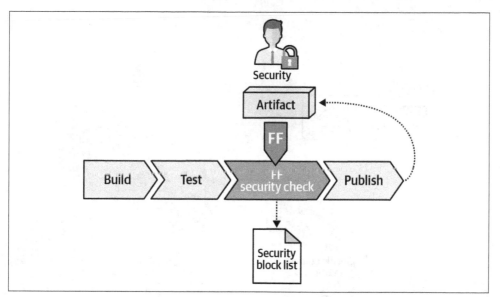

Figure 9-8. Security scanning during continuous integration

The fitness function shown in Figure 9-8 illustrates how teams can utilize holistic governance of important aspects of their ecosystem. Security is a critical fast-feedback requirement in organizations, and automating security checks provides the fastest possible feedback. Automation doesn't replace people in the feedback loop. Rather, it allows teams to automate regression and other automatable tasks, freeing people for more creative approaches that only a human can imagine.

Case study: Concurrency fitness function

PenultimateWidgets was using the Strangler Fig pattern (*https://oreil.ly/BhDNV*)—slowly replacing functionality one discrete behavior at a time. Thus, the team created a new microservice to handle a specific part of the domain. The new service runs in production, using the double-writing strategy but maintaining the source of truth in the legacy database. Because the team had not written this type of service before, the architects estimated based on preliminary data that the scaling factor should be 120 requests/second. However, the service frequently crashed, even though measurements showed that they could handle up to 300 requests/second. Does the team need to increase the auto-scaling factor or is something else creating the problem? The problem is illustrated in Figure 9-9.

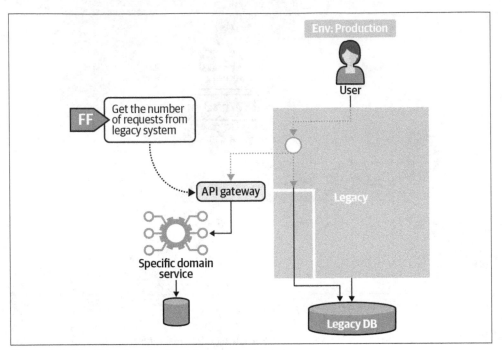

Figure 9-9. Verifying levels of concurrency

As shown in Figure 9-9, the team created a fitness function to measure the real performance in the production system. This fitness function:

1. Calculates the number of incoming calls in production to verify the maximum number of requests that the service needs to support and what would be the auto-scaling factor to guarantee availability with horizontal scaling

2. Create a New Relic Query to get the number of calls per second in production

3. Make new load and concurrency tests using the new number of requests per second

4. Monitor the memory and CPU, and define the stress point

5. Put that fitness function in the pipeline to guarantee availability and performance over time

After running the fitness function, the team realized that the average number of calls was 1,200 per second, greatly exceeding their estimate. Thus, the team updated the scaling factor to reflect reality.

Case study: Fidelity fitness function

The same team from the previous example faced a common problem when teams used the Strangler Fig pattern—how can they be sure that the new system replicates the behavior of the old system? They built what we call a *fidelity fitness function*, one that allows teams to selectively replace chunks of functionality one piece at a time. Most of these fitness functions are inspired by the example shown in Example 4-11, which allows the ability to run two versions of code side by side (which thresholds) to ensure the new replicates the old.

The fidelity fitness function the team implemented appears in Figure 9-10.

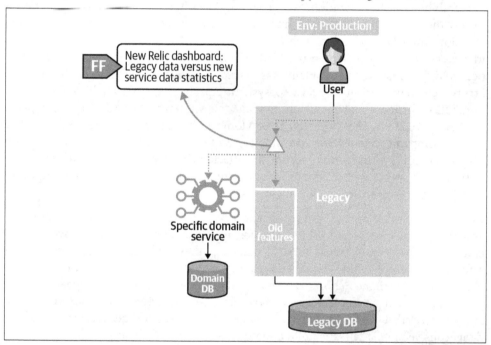

Figure 9-10. Fidelity fitness function to ensure equivalent responses

The team implemented the fitness function to ensure consistency. However, they realized a side benefit as well: they also identified some data that came from sources they had not documented, leading them to a better holistic understanding of data dependencies in the (poorly documented) legacy system.

Building Enterprise Fitness Functions

In an evolutionary architecture, the role of the enterprise architect revolves around *guidance* and *enterprise-wide fitness functions*. Microservices architectures reflect this changing model. Because each service is operationally decoupled from the others, sharing resources isn't a consideration. Instead, architects provide guidance around the purposeful coupling points in the architecture (such as service templates) and platform choices. Enterprise architecture typically owns this shared infrastructure function and constrains platform choices to those supported consistently across the enterprise.

Case Study: Zero-Day Security Vulnerability

What does a company do when a zero-day exploit is discovered in one of the development frameworks or libraries it uses? Many scanning tools exist to search for known vulnerabilities at the network packet level, but they often don't have the proper hooks to test the right thing in a timely manner. A dire example of this scenario affected a major financial institution a few years ago. On September 7, 2017, Equifax, a major credit scoring agency in the United States, announced that a data breach had occurred. Ultimately, the problem was traced to a hacking exploit of the popular Struts web framework in the Java ecosystem (Apache Struts vCVE-2017-5638). The foundation issued a statement announcing the vulnerability and released a patch on March 7, 2017. The Department of Homeland Security contacted Equifax and similar companies the next day, warning them of this problem, and they ran scans on March 15, 2017, which found *most* of the affected systems…most, not *all*. Thus, the critical patch wasn't applied to many older systems until July 29, 2017, when Equifax's security experts identified the hacking behavior that led to the data breach.

In a world with automated governance, every project runs a deployment pipeline, and the security team has a "slot" in each team's deployment pipeline where they can deploy fitness functions. Most of the time, these will be mundane checks for safeguards like preventing developers from storing passwords in databases and similar regular governance chores. However, when a zero-day exploit appears, having the same mechanism in place everywhere allows the security team to insert a test in every project that checks for a certain framework and version number; if it finds the dangerous version, it fails the build and notifies the security team. Increasingly, teams worry about software supply chain issues—what is the provenance of the libraries and frameworks of (particularly) open source tools? Unfortunately, numerous stories exist describing developer tools acting as an attack vector. Thus, teams need to pay attention to metadata about dependencies. Fortunately, a number of tools have appeared to address tracking and automating software supply chain governance, such as snyk (*https://snyk.io*) and Dependabot (*https://github.com/dependabot*), used by GitHub (*https://github.com*).

Teams configure deployment pipelines to awaken them for any change to the ecosystem: code, database schema, deployment configuration, and fitness functions. Changes to dependencies allow the security team to monitor possible vulnerabilities, providing a hook to the correct information at the proper time.

If each project uses a deployment pipeline to apply fitness functions as part of their build, enterprise architects can insert some of their own fitness functions. This allows each project to verify cross-cutting concerns, such as scalability, security, and other enterprise-wide concerns, on a continual basis, discovering flaws as early as possible. Just as projects in microservices share service templates to unify parts of technical architecture, enterprise architects can use deployment pipelines to drive consistent testing across projects.

Mechanisms like this allow enterprises to universally automate important governance tasks, and create opportunities to create governance around critical and important aspects of software development. The sheer number of moving parts in modern software requires automation to create assurances.

Carving Out Bounded Contexts Within Existing Integration Architecture

In "Reuse Patterns" on page 112, we discussed the issues around architects trying to achieve reuse without creating brittleness. A specific example of this issue often arises in reconciling enterprise-level reuse and isolation via bounded contexts and architecture quanta, often exemplified in a data layer, as illustrated in Figure 9-11.

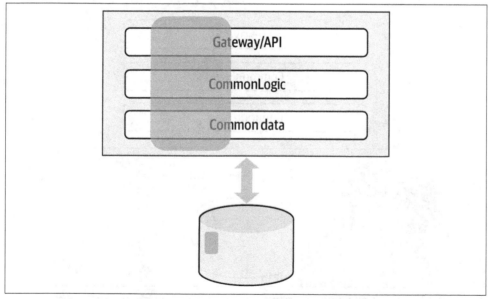

Figure 9-11. Bounded context identified within existing architecture layers

A common architecture pattern is the *layered architecture*, where architects partition components based on technical capabilities—presentation, persistence, and so on. The goal of the layered architecture is separation of concerns, which (hopefully) leads to higher degrees of reuse. *Technical partitioning* describes building architectures based on technical capabilities; it was the most common architecture style for many years.

However, after the advent of DDD, architects started designing architectures inspired by it, especially bounded context. In fact, the two most common new topologies architects build solutions with are *modular monoliths* and *microservices*, both heavily based on DDD.

However, these two patterns are fundamentally incompatible—layered architecture promotes separation of concerns and facilitates reuse across different contexts, which is one of the stated benefits of the layered approach. However, as we have illustrated, that kind of cross-cutting reuse is decried by both the connecting property of locality and the principle behind bounded context.

So how do organizations reconcile this conflict? By supporting separation of concerns without allowing the damaging side effects of cross-cutting reuse. This is in fact yet another example of having an architectural principle that requires governance, leading to fitness functions to augment the structure.

Consider the architecture illustrated in Figure 9-12.

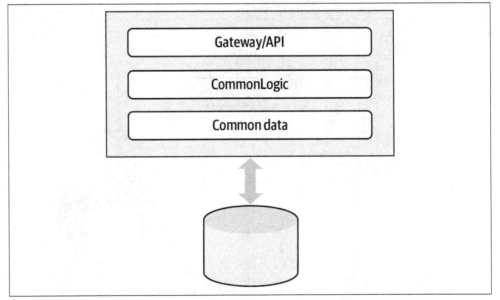

Figure 9-12. A traditional layered architecture, both components and monolithic database

In Figure 9-12, the architects have partitioned the architecture in terms of technical capabilities—the actual layers aren't important. However, during a DDD exercise, the team identifies the parts of an application with the integration architecture that should be isolated as a bounded context, illustrated in Figure 9-13.

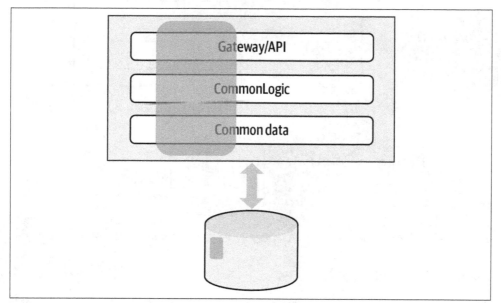

Figure 9-13. An embedded bounded context within another architecture

In Figure 9-13, the team has identified the bounded context (shaded area) within the technical layers. While further separating the parts of the domain based on technical features doesn't harm anything, teams also need to prevent applications from coupling to their implementation details.

Thus, the team builds fitness functions to prevent cross-bounded context communication, as illustrated in Figure 9-14.

The team builds fitness functions in each appropriate place to prevent accidental coupling. Of course, returning to a common theme in this book, we can't specify exactly what those fitness functions will look like—it will depend on the assets the teams want to protect. However, the overarching goal should be clear: prevent violating the bounded context by violating the locality principle of connascence.

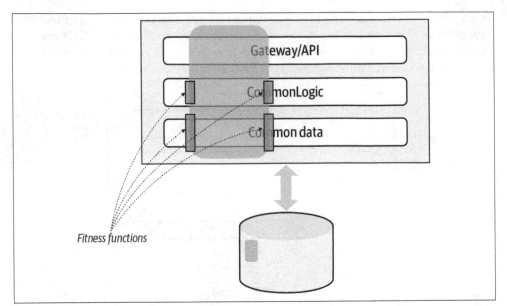

Figure 9-14. Carving out a bounded context within a layered architecture

Where Do You Start?

Many architects with existing architectures that resemble Big Balls of Mud struggle with where to start adding evolvability. While appropriate coupling and use of modularity are some of the first steps you should take, sometimes there are other priorities. For example, if your data schema is hopelessly coupled, determining how DBAs can achieve modularity might be the first step. Here are some common strategies and reasons to adopt the practices around building evolutionary architectures.

Low-Hanging Fruit

If an organization needs an early win to prove the approach, architects may choose the easiest problem that highlights the evolutionary architecture approach. Generally, this will be part of the system that is already decoupled to a large degree and hopefully not on the critical path to any dependencies. Increasing modularity and decreasing coupling allows teams to demonstrate other aspects of evolutionary architecture, namely fitness functions and incremental change. Building better isolation allows more focused testing and the creation of fitness functions. Better isolation of deployable units makes building deployment pipelines easier and provides a platform for building more robust testing.

Metrics are a common adjunct to the deployment pipeline in incremental change environments. If teams use this effort as a proof of concept, developers should gather appropriate metrics for both before and after scenarios. Gathering concrete data is the best way for developers to vet the approach; remember the adage that *demonstration defeats discussion*.

This "easiest first" approach minimizes risk at the possible expense of value, unless a team is lucky enough to have *easy* and *high value* align. This is a good strategy for companies that are skeptical and want to dip their toes in the metaphorical water of evolutionary architecture.

Highest Value First

An alternative approach to "easiest first" is "highest value first": find the most critical part of the system and build evolutionary behavior around it first. Companies may take this approach for several reasons. First, if architects are convinced that they want to pursue an evolutionary architecture, choosing the highest-value portion first indicates commitment. Second, for companies still evaluating these ideas, their architects may be curious as to how applicable these techniques are within their ecosystem. Thus, by choosing the highest-value part first, they demonstrate the long-term value proposition of evolutionary architecture. Third, if architects have doubts that these ideas can work for their application, vetting the concepts via the most valuable part of the system provides actionable data as to whether they want to proceed.

Testing

Many companies lament the lack of testing their systems have. If developers find themselves in a codebase with anemic or no testing, they may decide to add some critical tests before undertaking the more ambitious move to evolutionary architecture.

It is generally frowned upon for developers to undertake a project that only adds tests to a codebase. Management looks upon this activity with suspicion, especially if new-feature implementation is delayed. Rather, architects should combine increasing modularity with high-level functional tests. Wrapping functionality with unit tests provides better scaffolding for engineering practices such as test-driven development (TDD) but takes time to retrofit into a codebase. Instead, developers should add coarse-grained functional tests around some behavior before restructuring the code, allowing you to verify that the overall system behavior hasn't changed because of the restructuring.

Testing is a critical component to the incremental change aspect of evolutionary architecture, and fitness functions leverage tests aggressively. Thus, at least some level of testing enables these techniques, and a strong correlation exists between comprehensiveness of testing and ease of implementing an evolutionary architecture.

Infrastructure

New capabilities come slowly to some companies, and the operations group is a common victim of lack of innovation. For companies that have a dysfunctional infrastructure, getting those problems solved may be a precursor to building an evolutionary architecture. Infrastructure issues come in many forms. For example, some companies outsource all their operational responsibilities to another company and thus don't control that critical piece of their ecosystem; the difficultly of DevOps rises by orders of magnitude when saddled with the overhead of cross-company coordination.

Another common infrastructure dysfunction is an impenetrable firewall between development and operations, where developers have no insight into how code eventually runs. This structure is common in companies rife with politics across divisions, where each silo acts autonomously.

Lastly, architects and developers in some organizations have ignored good practices and consequently built massive amounts of technical debt that manifests within infrastructure. Some companies don't even have a good idea of what runs where and other basic knowledge of the interactions between architecture and infrastructure.

Infrastructure Always Impacts Architecture

Neal once did consulting work for a company that ran a hosted service for users. The company had a large number of servers (approximately 2,500 at the time), and had built silos *within* the operations group: one team installed hardware, another installed operating systems, and a third installed applications. Needless to say, when a developer wanted a resource, they cast a ticket into the black hole of operations, where more tickets were generated and bounced around for weeks until resources appeared. To exacerbate the problem, the company's CIO had left the year before, and the CFO was handling his department. Of course, the CFO was concerned primarily with cost savings, not modernizing what he viewed as merely overhead.

While investigating operation weaknesses, one of the developers mentioned that each server accommodated only about five users, which was shocking considering the simplicity of the application. Sheepishly, developers explained that they had abused HTTP session state to legendary degrees, essentially treating it as a huge in-memory database. Thus, they could host only a few users per server. The problem was that their operations group could not produce a realistic production-like environment for debugging purposes, and they absolutely forbade developers from debugging (or even extensive monitoring) for production, mostly because of political forces. Without the ability to interact with a realistic version of the application, developers couldn't untangle the mess they had gradually created.

Performing some back-of-the-envelope calculations, we ascertained that the company could likely run on an order of magnitude fewer servers, more like 250. Yet, the

---

company was too busy buying new servers, installing operating systems, and so on. The grand irony, of course, is that their cost-saving measures actually cost the company a huge sum.

Ultimately, the besieged developers created their own guerilla DevOps group and started managing servers themselves, bypassing the traditional operations organization entirely. A fight loomed in the future between the two groups, but in the short term, the developers started making progress in restructuring their application.

Ultimately, the advice parallels the annoying-but-accurate consultant's answer of *It Depends!* Only architects, developers, DBAs, DevOps, testing, security, and the other host of contributors can ultimately determine the best road map toward evolutionary architecture.

Case Study: Enterprise Architecture at PenultimateWidgets

PenultimateWidgets is considering revamping a major part of its legacy platform, and a team of enterprise architects generated a spreadsheet listing all the properties the new platform should exhibit: security, performance metrics, scalability, deployability, and a host of other properties. Each category contained 5 to 20 cells, each with some specific criteria. For example, one of the uptime metrics insisted that each service offer five nines (99.999) of availability. In total, they identified 62 discrete items.

But they realized some problems with this approach. First, would they verify each of these 62 properties on projects? They could create a policy, but who would verify that policy on an ongoing basis? Verifying all these things manually, even on an ad hoc basis, would be a considerable challenge.

Second, would it make sense to impose strict availability guidelines across every part of the system? Is it critical that the administrator's management screens offer five nines? Creating blanket policies often leads to egregious overengineering.

To solve these problems, the enterprise architects defined their criteria as fitness functions and created a deployment pipeline template for each project to start with. Within the deployment pipeline, the architects designed fitness functions to automatically check critical features such as security, leaving individual teams to add specific fitness functions (like availability) for their service.

Future State?

What is the future state of evolutionary architecture? As teams become more familiar with the ideas and practices, they will subsume them into business as usual and start using these ideas to build new capabilities, such as data-driven development.

Much work must be done around the more difficult kinds of fitness functions, but progress is already occurring as organizations solve problems and make many of their solutions freely available. In the early days of agility, people lamented that some problems were just too hard to automate, but intrepid developers kept chipping away and now entire data centers have succumbed to automation. For instance, Netflix has made tremendous innovations in conceptualizing and building tools like the Simian Army, supporting holistic continuous fitness functions (but not yet calling them that).

There are a couple of promising areas.

Fitness Functions Using AI

Gradually, large, open source, artificial intelligence frameworks are becoming available for regular projects. As developers learn to utilize these tools to support software development, we envision fitness functions based on AI that look for anomalous behavior. Credit card companies already apply heuristics such as flagging near-simultaneous transactions in different parts of the world; architects can start to build investigatory tools to look for odd behaviors in architecture.

Generative Testing

A practice common in many functional programming communities gaining wider acceptance is the idea of *generative testing*. Traditional unit tests include assertions of correct outcomes within each test case. However, with generative testing, developers run a large number of tests and capture the outcomes, then use statistical analysis on the results to look for anomalies. For example, consider the mundane case of boundary-checking ranges of numbers. Traditional unit tests check the known places where numbers break (negatives, rolling over numerical sizes, etc.) but are immune to unanticipated edge cases. Generative tests check every possible value and report on edge cases that break.

Why (or Why Not)?

No silver bullets exist, including in architecture. We don't recommend that every project take on the extra cost and effort of evolvability unless it benefits them.

Why Should a Company Decide to Build an Evolutionary Architecture?

Many businesses find that the cycle of change has accelerated over the past few years, as reflected in the aforementioned *Forbes* observation that every company must be competent at software development and delivery. Let's look at some reasons why using evolutionary architectures makes sense.

Predictable versus evolvable

Many companies value long-term planning for resources and other strategic matters; companies obviously value *predictability*. However, because of the dynamic equilibrium of the software development ecosystem, predictability has expired. Enterprise architects may still make plans, but they may be invalidated at any moment.

Even companies in staid, established industries shouldn't ignore the perils of systems that cannot evolve. The taxi industry was a multicentury, international institution when it was rocked by ride-sharing companies that understood and reacted to the implications of the shifting ecosystem. The phenomenon known as The Innovators Dilemma (*https://oreil.ly/1d6Zx*) predicts that companies in well-established markets are likely to fail as more agile startups address the changing ecosystem better.

Building evolvable architecture takes extra time and effort, but the reward comes when the company can react to substantive shifts in the marketplace without major rework. Predictability will never return to the nostalgic days of mainframes and dedicated operations centers. The highly volatile nature of the development world increasingly pushes all organizations toward incremental change.

Scale

For a while, the best practice in architecture was to build transactional systems backed by relational databases, using many of the features of the database to handle coordination. The problem with that approach is scaling—it becomes hard to scale the backend database. Lots of byzantine technologies spawned to mitigate this problem, but they were only Band-Aids to the fundamental problem of scale: coupling. Any coupling point in an architecture eventually prevents scale, and relying on coordination at the database level eventually hits a wall.

Amazon faced this exact problem. The original site was designed with a monolithic frontend tied to a monolithic backend modeled around databases. When traffic increased, the team had to scale up the databases. At some point, they reached the limits of database scale, and the impact on the site was decreasing performance—every page loaded more slowly.

Amazon realized that coupling everything to one *thing* (whether a relational database, enterprise service bus, etc.) ultimately limited scalability. By redesigning the architecture in more of a microservices style that eliminated inappropriate coupling, Amazon allowed its overall ecosystem to scale.

A side benefit of that level of decoupling is enhanced evolvability. As we have illustrated throughout the book, inappropriate coupling represents the biggest challenge to evolution. Building a scalable system also tends to correspond to an evolvable one.

Advanced business capabilities

Many companies look with envy at Facebook, Netflix, and other cutting-edge technology companies because they have sophisticated features. Incremental change allows well-known practices such as hypotheses and data-driven development. Many companies yearn to incorporate their users into their feedback loop via multivariate testing. A key building block for many advanced DevOps practices is an architecture that can evolve. For example, developers find it difficult to perform A/B testing if a high degree of coupling exists between components, making isolation of concerns more daunting. Generally, an evolutionary architecture allows a company better technical responsiveness to inevitable but unpredictable changes.

Cycle time as a business metric

In "Deployment Pipelines" on page 32, we made the distinction between *Continuous Delivery*, where at least one stage in the deployment pipeline performs a manual *pull*, and *continuous deployment*, where every stage automatically promotes to the next upon success. Building continuous deployment takes a fair amount of engineering sophistication—why would a company go quite that far?

Because cycle time has become a business differentiator in some markets. Some large conservative organizations view software as overhead and thus try to minimize cost. Innovative companies see software as a competitive advantage. For example, if AcmeWidgets has created an architecture where the cycle time is three hours, and PenultimateWidgets still has a six-week cycle time, AcmeWidgets has an advantage it can exploit.

Many companies have made cycle time a first-class business metric, mostly because they live in a highly competitive market. All markets eventually become competitive in this way. For example, in the early 1990s, some big companies were more aggressive in moving toward automating manual workflows via software and gained a huge advantage as all companies eventually realized that necessity.

Isolating architectural characteristics at the quantum level

Thinking of traditional nonfunctional requirements as fitness functions and building a well-encapsulated architectural quantum allows architects to support different characteristics per quantum, one of the benefits of a microservices architecture. Because the technical architecture of each quantum is decoupled from other quanta, architects can choose different architectures for different use cases. For example, developers on one small service may choose a microkernel architecture because they want to support a small core that allows incremental addition. Another team of developers may choose an event-driven architecture for their service because of scalability concerns. If both services were part of a monolith, architects would have to make trade-offs to attempt to satisfy both requirements. By isolating technical architecture at a small

---

quantum level, architects are free to focus on the primary characteristics of a singular quantum, not analyzing the trade-offs for competing priorities.

Adaptation versus evolution

Many organizations fall into the trap of gradually increasing technical debt and reluctance to make needed restructuring modifications, which in turns makes systems and integration points increasingly brittle. Companies try to pave over this brittleness with connection tools like service buses, which alleviates some of the technical headaches but doesn't address deeper logical cohesion of business processes. Using a service bus is an example of *adapting* an existing system to use in another setting. But as we've highlighted previously, a side effect of adaptation is increased technical debt. When developers adapt something, they preserve the original behavior and layer new behavior alongside it. The more adaptation cycles a component endures, the more parallel behavior there is, increasing complexity, hopefully strategically.

The use of feature toggles offers a good example of the benefits of adaptation. Often, developers use toggles when trying several alternatives via hypotheses-driven development, testing their users to see what resonates best. In this case, the technical debt imposed by toggles is purposeful and desirable. Of course, the engineering best practice around these types of toggles is to remove them as soon as the decision is resolved.

Alternatively, *evolving* implies fundamental change. Building an evolvable architecture entails changing the architecture in situ, protected from breakages via fitness functions. The end result is a system that continues to evolve in useful ways without an increasing legacy of outdated solutions lurking within.

Why Would a Company Choose Not to Build an Evolutionary Architecture?

We don't believe that evolutionary architecture is the cure for all ailments! Companies have several legitimate reasons to pass on these ideas. Here are some common reasons.

Can't evolve a Big Ball of Mud

One of the key "-ilities" architects neglect is *feasibility*—should the team undertake this project? If an architecture is a hopelessly coupled Big Ball of Mud, making it possible to evolve it cleanly will take an enormous amount of work—likely more than rewriting it from scratch. Companies loathe throwing anything away that has perceived value, but often a rework is more costly than a rewrite.

How can companies tell if they're in this situation? The first step to converting an existing architecture into an evolvable one is *modularity*. Thus, a developer's first task requires finding whatever modularity exists in the current system and restructuring the architecture around those discoveries. Once the architecture becomes less entangled, it becomes easier for architects to see underlying structures and make reasonable determinations about the effort needed for restructuring.

Other architectural characteristics dominate

Evolvability is only one of many characteristics architects must weigh when choosing a particular architecture style. No architecture can fully support conflicting core goals. For example, building high performance and high scale into the same architecture is difficult. In some cases, other factors may outweigh evolutionary change.

Most of the time, architects choose an architecture for a broad set of requirements. For example, perhaps an architecture needs to support high availability, security, and scale. This leads toward general architecture patterns, such as monolith, microservices, or event-driven patterns. However, a family of architectures known as *domain-specific architectures* attempt to maximize a single characteristic. Having built their architecture for such a specific purpose, evolving it to accommodate other concerns would present difficulties (unless developers are extraordinarily lucky and architectural concerns overlap). Thus, most domain-specific architectures aren't concerned with evolution because their specific purpose overrides other concerns.

Sacrificial architecture

Martin Fowler defined a sacrificial architecture (*https://oreil.ly/0RyeF*) as one designed to be thrown away. Many companies need to build simple versions initially to investigate a market or prove viability. Once proven, they can build the *real* architecture to support the characteristics that have manifested.

Many companies do this strategically. Often, companies build this type of architecture when creating a minimum viable product (*https://oreil.ly/SgSj8*) to test a market, anticipating building a more robust architecture if the market approves. Building a sacrificial architecture implies that architects aren't going to try to evolve it but rather replace it at the appropriate time with something more permanent. Cloud offerings make this an attractive option for companies experimenting with the viability of a new market or offering.

Planning on closing the business soon

Evolutionary architecture helps businesses adapt to changing ecosystem forces. If a company doesn't plan to be in business in a year, there's no reason to build evolvability into its architecture.

Summary

Building evolutionary architectures isn't a silver-bullet set of tools architects can download and run. Rather, it is a holistic approach to governance in architecture, based on the cumulative experience we have learned about software engineering. Real software engineering will rely on automation plus incremental change, both features of evolutionary architecture.

Remember that often turnkey tools won't exist for your ecosystem. So the key question is, "Is the information I need available somewhere?" If so, then a simple handcrafted scripting tool can gather and aggregate that disparate data to provide architectural value.

Architects don't have to implement an elaborate set of fitness functions. Just like domain testing via unit tests, architects should focus on high-value fitness functions that justify the effort to create and maintain them. There is no absolute end state for evolution in an architecture, only degrees of value added via these approaches.

To evolve a software system, architects must have confidence in the structural design and engineering practices working synergistically. Controlling coupling and automating verification is the key to building well-governed architectures that can evolve via domain, technical changes, or both.

Index

reporting atop the system of record antipattern, 189

business metric, cycle time as, 226

About the Authors

Neal Ford is director, software architect, and meme wrangler at ThoughtWorks, a software company and a community of passionate, purpose-led individuals who think disruptively to deliver technology to address the toughest challenges, all while seeking to revolutionize the IT industry and create positive social change. Before joining ThoughtWorks, Neal was the chief technology officer at The DSW Group, Ltd., a nationally recognized training and development firm.

Neal has a degree in computer science from Georgia State University specializing in languages and compilers and a minor in mathematics specializing in statistical analysis. He is an internationally recognized expert on software development and delivery, especially at the intersection of agile engineering techniques and software architecture. Neal has authored magazine articles, nine books (and counting), and dozens of video presentations and has spoken at hundreds of developer conferences worldwide. The topics of these works include software architecture, Continuous Delivery, functional programming, and cutting-edge software innovations, as well as a business-focused book and video on improving technical presentations. His primary consulting focus is the design and construction of large-scale enterprise applications. If you have an insatiable curiosity about Neal, visit his website at *nealford.com*.

Dr. Rebecca Parsons is ThoughtWorks' chief technology officer with decades-long applications development experience across a range of industries and systems. Her technical experience includes leading the creation of large-scale distributed object applications, the integration of disparate systems, and working with architecture teams. Separate from her passion for deep technology, Dr. Parsons is a strong advocate for diversity in the technology industry.

Before joining ThoughtWorks, Dr. Parsons worked as an assistant professor of computer science at the University of Central Florida where she taught courses in compilers, program optimization, distributed computation, programming languages, theory of computation, machine learning, and computational biology. She also worked as a Director's Postdoctoral Fellow at the Los Alamos National Laboratory researching issues in parallel and distributed computation, genetic algorithms, computational biology, and nonlinear dynamical systems.

Dr. Parsons received a Bachelor of Science degree in computer science and economics from Bradley University, a Master of Science in computer science from Rice University, and her PhD in computer science from Rice University. She is also the coauthor of *Domain-Specific Languages*, *The ThoughtWorks Anthology*, and *Building Evolutionary Architectures*, 1st edition.

Patrick Kua is an independent CTO coach, former CTO of N26, and former principal technical consultant at ThoughtWorks, having worked in the technology industry for over 20 years. His personal mission is to accelerate the growth of technical leaders, and he does that through one-on-one coaching, online and in-person technical leadership workshops, and his popular newsletter for leaders in tech, *Level Up* (*https://levelup.patkua.com*).

He is the author of *The Retrospective Handbook: A Guide for Agile Teams and Talking with Tech Leads: From Novices to Practitioners* and offers training via the *The Tech Lead Academy* (*https://techlead.academy*).

You can discover more about him at his website, *patkua.com*, or reach out to him on twitter at @patkua (*http://twitter.com/patkua*).

Pramod Sadalage is director of Data & DevOps at ThoughtWorks, where he enjoys the rare role of bridging the divide between database professionals and application developers. He is usually sent to clients with particularly challenging data needs that require new technologies and techniques. In the early 2000s he developed techniques to allow relational databases to be designed in an evolutionary manner based on version-controlled schema migrations.

He is coauthor of *Software Architecture: The Hard Parts*, coauthor of *Refactoring Databases*, coauthor of *NoSQL Distilled*, and author of *Recipes for Continuous Database Integration*, and he continues to speak and write about the insights he and his clients learn.

Colophon

The animal on the cover of *Building Evolutionary Architectures* is the open brain coral (*Trachyphyllia geoffroyi*). Also known as a "folded brain" or "crater" coral, this large-polyp stony (LPS) coral is native to the Indian Ocean.

Known for its distinctive folds, bright colors, and hardiness, this free-living coral subsists on the photosynthetic output of a surface layer of zooxanthellae during the day, while at night it extends tentacles from its polyps to steer prey, which include various plankton as well as small fish, into one of its mouths (some open brain corals have two or three of them).

Because of its striking appearance and easy-to-accommodate diet, *Trachyphyllia geoffroyi* is a popular choice for aquariums, where it thrives in the bottom layer of sand and/or silt resembling the shallow seafloors of its native habitat. They benefit from an environment with moderate water flow and rich with plant and animal matter to consume.

Trachyphyllia geoffroyi is listed on the IUCN Red List at Near Threatened status. Many of the animals on O'Reilly covers are endangered; all of them are important to the world.

The cover illustration is by Karen Montgomery, based on an antique line engraving from Jean Vincent Félix Lamouroux's *Exposition Methodique des genres de L'Ordre des Polypiers*. The cover fonts are Gilroy Semibold and Guardian Sans. The text font is Adobe Minion Pro; the heading font is Adobe Myriad Condensed; and the code font is Dalton Maag's Ubuntu Mono.

O'REILLY®

Learn from experts.
Become one yourself.

Books | Live online courses
Instant Answers | Virtual events
Videos | Interactive learning

Get started at oreilly.com.

Printed in the USA
CPSIA information can be obtained
at www.ICGtesting.com
JSHW051907200524
63489JS00009B/444